Lon

T0014442

Brazilian
Portuguese

Phrasebook & Dictionary

Acknowledgments
Product Editor Bridget Blair, Damian Kemp
Book Designer Michael Weldon, Fabrice Robin
Language Writers Yukiyoshi Kamimura, Marcia Monje de Castro
Cover Image Researcher Brendan Dempsey-Spencer

Thanks
James Hardy, Andi Jones, Wayne Murphy, Catherine Naghten,
Kirsten Rawlings

Published by Lonely Planet Global Limited
CRN 554153

6th Edition – September 2023
ISBN 978 1 78657 576 0
Text © Lonely Planet 2023
Cover Image Ilha de Boipeba, Aldo Pavan/4Corners Images ©

Printed in China   10 9 8 7 6 5 4 3 2 1

Contact lonelyplanet.com/contact

MIX
Paper from
responsible sources
FSC™ C02174
www.fsc.org

acknowledgments

The phrases in this book were translated by Marcia Monje de Castro, with special thanks to Yukiyoshi Kamimura for translating the Sustainable Travel section. Yukiyoshi Kamimura was also responsible for creating the illustrations. Wayne Murphy created the map.

make the most of this phrasebook ...

Anyone can speak another language! It's all about confidence. Don't worry if you can't remember your school language lessons or if you've never learnt a language before. Even if you learn the very basics (on the inside covers of this book), your travel experience will be the better for it. You have nothing to lose and everything to gain when the locals hear you making an effort.

finding things in this book

For easy navigation, this book is in sections. The Basics chapters are the ones you'll thumb through time and again. The Practical section covers basic travel situations like catching transport and finding a bed. The Social section gives you conversational phrases, pick-up lines, the ability to express opinions – so you can get to know people. Food has a section all of its own: gourmets and vegetarians are covered and local dishes feature. Safe Travel equips you with health and police phrases, just in case. Remember the colours of each section and you'll find everything easily; or use the comprehensive Index. Otherwise, check the two-way traveller's Dictionary for the word you need.

being understood

Throughout this book you'll see coloured phrases on the right-hand side of each page. They're phonetic guides to help you pronounce the language. You don't even need to look at the language itself, but you'll get used to the way we've represented particular sounds. The pronunciation chapter in Basics will explain more, but you can feel confident that if you read the coloured phrase slowly, you'll be understood.

communication tips

Body language, ways of doing things, sense of humour – all have a role to play in every culture. 'Local talk' boxes show you common ways of saying things, or everyday language to drop into conversation. 'Listen for ...' boxes supply the phrases you may hear. They start with the phonetic guide (because you'll hear it before you know what's being said) and then lead in to the language and the English translation.

contents

5

brazilian portuguese

Caribbean Sea · St Vincent — · — Barbados · Grenada — · —Trinidad & Tobago

Panama

Venezuela

Guyana

Suriname

French Guiana (Fr.)

NORTH ATLANTIC OCEAN

Colombia

Ecuador

Peru

B R A Z I L

Macapá

Belém

São Luís

Fortaleza

Teresina

Rio Gra do Nor

Paraíb

Pernam

Manaus

Alagoas

Sergipe

Salvador da Bahia

Rio Branco

Porto Velho

Palmas

Cuiabá

Brasília

Bolivia

Campo Grande

Belo Horizonte

Vitória

Chile

SOUTH PACIFIC OCEAN

Paraguay

Rio de Janeiro

São Paulo

Curitiba

Florianópolis

SOUTH ATLANTIC OCEAN

Argentina

Porto Alegre

Uruguay

▓ national language
For more details see the **introduction**.

ABOUT BRAZILIAN PORTUGUESE

Portuguese is spoken by around 190 million people worldwide, 89% of whom live in Brazil. Brazil, the largest country in South America, is the only Portuguese-speaking nation on the continent. Although the country is large, there's very little regional variation, so you'll have no trouble making yourself understood from top to bottom.

The Portuguese arrived in Brazil at the beginning of the 16th century. Speakers from the different regions in Portugal all brought their own dialectal variations. However, as Portuguese colonists came into contact with the Tupi tribes that lived along the Atlantic coast, the Tupi language, along with Portuguese, became the main languages of Brazil. This was mostly due to the Jesuits, who translated prayers and hymns into Tupi and in doing so recorded and promoted the indigenous language. This situation did not last and the use of Tupi was banned in 1759 when the Jesuits were expelled from Brazil and Portuguese was instated as the country's main language.

Portuguese spoken in Brazil was influenced by Tupi and the Bantu and Yoruba languages of African slaves who were brought to Brazil through till the middle of the 19th century. Over a similar period, European Portuguese also underwent linguistic change through

at a glance ...

language name:
Portuguese
name in language:
português porr·too·ges
language family:
Romance
key country: Brazil
**approximate number
of speakers:** 169 million
in Brazil, 190 million
Portuguese speakers
worldwide
close relatives:
Catalan, Galician, French
Italian, Occitan,
Romanian, Spanish
donations to English:
cashew, ipecac, macaw,
petunia, piranha, toucan

introduction

7

contact with French. Due to this divergence, Brazilian Portugue[se]
today differs from European Portuguese in approximately the san[e]
way that British English differs from American English. Europe[an]
and Brazilian Portuguese have different spelling, different pr[o]
nunciation and to some extent, different vocabulary. For examp[le]
in Portugal, the word for 'train' is *comboio* and in Brazil you'd s[ay]
trem.

This book will ensure not only that you have the right wor[ds]
at your disposal, but that you pronounce them as a true *brasile[iro]*
(if you're a man) or *brasileira* (if you're a woman). Need mo[re]
encouragement? Remember, the contact you make using Braz[il]
ian Portuguese will make your travels unique. Local knowledg[e]
new relationships and a sense of satisfaction are on the tip of yo[ur]
tongue, so don't just stand there, say something!

abbreviations used in this book

m	masculine	sg	singular	pol	polite
f	feminine	pl	plural	inf	informal

The pronunciation guide used in this book is based on the pronunciation of Brazilian Portuguese common in urban areas. There are small variations in pronunciation throughout the country, but they cause little difficulty when communicating.

vowel sounds

Vowel sounds are quite similar to those found in English, so you should be able to get talking with confidence. There are some differences of course: the *ay* sound, for example, is much shorter than the English version of it. But with every conversation you have, the sounds will become more familiar and you'll discover ways to make those same sounds yourself.

symbol	english equivalent	brazilian portuguese example
a	run	*camera*
aa	father	*padre*
ai	aisle	*pai*
aw	saw	*nó*
ay	day	*lei*
e	bet	*cedo*
ee	bee	*fino*
o	go	*gato*
oo	moon	*azul*
ow	how	*saudades*
oy	boy	*noite*

pronunciation

A characteristic feature of Brazilian Portuguese is the use of nasal vowels. Nasal vowels are pronounced as if you're trying to force the sound out of your nose rather than your mouth. It's easier than it sounds. English also has nasal vowels to some extent – when you say 'sing' in English, the 'i' is nasalised by the 'ng'. In our pronunciation guide, we've used ng after nasal vowels to indicate that it's nasal. The following is a list of the vowels that you'll normally see with ng in our phonetic guides.

symbol	english equivalent	brazilian portuguese example
ang	-	amanhã
ayng	-	pães
eng	-	tem
eeng	-	muito
ong	-	bom
oong	-	segundo
owng	-	fogão
oyng	-	nações

consonant sounds

The consonant sounds in Brazilian Portuguese are very similar to those of English, and even the rolled 'r' (rr), which doesn't exist in standard English varieties, will be familiar to most people (it's similar to the 'r' in Spanish). Two sounds (ly and ny) which might appear a little strange at first do actually occur in English (eg, 'million' and 'canyon'), but never at the beginning of a syllable as they do in Brazilian Portuguese.

symbol	english equivalent	brazilian portuguese example
b	big	*b*eber
d	dig	*d*ar/*d*edo
f	fun	*f*aca
g	go	*g*uia
h	hat	resto/serra
k	kick	*c*ama
l	loud	*l*ixo
ly	million	mura*lh*as
m	man	*m*acaco
n	no	*n*ada
ny	canyon	li*nh*a
p	pig	*p*adre
r	run	pa*r*a
rr	as the 'r' in run, but stronger and rolled	i*r*
s	so	gro*ss*o
sh	ship	*ch*ave
t	tin	*t*acho
v	very	*v*ago
w	win	m*u*ito
z	zoo	e*x*ame
zh	pleasure	*g*entes

word stress

Stress generally occurs on the second-to-last syllable of a word, though there are exceptions. When a word ends in a written -r or is pronounced with a nasalised vowel, the stress falls on the last syllable. Another exception: if a written vowel has an accent marked on it, the stress falls on the syllable containing that vowel.

In our transliteration system, we have indicated the stressed syllable with italics.

writing

Brazilian Portuguese is written with the latin alphabet, which is given below. For spelling purposes, pronunciation of letters is also provided:

alphabet			
a	a	n	e·ne
b	be	o	aw
c	se	p	pe
d	de	q	ke
e	e	r	e·he
f	e·fe	s	e·se
g	ge	t	te
h	a·gaa	u	oo
i	ee	v	ve
j	jo·ta	w	daa·bee·oo
k	kaa	x	hees
l	e·le	y	eep·see·lon
m	e·me	z	ze

Some letters have accent marks which denote stress, or variations in the sound usually represented. The accent marks used include those used on vowels: the acute (´), grave (`) and circumflex (^), indicating stress; and the tilde (~), indicating nasalisation. You'll also notice the tail (cedilla) sometimes used at the bottom of the letter 'c' – 'ç' is pronounced as s.

This chapter is arranged alphabetically and is designed to help you make your own sentences. If you can't find the exact phrase you need in this book, remember, a couple of well-chosen words, a little grammar and a gesture or two and you'll generally get the message across.

a/an

The Brazilian Portuguese words *um* and *uma* correspond to the English article 'a/an'. Whether you use the article *um* or *uma* depends upon the gender of the thing, person or concept talked about. If what you're referring to is masculine you use *um*, if it's feminine you use *uma*.

I'd like a pastry and a beer.
    Quero um pastel   ke·ro oom paas·tel
    e uma cerveja.   e oo·maa serr·ve·zhaa
    (lit: I-like a pastry and a beer)

Also see **gender**.

adjectives see describing things

any see some

articles see a/an and the

be

Brazilian Portuguese has two words which can be translated as 'be' in English: *ser* and *estar*. Learning to use them perfectly will take some time and effort, but the basic difference in their usage is not too difficult to grasp. They're both irregular verbs (just as 'be' is in English) so you need to remember by heart the various forms they take.

The verb *ser* refers to states that have a degree of permanency or durability about them.

I	am	Australian	*eu*	*sou*	*australiano* m
you sg	are	kind	*você*	*é*	*gentil* m&f
he/she	is	an artist	*ele/ela*	*é*	*artista* m&f
you pl	are	crazy	*vocês*	*são*	*loucos* m
we	are	students	*nós*	*somos*	*estudantes*
they	are	crazy	*eles/elas*	*são*	*loucos/ loucas* m/f

The verb *estar* generally refers to events which are temporary in nature.

I	am	on holiday	*eu*	*estou*	*de férias*
you sg	are	drunk	*você*	*está*	*bêbado* m
he/she	is	sick	*ele/ela*	*está*	*doente* m&f
you pl	are	lost	*vocês*	*estão*	*perdidos* m
we	are	travelling	*nós*	*estamos*	*viajando*
they	are	busy	*eles/elas*	*estão*	*ocupados/ ocupadas* m/f

comparing things

To compare one thing to another, use the words *mais* (more) and *menos* (less) in the following ways:

mais … do que …   mais … do ke …
more … than …

menos … do que …   me·nos … do ke …
less … than …

This shirt is nicer than that one.
   Esta camisa é mais   es·*taa* kaa·*mee*·zaa e mais
   bonita do que esta.   bo·*nee*·taa do ke es·taa
   (lit: this shirt is more nice of
     that this)

To refer to something as the most or least (eg, biggest) use
mais (more) and *menor* (less) in the following ways:

   o/a … mais … m/f   o/aa … mais …
   the … most …
   o/a … menor … m/f   o/aa … me·*nor* …
   the … least …

I'd like the cheapest room.
   Quero o quarto mais   *ke*·ro o *kwaar*·to mais
   barato.   baa·*raa*·to
   (lit: I-like the room most cheap)

demonstratives see this & that

describing things

Adjectives are generally placed after the noun. They vary in
form depending on the gender and number of the noun that
they describe:

the pretty young woman
   a jovem bonita   aa *zho*·veng bo·*nee*·taa
   (lit: a young-woman beautiful)
the pretty young women
   as jovens bonitas   as *zho*·vengs bo·*nee*·taas
   (lit: the young-girls beautiful)
the handsome young man
   o rapaz bonito   o haa·*paas* bo·nee·to
   (lit: a young-man handsome)
the handsome young men
   os rapazess bonitos   os haa·*paa*·zes bo·*nee*·tos
   (lit: the young-men handsome)

Here are the various endings that adjectives take to agree with the nouns that they describe:

	singular	plural
masculine	-o	-os
feminine	-a	-as

feminine see gender

gender

All nouns are either masculine or feminine. They determine the endings used on adjectives that describe them as well as which forms of the Portuguese equivalents of the articles 'a/ an' and 'the' are used. The gender that a given noun takes is often arbitrary. For example, there's no reason why the noun *sol* 'sun' is masculine while *praia* 'beach' is feminine. The dictionary will tell you what gender a noun is, but here are some guidelines for taking a guess at the gender of a noun (there are exceptions though):

often masculine	often feminine
nouns referring to male persons (or male animals)	nouns referring to female persons (or female animals)
nouns ending in -o	nouns ending in -a
nouns ending in -ema, -oma and -ama	nouns ending with -dade

Also see **a/an**, **the** and **describing things**.

have

Possession can be indicated using the verb *ter* 'to have' which is an irregular verb.

I have a flight at 6pm.
> *Tenho um vôo às seis*   te·nyo oom *vo*·o aas says
> *da noite.*   da *noy*·te
> (lit: I-have a flight at-the six
> of-the night)

I	have	a ticket	eu	tenho	uma pasagem
you sg	have	the bill	você	tem	a conta
he/she	has	water	ele/ela	tem	água
we	have	the key	nós	temos	a chave
you pl	have	a letter	vocês	têm	uma carta
they	have	the menu	eles/elas	têm	o cardápio

masculine see gender

more than one

You can make a noun plural by adding -*s*:

book	livro m	books	livros m pl
bed	cama f	beds	camas f pl

If the noun ends in -*s*, -*z* or -*r*, and the final syllable is stressed, then the plural is formed by adding -*es*:

singular	plural	singular	plural
portuguese	português	portuguese	portuguêses
youth	rapaz m	youths	rapazes m pl
flower	flor f	flowers	flores f pl

Remember when using plural nouns to change the articles and adjectives used with these nouns to their corresponding plural forms too.

There are some exceptions and additional rules for making nouns plural – they can't all be covered here, so consult a grammar of Portuguese if you'd like to know more.

Also see **a/an**, **describing things**, **some**, and **the**.

my & your

Like English, Brazilian Portuguese uses pronouns to indicate possession. In the table below are the equivalents for the English possessive pronouns. To express possession you place them before the noun they describe and make them agree in number (plural or singular) and gender (masculine or feminine) with the noun.

	singular		plural	
	masculine	feminine	masculine	feminine
	map	letter	maps	letters
my	meu mapa	minha carta	meus mapas	minhas cartas
your sg&pl	seu mapa	sua carta	seus mapas	suas cartas
his/her/its	seu mapa	sua carta	seus mapas	suas cartas
our	nosso mapa	nossa carta	nossos mapas	nossas cartas
their	seu mapa	sua carta	seus mapas	suas cartas

Here's how you'd use possessive pronouns to say that something is yours.

It's my ticket.
  É a minha pasagem.   e a *mee*·nya pa·*saa*·zheng
  (lit: it-is the my ticket)

A simple statement of possession (eg, 'It's mine') is formed by using *É* ('it-is') with the possessive pronoun (to agree with the thing possessed).

It's mine.
É meu.   e me·oo
(lit: it-is mine)

negative

To make a sentence negative, just add the word *não* (no), before the main verb:

I don't want to walk any more.
Não quero andar mais.   nowng ke·ro ang·daar mais
(lit: no I-want to-walk more)

The double negative isn't only acceptable, but correct:

I can't see anything.
Não vejo nada.   nowng ve·zho naa·daa
(lit: no I-see nothing)

negative words		
never	*nunca*	*noong·kaa*
no/not	*não*	nowng
nobody	*ninguém*	neeng·geng
none sg	*nenhum/* *nenhuma* m/f	neng·ee·oom/ neng·ee·oo·maa
nor	*nem*	neng

nouns see gender

number see more than one

planning ahead

The future is usually expressed by using the present tense of
the verb *ir*, (go), plus another verb. It's equivalent to 'going
to …' in English:

I'm going to come back next week.

Vou voltar na semana	vo vol·*taarr* na se·*ma*·naa
que vem.	ke veng
(lit: I-go to-come-back	
in-the week which comes)	

I	vou	we	vamos
you sg	vai	you pl	vão
he/she/it	vai	they	vão

Just like in English, you'd also be understood when expressing
your plans, if you use the present tense with some indication
of time referring to the future:

I'm going to Rio tomorrow.

Vou para o Rio	vo *paa*·ra o *hee*·o
amanha.	aa·*ma*·nyang
(lit: I-go to the Rio tomorrow)	

plural see **more than one**

pointing something out

The easiest way to point something out in Portuguese is to
start your phrase with *É …* (lit: It-is …).

That's a beautiful building.

É um edifício bonito.	e oom e·dee·*fee*·syo bo·*nee*·to
(lit: it-is a building beautiful)	

Also see **this & that**.

possession see have, my & your and somebody's

There are a number of ways to indicate possession in Brazilian Portuguese. The easiest way is by using the verb *ter* (see **have**). You could also use possessive pronouns (see **my & your**) or, simplest of all, use the preposition *de* (of) followed by the possessor (see **somebody's**).

To find out who's the owner of something, you can use the simple phrases *De quem é isto …?* (of whom it-is this …?) for a single thing, or *De quem são estes/estas …? m/f* (of whom are-they these …?) for plural things:

Whose seat is this?

De quem é este assento?   de keng e *es·*te aa·*seng·*to
(lit: of whom it-is this seat)

pronouns

Subject pronouns corresponding to 'I', 'you', 'he', 'she', 'it', 'we' and 'they' are often omitted, as verb endings make it clear who the subject is. Use them if you want to emphasise the subject.

	singular			plural	
I	*eu*	e·oo	**we**	*nós*	nos
you	*você*	vo·se	**you**	*vocês*	vo·ses
he /it m	*ele*	e·le	**they** m or m&f	*eles*	e·les
she/it f	*ela*	e·laa	**they f**	*elas*	e·laas

Note that unlike in other romance languages (and even the Portuguese spoken in Portugal), Brazilian Portuguese does not commonly distinguish between formal and informal forms of 'you'.

question words

who	*quem*	keng
Who are you?	*Quem é você?*	keng e *vo*·se
what	*(o) que*	(o) ke
What's wrong?	*O que é que há?*	o ke e ke a
which/what	*qual/quais* sg/pl	kwow/kais
What's the best restaurant in the city?	*Qual é o melhor restaurante da cidade?*	kwow e o me·*lyorr* hes·tow·*rang*·te daa see·*daa*·de
where	*onde*	*ong*·de
Where is the Australian Embassy?	*Onde fica a embaixada Australiana?*	*ong*·de fee·kaa aa eng·bai·*shaa*·daa ows·traa·lee·*a*·na
when	*quando*	*kwang*·do
When is the flight?	*Quando sai o vôo?*	*kwang*·do sai o *vo*·o
how/by what means	*como é que*	*ko*·mo e ke
How do I find the bus station?	*Como é que vou para a rodoviária?*	*ko*·mo e ke vow *paa*·raa aa ho·do·vee·*aa*·ryaa
how much/ how many?	*quanto/a* m/f *quantos/quantas* m/f pl	*kwang*·to/*kwang*·taa *kwang*·tos/ *kwang*·taas
How much is it?	*Quanto custa?*	*kwang*·to *koos*·taa
why	*por que*	porr ke
Why are we stopping here?	*Por que estamos parando aqui?*	porr ke es·*ta*·mos paa·*raang*·do aa·*kee*

some

The plural forms of the words for 'a/an' (*um* and *uma*) are used to express the English 'some'. If what you're referring to is masculine plural, use *uns*, and if it's feminine plural, use *umas*.

I'd like some headache pills.
> *Quero uns comprimidos*   ke·ro oongs kong·pree·*mee*·dos
> *para dor de cabeça.*   paa·raa dorr de kaa·*be*·saa
> (lit: I-like some pills for
> pain of head)

I've had a few to drink.
> *Tomei umas e outras.*   to·*may* oo·maas e o·traas
> (lit: I-drank some and
> others)

Also see **a/an** and **gender**.

somebody's

The simplest way of indicating possession is by using the preposition *de* (from), followed by the person who's the owner of the thing. You can only do this with proper nouns (for people or places).

It's Carla's backpack.
> *É a mochila de Carla.*   e aa mo·*shee*·laa de *karr*·laa
> (lit: it-is the backpack
> of Carla)

See also **possession**.

the

There are four words that correspond to the English article 'the'. The form you use is determined by the gender and number of the noun the article is used with:

masculine	o sg	o trem o treng	the train
	os pl	os trens os treng	the trains
feminine	a sg	a mochila a mo·shee·la	the backpack
	as pl	as mochilas a mo·shee·la	the backpacks

Also see **gender** and **more than one**.

this & that

To refer to or point at a person or object, use one of the following forms (known as demonstratives) before the noun, depending on whether the person or object you're referring to is close or further away, masculine or feminine, and singular or plural:

	singular		plural	
	masculine	feminine	masculine	feminine
close	este	esta	estes	estas
away	aquele	aquela	aqueles	aquelas

Is this seat free?

Este lugar está vago?   es·te loo·gaarr es·taa vaa·go
(lit: this seat it-is free)

This view is wonderful.

Esta vista é	es·taa *vees*·taa e
maravilhosa.	maa·raa·vee·*lyo*·zaa
(lit: this view it-is wonderful)	

These forms can also be used on their own without an accompanying noun – meaning 'this (one)', 'that (one)', 'these' and 'those'.

Does this market open every day?

Este mercado abre todos	es·te merr·*kaa*·do *aa*·bre *to*·dos
os dias?	os *dee*·aas
(lit: this market open all	
the days)	

Those are Brazilian.

Aqueles são brasileiros.	a·*ke*·les sowng braa·zee·*lay*·ros
(lit: those they-are	
Brazilians)	

Also see **pointing something out**.

verbs

Brazilian Portuguese has three types of verbs: those ending in *-ar* (eg, *morar*, 'to live'), those ending in *-er* (eg, *comer*, 'to eat') and those ending in *-ir* (eg, *partir*, 'to leave'). Despite this, the present tense verb endings for each person ('I', 'you', 'we' etc) are very similar for all three so you can recognise them easily:

	-ar	-er	-ir
I	-o		
you/he/she/it	-a	-e	
we	-amos	-emos	-imos
you/they	-am	-em	

As in any language, some verbs are irregular in Brazilian Portuguese. The most important ones are *ser*, *estar* and *ter* (see **be** and **have**).

word order

Generally, the word order of a sentence is the same as in English (subject-verb-object).

I'd like a room.
> *Eu quero um quarto.*　　　*e·oo ke·ro oom kwaarr·to*
> (lit: I I-like a room)

yes/no questions

When asking a question, simply make a statement, but raise your intonation inquisitively towards the end of the sentence, as you would in English.

Do you speak English?
> *Você fala inglês?*　　　*vo·se faa·laa eeng·gles*
> (lit: you speak-you English)

If what you're doing is really making a statement but you're requesting confirmation or agreement, you can put the tag *não é* (lit: not it-is) on the end.

John lives in Rio, doesn't he?
> *João mora no Rio,*　　　*zho·owng mo·raa no hee·o*
> *não é?*　　　nowng e
> (lit: John lives-he in Rio
>   not it-is)

In rapid everyday speech the tag *não é* sounds more like ne.

language difficulties
dificuldades com a lingua

Do you speak (English)?
Você fala (inglês)?
vo·*se* faa·laa (eeng·*gles*)

Does anyone speak (English)?
Alguém aqui fala (inglês)?
ow·*geng* aa·*kee* faa·laa (eeng·*gles*)

Do you understand?
Você entende?
vo·*se* eng·*teng*·de

Yes, I understand.
Sim, entendo.
seeng eng·*teng*·do

No, I don't understand.
Não, não entendo.
nowng nowng eng·*teng*·do

I speak (English).
Eu falo (inglês).
e·oo faa·lo (eeng·*gles*)

I don't speak (Portuguese).
Eu não falo (português).
e·oo faa·lo (porr·too·*ges*)

I speak a little.
Eu falo um pouquinho.
e·oo faa·lo oom po·*kee*·nyo

I (don't) understand.
Eu (não) entendo.
e·oo (nowng) eng·*teng*·do

What does 'bem-vindo' mean?
O que quer dizer 'bem-vindo'?
o ke kerr dee·*zerr* beng *veeng*·do

How do you ...?	*Como se ...?*	*ko*·mo se ...
pronounce this	*pronuncia isto*	pro·noong·*see*·aa *ees*·to
write 'ajuda'	*escreve 'ajuda'*	es·*kre*·ve aa·*zhoo*·daa

Could you please ...?	*Você poderia ... por favor?*	vo·*se* po·de·*ree*·aa ... porr faa·*vorr*
repeat that	*repetir isto*	he·pe·*teerr ees*·to
speak more slowly	*falar mais devagar*	faa·*laarr* mais de·vaa·*gaarr*
write it down	*escrever num papel*	es·kre·*verr* noom paa·*pel*

false friends

Beware of false friends – words which can look and sound like English words but have a different meaning altogether.

atualmente   ak·twow·*meng*·te   nowadays
  not 'actually' which is *na verdade*, na verr·*da*·de

longe   *long*·zhe   far away
  not 'long' which is *comprido* m, kong·*pree*·do or
  comprida f, kong·*pree*·daa

magazine   ma·ga·*zeen*   department store
  not 'magazine' which is *revista*, he·*vees*·ta

novela   no·*ve*·la   soap opera
  not 'novel' which is *romance*, ho·*mang*·se

pretender   pre·*teng*·de   intend
  not 'pretend' which is *fingir*, feeng·*geer*

puxar   poo·*shaarr*   pull
  not 'push' which is *empurrar*, eng·poo·raarr

sorte   *sorr*·te   luck
  not 'sort' which is *typo*, *tee*·po

numbers & amounts
números & quantidades

cardinal numbers

números cardinais

0	zero	ze·ro	6	seis	says
1	um	oom	7	sete	se·te
2	dois	doys	8	oito	oy·to
3	três	tres	9	nove	naw·ve
4	quatro	kwaa·tro	10	dez	dez
5	cinco	seeng·ko			

11	onze	ong·ze
12	doze	do·ze
13	treze	tre·ze
14	quatorze	kaa·torr·ze
15	quinze	keeng·ze
16	dezesseis	de·ze·says
17	dezesete	de·ze·se·te
18	dezoito	de·zoy·to
19	dezenove	de·ze·naw·ve
20	vinte	veeng·te
21	vinte e um	veeng·te e oom
22	vinte e dois	veeng·te e doys
30	trinta	treeng·taa
40	quarenta	kwaa·reng·taa
50	cinquenta	seen·kweng·taa
60	sessenta	se·seng·taa
70	setenta	se·teng·taa
80	oitenta	oy·teng·taa
90	noventa	no·veng·taa
100	cem	seng
200	duzentos	doo·zeng·tos
1,000	mil	mee·oo
1,000,000	um milhão	oom mee·lyowng

ordinal numbers

1st	*primeiro/primeira* m/f	pree·*may*·ro/pree·*may*·raa
2nd	*segundo/segunda* m/f	se·*goong*·do/se·*goong*·daa
3rd	*terceiro/terceira* m/f	terr·*say*·ro/terr·*say*·raa
4th	*quarto/quarta* m/f	kwaarr·to/kwaarr·taa
5th	*quinto/quinta* m/f	*keeng*·to/*keeng*·taa

fractions

a quarter	*um quarto*	oom *kwaarr*·to
a third	*um terço*	oom *terr*·so
a half	*metade*	me·*taa*·de
three-quarters	*três quartos*	tres *kwaarr*·tos
all (of it)	*inteiro/inteira* m/f	eeng·*tay*·ro/eeng·*tay*·ra
all (of them)	*tudo/tuda* m/f	*too*·do/*too*·daa
none	*nenhum*	ne·*yoom*

useful amounts

How much?	*Quanto?*	*kwang*·to
How many?	*Quantos/Quantas?* m/f	*kwang*·tos/*kwan*·taas
Please give me …	*Por favor me dê …*	porr faa·*vorr* me de …
a few	*alguns*	ow·*goons*
(just) a little	*(só) um pouquinho*	(saw) oom po·*kee*·nyo
a lot	*muito*	*mweeng*·to
less	*menos*	*me*·nos
many	*muitos/muitas* m/f	*mweeng*·tos/*mweeng*·taas
more	*mais*	mais
some	*um pouco*	oom *po*·ko

telling the time

The 24-hour clock is usually used when telling the time in Brazilian Portuguese. Alternatively, you can add *da manhã* (in the morning), *da tarde* (in the afternoon), or *da noite* (in the evening) to specify the exact time.

Time is given using a plural form of the verb 'be', *ser* (*são*), except in the case of 1 o'clock, when the singular form (*é*) is used.

What time is it?	*Que horas são?*	ke *aw*·raas sowng
It's (one) o'clock.	*É (um) hora.*	e (oom) *aw*·raa
It's (ten) o'clock.	*São (dez) horas.*	sowng (des) *aw*·raas
Five past (ten).	*(Dez) e cinco.*	(des) e *seeng*·ko
Quarter past (ten).	*(Dez) e quinze.*	(des) e *keeng*·ze
Half past (ten).	*(Dez) e meia.*	(des) e *may*·aa

After the half hour, state the number of minutes to the next hour until that hour arrives.

Quarter to (ten).	*Quinze para as (dez).*	*keeng*·ze *paa*·raa aas (des)
Twenty to (ten).	*Vinte para as (dez).*	*veeng*·te *paa*·raa aas (des)
in the morning	*da manhã*	daa ma·*nyang*
in the afternoon	*da tarde*	daa *taarr*·de
in the evening	*da noite*	daa *noy*·te
At what time ...?	*A que horas ...?*	aa ke *aw*·raas ...
At (ten).	*Às (dez).*	aas (des)
At (7.57pm).	*Às (sete e cinquenta e sete da noite).*	aas (*se*·te e seeng·*kweng*·taa e *se*·te daa *noy*·te)

days of the week

Monday	*segunda-feira*	se·*goong*·daa·*fay*·raa
Tuesday	*terça-feira*	terr·saa·*fay*·raa
Wednesday	*quarta-feira*	kwaarr·taa·*fay*·raa
Thursday	*quinta-feira*	keeng·taa·*fay*·raa
Friday	*sexta-feira*	ses·taa·*fay*·raa
Saturday	*sábado*	*saa*·baa·doo
Sunday	*domingo*	do·*meeng*·go

the calendar

o calendário

months

January	*janeiro*	zha·*nay*·ro
February	*fevereiro*	fe·ve·*ray*·ro
March	*março*	*marr*·so
April	*abril*	aa·*bree*·oo
May	*maio*	*maa*·yo
June	*junho*	*zhoo*·nyo
July	*julho*	*zhoo*·lyo
August	*agosto*	aa·*gos*·to
September	*setembro*	se·*teng*·bro
October	*outubro*	o·*too*·bro
November	*novembro*	no·*veng*·bro
December	*dezembro*	de·*zeng*·bro

dates

What date is it today?
Qual é a data de hoje? kwow e aa *daa*·taa de o·zhe

It's (18 October).
Hoje é dia (dezoito de outubro). o·zhe e *dee*·aa (de·*zoy*·to de o·*too*·bro)

seasons

summer	*verão* m	ve·*rowng*
autumn	*outono* m	o·*to*·no
winter	*inverno* m	een·*verr*·no
spring	*primavera* f	pree·maa·*ve*·raa
... season	*época* f *de* ...	*e*·po·kaa de ...
dry	*seca*	*se*·kaa
monsoon	*monção*	mong·*sowng*
wet	*chuvas*	*shoo*·vaas

present

now	*agora*	aa·*go*·raa
this ...		
afternoon	*esta tarde*	es·taa *taarr*·de
morning	*esta manhã*	es·taa ma·*nyang*
month	*este mês*	*es*·te mes
week	*esta semana*	es·taa se·*ma*·naa
year	*este ano*	*es*·te *a*·no
today	*hoje*	o·zhe
tonight	*hoje à noite*	o·zhe aa *noy*·te

past

(three days) ago	*(três dias) atrás*	(tres *dee*·aas) aa·*traas*
day before	*antes de*	*ang*·tes de
yesterday	*ontem*	*ong*·teng
yesterday	*ontem*	*ong*·teng
last ...		
month	*mês passado*	mes paa·*saa*·do
night	*noite passada*	*noy*·te paa·*saa*·daa
week	*semana*	se·*ma*·naa
	passada	paa·*saa*·daa
year	*ano passado*	*a*·no paa·*saa*·do

since (May)	desde (Maio)	des·de (maa·yo)
yesterday ...	ontem ...	ong·teng ...
afternoon	à tarde	aa taarr·de
evening	à noite	aa noy·te
morning	de manhã	de ma·nyang

future

day after	depois de	de·poys de
tomorrow	amanhã	aa·ma·nyang
in (six days)	daqui a	daa·kee aa
	(seis dias)	(says dee·aas)
tomorrow	amanhã	aa·ma·nyang
next ...	... que vem	... ke veng
month	mês	mes
week	semana	se·ma·naa
year	ano	a·no
tomorrow ...	amanhã ...	aa·ma·nyang ...
afternoon	à tarde	aa taarr·de
evening	à noite	aa noy·te
morning	de manhã	de ma·nyang
until (June)	até (junho)	aa·te (zhoo·nyo)

during the day

afternoon	tarde f	taar·de
day	dia m	dee·aa
evening	noite f	noy·te
midday	meio dia m	may·oo dee·a
midnight	meia noite f	may·aa noy·te
morning	manhã f	ma·nyang
night	noite f	noy·te
sunrise	nascer m do sol	naa·serr do sol
sunset	pôr m do sol	porr do sol

How much is it?
Quanto custa? — kwang·to koos·taa

Can you write down the price?
Você pode escrever o preço? — vo·se po·de es·kre·verr o pre·so

That's too expensive.
Está muito caro. — es·taa mweeng·to kaa·ro

I don't want to pay the full price.
*Não quero pagar o
preço todo.* — nowng ke·ro paa·gaarr o
pre·so to·do

Do you accept …?	*Vocês aceitam …?*	vo·ses aa·say·tang …
credit cards	*cartão de crédito*	kaarr·towng de kre·dee·to
debit cards	*saque eletrônico*	sa·kee e·le·tro·nee·ko
travellers cheques	*traveller cheque*	tra·ve·ler she·kee
I'd like to …	*Gostaria de …*	gos·taa·ree·aa de …
cash a cheque	*descontar um cheque*	des·kon·taarr oom she·kee
change a travellers cheque	*trocar traveller cheques*	tro·kaarr traa·ve·ler she·kes
change money	*trocar dinheiro*	tro·kaar dee·nyay·ro
get a cash advance	*fazer um saque adiantado*	fa·zerr oom saa·ke aa·dee·an·taa·do
withdraw money	*retirar dinheiro*	he·tee·raarr dee·nyay·ro

Can I use my credit card to withdraw money?
Posso usar o meu — po·so oo·*zaarr* o *me*·oo
cartão de crédito para — kaar·*towng* de *kre*·dee·to *paa*·raa
retirar dinheiro? — he·tee·*raarr* dee·*nyay*·ro

Where's …?	*Onde tem …?*	ong·de teng …
an automatic	*um caixa*	oom *kai*·shaa
teller machine	*automático*	ow·to·*maa*·tee·ko
a foreign	*uma loja de*	*oo*·maa *lo*·zhaa de
exchange office	*câmbio*	*kam*·bee·o

What's the …?	*Qual …?*	kwow …
exchange rate	*o câmbio do*	o *kang*·byo do
	dia	*dee*·aa
charge for	*a taxa*	aa *taa*·shaa
that	*cobrada*	ko·*braa*·daa

I'd like …, please.	*Gostaria de …*	gos·taa·*ree*·aa …
a refund	*ser*	serr
	reembolsado	he·eng·bol·*saa*·do
my change	*ter o meu troco*	terr o *me*·oo *tro*·ko
to return this	*devolver isto*	de·vol·*verr* ees·to

Could I have a …,	*Pode me dar …,*	*po*·de me daarr …
please?	*por favor?*	porr faa·*vorr*
bag	*um saco*	oom *saa*·ko
receipt	*o recibo*	o he·*see*·bo

getting around

andando por aí

Which ... goes to (Niterói)?	*Qual o ... que vai para (Niterói)?*	kwow o ... ke vai *paa*·raa (nee·te·*roy*)
boat	*barco*	*baarr*·ko
bus	*ônibus*	*o*·nee·boos
plane	*avião*	aa·vee·*owng*
train	*trem*	treng

When's the ... (bus)?	*Quando sai o ... (ônibus)?*	*kwang*·do sai o ... (*o*·nee·boos)
first	*primeiro*	pree·*may*·ro
last	*último*	*ool*·tee·mo
next	*próximo*	*pro*·see·mo

What time does it leave?
A que horas sai? — aa ke *aw*·raas sai

What time does it get to (Paraty)?
A que horas chega em (Paraty)? — aa ke *aw*·raas *she*·gaa eng (paa·*raa*·tee)

How long will it be delayed?
Quanto tempo vai atrasar? — *kwang*·to *teng*·po vai aa·*traa*·zaarr

Is this seat free?
Este lugar está vago? — *es*·te loo·*gaarr* es·*taa* vaa·go

That's my seat.
Este é o meu lugar. — *es*·te e o *me*·oo loo·*gaarr*

Please tell me when we get to (Búzios).
Por favor me avise quando chegarmos à (Búzios). — porr faa·*vor* me aa·*vee*·ze *kwang*·do she·*gaarr*·mos aa (*boo*·zee·os)

Please stop here.
Por favor pare aqui.   por faa·*vorr* paa·re aa·*kee*

How long do we stop here?
Quanto tempo ficaremos   kwang·to teng·po fee·ka·*re*·mos
parados aqui?   paa·*raa*·dos aa·*kee*

tickets

passagem

Where do I buy a ticket?
Onde que eu compro a   ong·de ke e·oo kong·pro aa
passagem?   paa·*sa*·zheng

Do I need to book?
Preciso reservar?   pre·*see*·zo he·zer·*vaarr*

A ... ticket (to Petrópolis).	*Uma passagem de ... (para Petrópolis).*	oo·maa paa·*sa*·zheng de ... (*paa*·raa pe·*tro*·po·lees)
1st-class	*primeira classe*	pree·*may*·raa *klaa*·se
2nd-class	*segunda classe*	se·*goom*·daa *klaa*·se
child's	*criança*	kree·*ang*·sa
one-way	*ida*	ee·daa
return	*ida e volta*	ee·daa e *vol*·taa
student's	*estudante*	es·too·*dang*·te

I'd like a/an ... seat.	*Gostaria de um lugar ...*	gos·taa·*ree*·aa de oom loo·*gaarr* ...
aisle	*no corredor*	no ko·he·*dorr*
(non-)smoking	*na área de (não) fumantes*	na aa·re·aa de (nowng) foo·*mang*·tes
window	*na janela*	naa zhaa·*ne*·laa

Is there (a) ...?	*Tem ...?*	teng ...
air-	*ar*	aarr
conditioning	*condicionado*	kong·dee·syo·*naa*·do
blanket	*cobertor*	ko·berr·*torr*
toilet	*banheiro*	ba·*nyay*·ro

I'd like to ... my ticket, please.	Gostaria de ... minha passagem, por favor.	gos·taa·*ree*·aa de ... *mee*·nya paa·*saa*·zheng porr faa·*vor*
cancel	cancelar	kang·se·*laarr*
change	trocar	tro·*kaarr*
confirm	confirmar	kong·feerr·*maarr*

How long does the trip take?

Quanto tempo de viagem? kwang·to teng·po de vee·*aa*·zheng

Is it a direct route?

É uma rota direta? e oo·maa ho·taa dee·*re*·taa

---

listen for ...

aa·traa·*zaa*·do	atrasado	**delayed**
aa·*zheng*·te de vee·*aa*·zhengs	agente de viagens	**travel agent**
bee·lye·te·*ree*·aa	bilheteria	**ticket window**
es·te/aa·*ke*·le	este/aquele	**this/that one**
kang·se·*laa*·do	cancelado	**cancelled**
o·*raa*·ryo	horário	**timetable**
plaa·taa·*forr*·maa	plataforma	**platform**
shay·o	cheio	**full**

luggage

bagagem

Where can I find ...?	Onde posso encontrar ...?	ong·de po·so eng·kon·*traarr* ...
a luggage locker	um guarda volumes	oom *gwaarr*·daa vo·*loo*·mes
a trolley	um carrinho	oom kaa·*hee*·nyo
the baggage counter	o balcão de bagagem	o baal·*kowng* de baa·*gaa*·zheng
the left-luggage office	o balcão de guarda volumes	o baal·*kowng* de *gwaarr*·daa vo·*loo*·mes

My luggage	Minha	*mee*·nya
has been ...	bagagem foi ...	baa·*gaa*·zheng foy ...
damaged	danificada	da·nee·fee·*kaa*·daa
lost	perdida	perr·*dee*·daa
stolen	roubada	ho·*baa*·daa

That's (not) mine.
Isto (não) é meu.   ees·to (nowng) e me·oo

Can I have some coins/tokens?
Pode me dar umas   *po*·de me daarr oo·maas
moedas/fichas?   mo·e·daas/*fee*·shaas

plane

avião

Where does flight (RG 615) arrive/depart?
De onde sai/chega o vôo   de *ong*·de sai/*she*·gaa o *vo*·o
(RG 615)?   (*e*·he ge say·*sen*·tos e *keen*·ze)

Where's ...?	Onde fica ...?	*ong*·de *fee*·kaa ...
arrivals	portão de	porr·*towng* de
	chegada	she·*gaa*·daa
departures	portão de	porr·*towng* de
	partida	paarr·*tee*·daa
gate (20)	portão (vinte)	porr·*towng* (*veeng*·te)
the airport	o ônibus do	o *o*·nee·boos do
shuttle	aeroporto	aa·e·ro·*porr*·to

For phrases about getting through customs, see **border crossing**, page 49.

PRACTICAL

40

boat

barco

What's the sea like today?
Como está o mar hoje? ko·mo es·*taa* o maarr o·zhe

Are there life jackets?
Tem colete salva-vidas? teng ko·*le*·te sow·vaa·vee·daas

What island/beach is this?
Que ilha/praia é esta? ke ee·*lyaa*/prai·aa e es·taa

I feel seasick.
Estou enjoado/ es·to eng·zho·*aa*·do/
enjoada. m/f eng·zho·*aa*·daa

cabin	cabine f	kaa·*bee*·ne
car deck	deck m de carro	de·kee de *kaa*·ho
captain	capitão m	kaa·pee·*towng*
deck	deck m	de·kee
ferry	barca f	*baarr*·kaa
hammock	rede f	*he*·de
lifeboat	barco m	*baarr*·ko
	salva-vidas	sow·vaa·vee·daas
life jacket	colete m	ko·*le*·te
	salva-vidas	sow·vaa·vee·daas
yacht	iate m	ee·*aa*·te

transport

41

bus & coach

How often do buses come?
*Qual a frequência dos
ônibus?*
kwow aa fre·*kweng*·see·aa dos
o·nee·boos

Is this the bus to (Campinas)?
*Este ônibus vai para
(Campinas)?*
es·te o·nee·boos vai *paa*·raa
(kang·*pee*·naas)

Does it stop at (Ilheús)?
Ele para em (Ilheús)?
e·le *paa*·raa eng (ee·*lye*·oos)

What's the next stop?
*Qual é a próxima
parada?*
kwow e aa *pro*·see·maa
paa·*raa*·daa

I'd like to get off at (Ipanema).
*Gostaria de saltar
em (Ipanema).*
gos·taa·*ree*·aa de sow·*taarr*
eng (ee·paa·*ne*·maa)

city/local bus	*ônibus* m *local*	o·nee·boos lo·*kow*
intercity bus	*ônibus* m	o·nee·boos
	inter urbano	eeng·terr oorr·*ba*·no

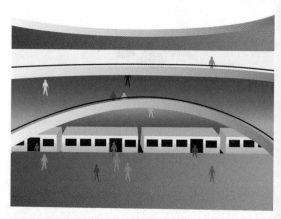

train

What station is this?
Que estação é esta?   ke es·taa·*sowng* e es·taa

What's the next station?
Qual é a próxima   kwow e aa *pro*·see·maa
estação?   es·taa·*sowng*

Does it stop at (Ouro Preto)?
Ele pára em (Ouro Preto)?   e·le *paa*·raa eng (*o*·ro *pre*·to)

Do I need to change?
Preciso trocar de trem?   pre·*see*·so tro·*kaarr* de treng

Is it direct/express?
É direto/rápido?   e dee·*re*·to/*haa*·pee·do

Which carriage   *Qual o vagão …?*   kwow o vaa·*gowng* …
is …?
  1st class   *de primeira*   de pree·*may*·raa
    classe   *klaa*·se
  for (Sabará)   *para (Sabará)*   *paa*·raa (saa·baa·*raa*)

taxi

I'd like a taxi …   *Gostaria de*   gos·taa·*ree*·aa de
  marcar um   maarr·*kaarr* oom
  táxi …   *taak*·see …
  at (9am)   *para as*   *paa*·raa aas
    (nove da   (*naw*·ve daa
    manhã)   ma·*nyang*)
  now   *agora*   aa·*go*·raa
  tomorrow   *amanhã*   aa·ma·*nyang*

Where's the taxi rank?
Onde fica a fila de   ong·de *fee*·kaa aa *fee*·laa de
táxi?   *taak*·see

Is this taxi free?
Este táxi está livre?   es·te *taak*·see es·*taa lee*·vre

Please put the meter on.
Por favor ligue o taxímetro.
porr fa·*vorr* lee·ge o taak·*see*·me·tro

How much is it to …?
Quanto custa até …?
kwang·to koos·taa aa·te …

Please take me to (this address).
Me leve para este endereço por favor.
me *le*·ve *paa*·raa *es*·te eng·de·*re*·so porr faa·*vorr*

Please …	*Por favor …*	porr faa·*vorr* …
slow down	*vai mais devagar*	vai *mais* de·vaa·*gaarr*
stop here	*pare aqui*	*paa*·re aa·*kee*
wait here	*espere aqui*	es·*pe*·re aa·*kee*

car & motorbike

hire

I'd like to hire a/an …	*Gostaria de alugar …*	gos·taa·*ree*·aa de aa·loo·*gaarr* …
4WD	*um carro quatro por quatro*	oom *kaa*·ho *kwaa*·tro porr *kwaa*·tro
automatic	*um automático*	oom ow·to·*maa*·tee·ko
car	*um carro*	oom *kaa*·ho
manual	*um manual*	oom ma·noo·*ow*
motorbike	*uma motocicleta*	*oo*·ma mo·to·see·*kle*·ta
with …	*com …*	kong …
a driver	*motorista*	mo·to·*rees*·taa
air-conditioning	*ar condicionado*	aarr kong·dee·syo·*naa*·

How much for daily/weekly hire?
Quanto custa para alugar por dia/ semana?
kwang·to koos·taa paa·raa aa·loo·*gaarr* porr dee·aa/ se·*ma*·naa

Does that include insurance/mileage?
Inclui seguro e kilometragem?
eeng·*kloo*·ee se·*goo*·ro e kee·lo·me·*traa*·zheng

Do you have a guide to the road rules in English?
Você teria um guia de ruas em inglês?
vo·*se* te·*ree*·aa oom *gee*·aa de *hoo*·aas eng eeng·*gles*

Do you have a road map?
Você teria um mapa de ruas?
vo·*se* te·*ree*·aa oom *maa*·paa de *hoo*·aas

on the road

Is this the road to (Salvador)?
Esta é a estrada para (Salvador)?
es·*taa* e aa es·*traa*·daa paa·raa (sow·*vaa*·dorr)

Where's a petrol station?
Onde tem um posto de gasolina?
ong·de teng oom *pos*·to de gaa·zo·*lee*·naa

Please fill it up.
Enche o tanque, por favor.
eng·she o *tang*·ke porr faa·*vorr*

I'd like (30) litres.
Coloque (trinta) litros.
ko·*lo*·ke (*treen*·ta) *lee*·tros

diesel	*diesel* m	*dee*·sel
LPG	*gás* m	gas
unleaded	*gasolina* f *comum*	gaa·zo·*lee*·naa ko·*moong*

Can you check the ...?	Pode checar ...?	po·de she·kaarr ...
oil	o óleo	o o·lyo
tyre pressure	os pneus	os pee·ne·oos
water	a água	aa aa·gwaa

What's the speed limit?
Qual o limite de velocidade?
kwow o lee·mee·te de ve·lo·see·daa·de

(How long) Can I park here?
(Quanto tempo) Posso estacionar aqui?
(kwang·to teng·po) po·so es·taa·syo·naarr aa·kee

Do I have to pay?
Tem que pagar?
teng ke paa·gaarr

problems

The car has broken down (at Manaus).
O carro quebrou (em Manaus).
o kaa·ho ke·bro (eng maa·nows)

The motorbike won't start.
A motocicleta náo está pegando.
a mo·to·se·kle·taa nowng es·ta pe·gang·do

I need a mechanic.
Preciso de um mecânico.
pre·see·so de oom me·ka·nee·ko

I've had an accident.
 Sofri um acidente.   so-*free* oom aa-see-*deng*-te

I have a flat tyre.
 Meu pneu furou.   *me*-oo pee-*ne*-oo foo-*ro*

I've lost my car keys.
 Perdi a chave do carro.   perr-*dee* a *shaa*-ve do *kaa*-ho

I've locked the keys inside.
 Tranquei a chave dentro   trang-*kay* aa *sha*-ve *deng*-tro
 do carro.   do *kaa*-ho

I've run out of petrol.
 Estou sem gasolina.   es-*to* seng gaa-zo-*lee*-naa

Can you fix it (today)?
 Você pode consertar   vo-*se po*-de kong-serr-*taarr*
 (hoje)?   (*o*-zhe)

How long will it take?
 Quanto tempo vai levar?   *kwang*-to *teng*-po vai le-*vaarr*

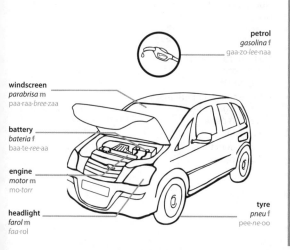

petrol
gasolina f
gaa-zo-*lee*-naa

windscreen
parabrisa m
paa-raa-*bree*-zaa

battery
bateria f
baa-te-*ree*-aa

engine
motor m
mo-*torr*

headlight
farol m
faa-rol

tyre
pneu f
pee-*ne*-oo

bicycle

I'd like ...	Queria ...	ke·*ree*·aa ...
my bicycle repaired	consertar a minha bicicleta	kong·serr·*taarr* a *mee*·nyaa bee·see·*kle*·taa
to buy a bicycle	comprar uma bicicleta	kong·*praarr* oo·maa bee·see·*kle*·taa
to hire a bicycle	alugar uma bicicleta	aa·loo·*gaarr* oo·maa bee·see·*kle*·taa

I'd like a ... bike.	Queria uma bicicleta ...	ke·*ree*·aa oo·maa bee·see·*kle*·taa ...
mountain	de montanha	de mong·*ta*·nya
racing	de corrida	de ko·*hee*·daa
second-hand	de segunda mão	de se·*goong*·daa mowng

How much is it per ...?	Quanto custa por ...?	*kwang*·to *koos*·taa porr ...
day	dia	*dee*·aa
hour	hora	*aw*·raa

Do I need a helmet?
Preciso usar capacete?
pre·*see*·so oo·*zaarr* kaa·paa·*se*·te

Is there a bicycle-path map?
Existe algum mapa de rotas para bicicleta?
e·*zees*·te ow·*goom maa*·paa de ho·taas paa·raa bee·see·*kle*·taa

I have a puncture.
Furou o pneu.
foo·*ro* o pee·*ne*·oo

border crossing
cruzando a fronteira

I'm …	Estou …	es·to …
in transit	em trânsito	eng trang·zee·to
on business	à negócios	aa ne·go·syos
on holiday	à turismo	aa too·rees·mo
I'm here for …	Vou ficar por …	vo fee·kaarr porr …
(10) days	(dez) dias	(dez) dee·aas
(two) months	(dois) meses	(doys) me·ses
(three) weeks	(três) semanas	(tres) se·ma·naas

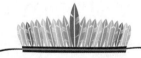

listen for …

eng groo·po	em grupo	**group**
kong aa faa·mee·lya	com a família	**family**
paa·saa·porr·te	passaporte	**passport**
so·zee·nyo	sozinho	**alone**
vees·to	visto	**visa**

I'm going to (Recife).
Estou indo para
(Recife).
es·to eeng·do paa·raa
(he·see·fe)

I'm staying at the (Ipanema Hotel).
Estou no (Hotel Ipanema). es·to no (o·tel ee·pa·nee·maa)

The child is on this passport.
As criança está
neste passaporte.
aas kree·ang·saa es·taa
nes·te paa·saa·porr·te

I have nothing to declare.

Não tenho nada a declarar.	nowng te·nyo naa·daa aa de·klaa·raarr	

I have something to declare.
Tenho algo a declarar. — te·nyo ow·go aa de·klaa·rarr

Do I have to declare this?
Preciso declarar isto? — pre·see·so de·klaa·raarr ees·to

That's (not) mine.
Isto (não) é meu. — ees·to (nowng) e me·oo

I didn't know I had to declare it.
Não sabia que tinha que declarar isto. — nowng saa·bee·aa ke tee·nyaa ke de·klaa·raarr ees·to

directions
direções

Where's ...?	Onde fica ...?	ong·de fee·kaa ...
a bank	o banco	o bang·ko
a market	o mercado	o merr·kaa·do
the tourist office	a secretaria de turismo	aa se·kre·taa·ree·aa de too·rees·mo

Can you show me (on the map)?
Você poderia me mostrar (no mapa)? — vo·se po·de·ree·aa me mos·traarr (no maa·paa)

What's the address?
Qual é o endereço? — kwow e o eng·de·re·so

How far is it?
Qual a distância daqui? — kwow aa dees·tang·syaa daa·kee

How do I get there?
Como é que eu chego lá? — ko·mo e ke e·oo she·go laa

It's ...	Fica ...	fee·kaa ...
behind ...	atrás ...	aa·traaz ...
close	perto	perr·to
here	aqui	a·kee
in front of ...	na frente de ...	naa freng·te de ...
near ...	perto ...	perr·to ...
next to ...	ao lado de ...	ow laa·do de ...
on the corner	na esquina	na es·kee·naa
opposite ...	do lado oposto ...	do laa·do o·pos·to ...
straight ahead	em frente	eng freng·te
there	lá	laa

north	norte	norr·te
south	sul	sool
east	leste	les·te
west	oeste	o·es·te

directions

51

by bus	de ônibus	de o·nee·boos
by taxi	de táxi	de taak·see
by train	de trem	de treng
on foot	a pé	aa pe

Turn ...	Vire ...	vee·re ...
at the corner	à esquina	aa es·kee·naa
at the	no sinal de	no see·now de
traffic lights	trânsito	trang·zee·to
left	à esquerda	aa es·kerr·daa
right	à direita	aa dee·ray·taa

What ... is this?	Que ...?	ke ...
avenue	avenida	aa·ve·nee·daa
	é esta	e es·taa
lane	travessa é esta	traa·ve·saa e es·taa
street	rua é esta	hoo·aa e es·taa
village	vilarejo	vee·laa·re·zho
	é este	e es·te

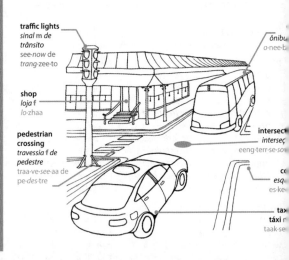

traffic lights
sinal m *de trânsito*
see·now de trang·zee·to

shop
loja f
lo·zhaa

pedestrian crossing
travessia f *de pedestre*
traa·ve·see·aa de pe·des·tre

ônibu
o·nee·b

interse
interse
eeng·terr·se·so

c
esq
es·ke

ta
táxi
taak·se

PRACTICAL

finding accommodation

buscando hospedagem

Where's a …?	Onde tem …?	ong·de teng …
bed and breakfast	uma pensão	oo·maa peng·sowng
camping ground	um local para acampamento	oom lo·kow paa·raa aa·kang·paa·meng·to
guesthouse	uma hospedaria	oo·maa os·pe·daa·ree·a
hotel	um hotel	oom o·tel
room	um quarto	oom kwaarr·to
youth hostel	um albergue da juventude	oom ow·berr·ge daa zhoo·veng·too·de

Can you recommend somewhere …?	Você pode recomendar algum lugar …?	vo·se po·de he·ko·meng·daarr ow·goom loo·gaarr …
cheap	barato	baa·raa·to
good	bom	bong
luxurious	de luxo	de loo·sho
nearby	perto daqui	perr·to daa·kee
romantic	romântico	ho·mang·tee·ko

What's the address?
Qual é o endereço? kwow e o en·de·re·so

For responses, see **directions**, page 51.

booking ahead & checking in

Do you have a ... room?	Tem um quarto de ...?	teng oom *kwaarr*·to de ...
double	casal	kaa·*zow*
single	solteiro	sol·*tay*·ro
twin	duplo	*doo*·plo

How much is it per ...?	Quanto custa por ...?	*kwang*·to *koos*·taa porr ...
night	noite	*noy*·te
person	pessoa	pe·*so*·aa
week	semana	se·*ma*·naa

I'd like to book a room, please.
*Eu gostaria de fazer
uma reserva, por favor.*
e·oo gos·taa·*ree*·aa de faa·*zerr*
oo·maa he·*zerr*·vaa porr faa·*vorr*

I have a reservation.
Eu tenho uma reserva.
e·oo *te*·nyo oo·maa he·*zerr*·vaa

My name's ...
Meu nome é ...
me·oo *no*·me e ...

For (three) nights/weeks.
*Para (três) noites/
semanas.*
paa·raa (tres) *noy*·tes/
se·*ma*·naas

From (July 2) to (July 6).
*De (dois de julho) até
(seis de julho).*
de (doys de *zhoo*·lyo) aa·*te*
(says de *zhoo*·lyo)

Can I see it?
Posso ver?
po·so verr

I'll take it.
Eu fico com ele.
e·oo *fee*·ko kong e·lee

signs

Banheiro	ba·*nyay*·ro	**Bathroom/ Toilet**
Não Tem Vaga	nowng teng *vaa*·gaa	**No Vacancy**
Tem Vaga	teng *vaa*·gaa	**Vacancy**

Do I need to pay upfront?

Tem que pagar	teng ke paa-*gaarr*	
adiantado?	aa-dee-ang-*taa*-do	

Can I pay ...?

	Posso pagar	po-so paa-*gaarr*
	com ...?	kong ...
by credit	*cartão de*	kaarr-*towng* de
card	*crédito*	kre-dee-to
by travellers	*travellers cheque*	tra-ve-lers she-kee
cheque		
in (US)	*dólar*	do-laarr
dollars	*(americano)*	(aa-me-ree-ka-no)

For other methods of payment, see **money**, page 35.

For other methods of payment, see **money**, page 35.

---

listen for ...

paa-raa *kwang*-taas	*Para quantas*	**How many**
noy-tes	*noites?*	**nights?**
he-se-pee-*sowng*	*recepção*	**reception**
paa-saa-*porr*-te	*passaporte*	**passport**
shaa-ve	*chave*	**key**
shay-o	*cheio*	**full**

---

requests & queries

pedidos & perguntas

When/Where is breakfast served?

Onde/Quando é servido	ong-de/*kwang*-do e serr-*vee*-do
o café da manhã?	o kaa-*fe* daa ma-*nyang*

Please wake me at (seven).

Por favor me acorde	porr faa-*vor* me aa-*kor*-de
às (sete).	aas (se-te)

Can I use the ...?

	Posso usar ...?	po-so oo-*zaarr* ...
kitchen	*a cozinha*	aa ko-*zee*-nyaa
laundry	*a lavanderia*	aa laa-vang-de-*ree*-aa
telephone	*o telefone*	o te-le-*fo*-ne

accommodation

Do you have a/an ...?	Tem ...?	teng ...
elevator	elevador	e·le·vaa·dorr
laundry service	serviço de lavanderia	serr·vee·so de laa·vang·de·ree·aa
message board	quadro de recados	kwaa·dro de he·kaa·dos
safe	cofre	ko·fre
swimming pool	piscina	pee·see·na

Do you ... here?	Vocês ...?	vo·ses ...
arrange tours	organizam passeios	orr·ga·nee·zang paa·say·os
change money	trocam dinheiro	tro·kang dee·nyay·ro

Could I have ..., please?	Pode me dar ..., por favor?	po·de me daarr ... porr faa·vorr
a mosquito net	um mosquiteiro	oom mos·kee·tay·ro
a receipt	um recibo	oom he·see·bo
an extra blanket	um outro cobertor	oom o·tro ko·berr·torr
my key	minha chave	mee·nyaa shaa·ve

local talk

dive	porcaria f	porr·kaa·ree·aa
rat-infested	infestado de rato	eeng·fes·taa·do de haa·to
top spot	ótimo lugar m	o·tee·mo loo·gaarr

Is there a message for me?
Tem recado para mim?   teng he·kaa·do paa·raa meeng

Can I leave a message for someone?
Posso deixar um
recado para alguém?   po·so day·shaarr oom
he·kaa·do paa·raa ow·geng

I'm locked out of my room.
Fiquei preso/presa fora
do quarto. m/f   fee·kay pre·so/pre·saa fo·raa
do kwaarr·to

complaints

It's too …	É muito …	e *mweeng*·to …
bright	*claro*	*klaa*·ro
cold	*frio*	*free*·o
dark	*escuro*	es·*koo*·ro
expensive	*caro*	*kaa*·ro
noisy	*barulhento*	baa·roo·*lyeng*·to
small	*pequeno*	pe·*ke*·no

This (pillow) isn't clean.
*Este (travesseiro) está   es·*te (traa·ve·*say*·ro) es·*taa*
sujo.   *soo*·zho

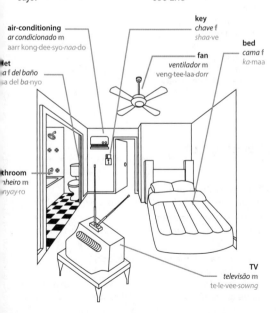

air-conditioning
ar condicionado m
aarr kong·dee·syo·*naa*·do

key
chave f
shaa·ve

bed
cama f
ka·maa

et
a f *del baño*
·a del *ba*·nyo

fan
ventilador m
veng·tee·laa·*dorr*

throom
heiro m
nyay·ro

TV
televisão m
te·le·vee·*sowng*

accommodation

57

The … doesn't	O … não está	o … nowng es·*taa*
work.	*funcionando.*	foong·syo·*nang*·do
air-	*ar*	aarr
conditioning	*condicionado*	kong·dee·syo·*naa*·do
fan	*ventilador*	veng·tee·laa·*dorr*
toilet	*banheiro*	ba·*nyay*·ro

Who is it?
  Quem é?   keng e
Just a moment.
  Um minutinho.   oom mee·noo·*tee*·nyo
Come in.
  Pode entrar.   po·de eng·*traarr*
Come back later, please.
  Volte mais tarde,   *vol*·te mais *taarr*·de
  por favor.   porr faa·*vorr*

checking out

fazendo o check out

What time is checkout?
  A que horas é o check out?   aa ke *aw*·raas e o shek owt
Can I have a late checkout?
  Posso fazer o check out   po·so faa·*zerr* o shek owt
  mais tarde?   mais *taar*·de
Can you call a taxi for me (for 11 o'clock)?
  Pode chamar um   po·de shaa·*maarr* oom
  taxi para mim   *taak*·see paa·ra meeng
  (para às onze horas)?   (*paa*·raa aas *ong*·ze *aw*·raas)

PRACTICAL

58

I'm leaving now.
Estou indo embora
agora.
es·*to eeng*·do eng·*bo*·raa
aa·*go*·raa

Can I leave my bags here?
Posso deixar minhas
malas aqui?
po·so day·*shaarr* mee·nyaas
maa·laas aa·*kee*

There's a mistake in the bill.
Houve um erro na conta.
o·ve oom e·ho naa *kong*·taa

I'll be back …	*Estarei de volta …*	es·taa·*ray* de *vol*·taa …
in (three) days	*em (três) dias*	eng (tres) *dee*·aas
on (Tuesday)	*na (terça-feira)*	naa (*terr*·saa·*fay*·raa)

Could I have	*Pode devolver …,*	po·de de·vol·*verr* …
my …, please?	*por favor?*	por faa·*vorr*
deposit	*o meu*	o *me*·oo
	depósito	de·*po*·zee·to
passport	*o meu*	o *me*·oo
	passaporte	paa·saa·*porr*·te
valuables	*os meus*	os *me*·oos
	objetos de	o·bee·*zhe*·tos de
	valor	vaa·*lorr*

I had a great stay, thank you.
Foi ótima a estadia,
obrigado/obrigada. m/f
foy o·tee·ma aa es·taa·*dee*·aa
o·bree·*gaa*·do/o·bree·*gaa*·daa

I'll recommend it to my friends.
Vou recomendar aos
meus amigos.
vo he·ko·meng·*daarr* ows
me·oos aa·*mee*·gos

camping

Do you have …?	Tem …?	teng …
a laundry	uma lavanderia	oo·maa laa·vang·de·ree·aa
a site	um lugar	oom loo·gaarr
electricity	eletricidade	e·le·tree·see·daa·de
shower facilities	chuveiro	shoo·vay·ro
tents for hire	barracas para alugar	baa·haa·kaas paa·raa aa·loo·gaar

How much is it per …?	Quanto custa por …?	kwang·to koos·taa porr …
person	pessoa	pe·so·aa
tent	barraca	baa·haa·kaa
vehicle	veículo	ve·ee·koo·lo

Can I …?	Posso …?	po·so …
camp here	acampar aqui	da·kang·paarr aa·kee
park next to my tent	estacionar ao lado da minha barraca?	es·taa·see·o·naarr ow laa·do daa mee·nyaa baa·haa·kaa

Who do I ask to stay here?
A quem eu peço para ficar aqui?
aa keng e·oo pe·so paa·raa fee·kaarr aa·kee

Is the water drinkable?
A água é potável?
a aa·gwaa e po·taa·vel

Is it coin-operated?
Isto funciona com moedas?
ees·to foong·syo·naa kong mo·e·daas

Could I borrow (a mallet)?
Posso pegar (um isqueiro) emprestado?
po·so pe·gaarr (oom ees·kay·ro) eng·pres·taa·do

renting

I'm here about the … for rent.

Estou aqui por causa do …   es·to aa·*kee* porr *kow*·zaa do …
para alugar.   paa·raa aa·loo·*gaarr*

Do you have a/an … for rent?

Você tem … para   vo·*se* teng … *paa*·raa
alugar?   aa·loo·*gaarr*

apartment	*apartamento* m	aa·paarr·taa·*meng*·to
cabin	*cabine* f	kaa·*bee*·ne
house	*casa* f	*kaa*·zaa
room	*quarto* m	*kwaarr*·to
(partly)	*(parcialmente)*	(paarr·see·ow·*meng*·te)
furnished	*mobiliado/*	mo·bee·*lyaa*·do/
	mobiliada m/f	mo·bee·*lyaa*·daa
unfurnished	*sem mobília*	seng mo·*bee*·lyaa

tongue torture

Tongue twisters are very popular in Brazil, and they're not a bad way to get your mouth around a new language. Try these for a bit of r practice:

O rato roeu a roupa do rei de Roma.
o *haa*·to ro·e·oo aa *ho*·paa do re de *ro*·maa
(The rat chewed the clothes of the king of Rome.)

Três pratos de trigo para três tigres tristes.
tres *praa*·tos de *tree*·go paa·raa tres *tee*·gres *trees*·tes
(Three plates of wheat for three sad tigers.)

staying with locals

Can I stay at your place?

Posso ficar na sua casa?	po·so fee·*kaarr* naa *soo*·aa *kaa*·zaa

Is there anything I can do to help?

Posso ajudar em alguma coisa?	po·so aa·zhoo·*daarr* eng ow·*goo*·maa *koy*·zaa

I have my own ...	Tenho o meu próprio ...	*te*·nyo o *me*·oo pro·pree·o ...
mattress	colchão	kol·*showng*
sleeping bag	saco de dormir	*saa*·ko de dorr·*meerr*

Can I ...?	Posso ...?	po·so ...
bring anything for the meal	trazer alguma coisa para a refeição	traa·*zerr* ow·*goo*·maa *koy*·zaa paa·raa aa he·fay·*sowng*
do the dishes	lavar a louça	laa·*varr* aa *lo*·saa
set/clear the table	arrumar/ limpar a mesa	aa·hoo·*maarr*/ *leeng*·paarr aa *me*·zaa
take out the rubbish	jogar o lixo fora	zho·*gaarr* o *lee*·sho *foo*·raa

Thanks for your hospitality.

Obrigado/Obrigada pela hospitalidade. m/f	o·bree·*gaa*·do/o·bree·*gaa*·daa pe·laa os·pee·taa·lee·*daa*·de

For dining-related expressions, see **eating out,** page 141.

looking for ...

procurando por ...

Where's ...?	Onde fica ...?	ong·de fee·kaa ...
a bookshop	a livraria	aa lee·vraa·ree·aa
a department store	a loja de departamentos	aa lo·zhaa de de·paarr·taa·meng·tos
a supermarket	o supermercado	o soo·perr·merr·kaa·do

Where can I buy (a padlock)?
Onde posso comprar (um cadeado)? ong·de po·so kong·praarr (oom kaa·de·aa·do)

or more shops, see the **dictionary** and for phrases on asking and giving directions, see **directions**, page 51.

making a purchase

fazendo compras

I'd like to buy (an adaptor plug).
Gostaria de comprar (um adaptador). gos·taa·ree·aa de kong·praarr (oom aa·daa·pee·taa·dorr)

How much is it?
Quanto custa? kwang·to koos·taa

Can you write down the price?
Você pode escrever o preço? vo·se po·de es·kre·verr o pre·so

Do you have any others?
Você tem outros? vo·se teng o·tros

Can I look at it?
Posso ver? po·so verr

I'm just looking.
Estou só olhando. es·to so o·lyang·do

Do you accept …?	Vocês aceitam …?	vo·ses aa·say·tang …
credit cards	cartão de crédito	kaarr·towng de kre·dee·to
debit cards	saque eletrônico	sa·kee e·le·tro·nee·ko
travellers cheques	traveller cheque	tra·ve·ler she·kee
Could I have a …, please?	Pode me dar um …, por favor?	po·de me daarr oom porr faa·vorr
bag	saco	saa·ko
receipt	recibo	he·see·bo

Could I have it wrapped?
Pode embrulhar? — po·de eng·broo·lyaarr

Does it have a guarantee?
Tem garantia? — teng gaa·rang·tee·aa

Can I have it sent overseas?
Vocês podem enviar para o exterior? — vo·ses po·deng eng·vee·aar paa·raa o es·te·ree·orr

Can you order it for me?
Pode fazer o pedido para mim? — po·de faa·zerr o pe·dee·do paa·raa meeng

Can I pick it up later?
Posso pegar mais tarde? — po·so pe·gaarr mais taarr·de

It's faulty.
Está com defeito. — es·taa kong de·fay·to

I'd like …, please.	Gostaria de …	gos·taa·ree·aa de …
a refund	ser reembolsado	serr he·eng·bol·saa·do
my change	ter o meu troco	terr o me·oo tro·ko
to return this	devolver isto	de·vol·verr ees·to

PRACTICAL

bargaining

That's too expensive.
Está muito caro.   es·*taa* mweeng·to kaa·ro

Can you lower the price?
Pode baixar o preço?   po·de bai·*shaarr* o *pre*·so

I don't want to pay the full price.
Não quero pagar o   nowng *ke*·ro paa·*gaarr* o
preço todo.   *pre*·so to·do

Do you have something cheaper?
Tem uma coisa mais   teng oo·maa koy·zaa mais
barata?   baa·*raa*·taa

I'll give you (fifty reals).
Dou (cinquenta reais).   do (seen·*kweng*·taa he·*ais*)

local talk

bargain	*pechincha* f	pe·*sheeng*·shaa
rip-off	*roubo* m	*ho*·bo
sale	*liquidação* f	lee·kee·daa *sowng*
specials	*preço* m	*pre*·so
	especial	es·pe·see·*ow*

clothes

roupas

Can I try it on?
Posso experimentar?   po·so es·pe·ree·meng·*taarr*

My size is (14).
Meu número é (quatorze).   me·oo noo·me·ro e (kaa·*torr*·ze)

It doesn't fit.
Não cabe.   nowng kaa·be

For clothing items, see the **dictionary**.

shopping

65

repairs

Can I have my (backpack) repaired here?

Vocês consertam a (mochila)?	vo·ses kong·serr·tang aa (mo·shee·laa)	

When will my ... be ready? *Quando ...?* kwang·do ...

camera	fica pronta a câmera	fee·kaa prong·taa aa ka·me·raa
(sun)glasses	ficam prontos os óculos (de sol)	fee·kang prong·tos os o·koo·los (de sol)
shoes	fica pronto o sapato	fee·kaa prong·to o saa·paa·to

darn holes

buttons	botões m pl	bo·toyngs
needle	agulha f	aa·goo·lyaa
scissors	tesoura f	te·zo·raa
thread	linha f	lee·nya

hairdressing

I'd like (a) ... *Gostaria de ...* gos·taa·ree·aa de ...

blow wave	secar	se·kaarr
colour	pintar	peeng·taarr
haircut	cortar	korr·taarr
my beard trimmed	aparar a barba	aa·paa·raarr aa baarr·baa
shave	fazer a barba	faa·zerr aa baarr·baa
trim	aparar	aa·paa·raarr

Don't cut it too short.
Não corta muito.   nowng *korr*·taa *mweeng*·to

Shave it all off!
Raspa tudo!   haas·paa too·do

Please use a new blade.
Por favor use uma   por fa·*vorr* oo·ze oo·maa
gilete nova.   zhee·*le*·te *no*·vaa

I should never have let you near me!
Não deveria nunca   nowng de·ve·*ree*·aa *noong*·kaa
ter deixado você   terr day·*shaa*·do vo·*se*
chegar perto de mim!   she·*gaarr perr*·to de meeng

For colours, see the **dictionary**.

books & reading

livros e leitura

Do you have …?	*Tem …?*	teng …
a book by	*algum livro*	ow·*goom* lee·vro
(Jorge	*do (Jorge*	do (*zhorzh*
Amado)	*Amado)*	aa·*maa*·do)
an entertain-	*um guia de*	oom *gee*·aa de
ment guide	*entretenimento*	eng·tre·te·nee·*meng*·to

shopping

I'd like a …	Gostaria de comprar um …	gos·taa·*ree*·aa de kong·*praarr* oom …
dictionary	dicionário	dee·see·o·*naa*·ryo
newspaper	jornal	zhorr·*now*
(in English)	(em inglês)	(eng eeng·*gles*)
notepad	bloco de notas	*blo*·ko de *no*·taas

Is there an English-language …?	Tem uma … de língua inglesa?	teng oo·maa … de *leeng*·gwaa eeng·*gle*·sa
bookshop	livraria	lee·vraa·*ree*·aa
section	seção	se·*sowng*

Can you recommend a book for me?
Você poderia me recomendar algum livro?
vo·*se* po·de·*ree*·aa me he·ko·meng·*daarr* ow·*goom* lee·vro

Do you have Lonely Planet guidebooks?
Vocês tem os guias de viagem do Lonely Planet?
vo·*ses* teng os *gee*·aas de vee·*aa*·zheng do *lo*·ne·lee *pla*·ne·tee

music

I'd like a …	Gostaria de comprar …	gos·taa·*ree*·aa de kong·*praarr* …
CD	um CD	oom se·*de*

I'm looking for something by (Caetano Veloso).
Estou procurando por alguma coisa (do Caetano Veloso).
es·*to* pro·koo·*rang*·do porr ow·*goo*·maa koy·zaa (do kaa·e·*ta*·no ve·*lo*·zo)

What's his/her best recording?
Qual é o melhor disco dele/dela? m/f
kwow e o me·*lyorr dees*·ko *de*·le/*de*·laa

Can I listen to this?
Posso escutar?
po·so es·koo·*taarr*

Souvenir hunters will find music, local crafts and musical instruments worthy mementos of their trip. Artisan fairs (*feira de artesanato*) are common weekend events in larger cities and offer a good range of souvenirs.

regional souvenirs

Is there a souvenir typical of this region?

Tem algum lenbrança	teng al·*goom* leng·*braan*·sa
específico desta	es·pe·see·*fee*·ko *des*·ta
região ?	re·*zhowng*

artesanato indígena – Indian handicrafts, including wooden and woven items

artigos de couro – leather goods

bikini fio dental – 'dental floss' bikini – the original string bikini. The name says it all.

jóia – jewellery

pedras preciosas – gemstones

rede – cotton hammocks, usually dyed in bright colours

musical instruments

The instruments that feature in traditional Brazilian music make great souvenirs.

berimbau – a stringed instrument commonly used in *capoeira* performances. It consists of a bow with metal string attached to a dried gourd which acts as a resonating chamber. A rod and a ring or coin is struck against the string to produce sound.

pandeiro – originally from East Africa, the tambourine is considered an essential part of Brazilian rhythm and is common throughout the country

reco-reco – a grooved piece of bamboo or iron also used in *capoeira*. A rod is scraped against the grooves to produce the rasping sound.

photography

I need … film for this camera.	Preciso de filme … para esta câmera.	pre·see·zo de feel·me … paa·raa es·taa ka·me·raa
APS	sistema APS	sees·te·maa aa pe e·se
B&W	Preto e Branco	pre·to e brang·ko
colour	colorido	ko·lo·ree·do
slide	de slide	de ees·lai·de
(200) speed	(duzentos) velocidade	(doo·zeng·tos) ve·lo·see·daa·de

I need a passport photo taken.
Preciso tirar foto para passporte. pre·see·zo tee·raarr fo·to paa·raa paa·saa·porr·te

When will it be ready?
Quando fica pronto? kwang·do fee·kaa prony·lo

How much is it?
Quanto custa? kwang·to koos·taa

I'm not happy with these photos.
Não gostei destas fotos. nowng gos·tay des·taas fo·tos

communications
comunicações

post office
correios e telégrafos

want to send a …	*Quero enviar …*	*ke·ro eng·vee·aarr …*
fax	*um fax*	oom faks
letter	*uma carta*	*oo·maa kaarr·taa*
parcel	*uma encomenda*	*oo·maa eng·ko·meng·daa*
postcard	*um cartão postal*	oom kaarr·*towng* pos·*tow*
want to buy …	*Quero comprar …*	*ke·ro kong·praarr …*
an aerogram	*um aerograma*	oom aa·e·ro·*gra*·maa
an envelope	*um envelope*	oom eng·ve·*lo*·pe
stamps	*selos*	*se·los*

airmail	*via aéreo/ aérea* m/f	*vee·aa aa·e·re·o/ aa·e·re·aa*
customs declaration	*declaração* f *da alfândega*	de·*klaa*·raa·*sowng* daa aal·*fang*·de·gaa
domestic	*doméstico*	do·*mes*·tee·ko
express	*rápido/ rápida* m/f	*haa*·pee·do/ *haa*·pee·daa
fragile	*frágil*	*fraa*·zheel
international	*internacional*	eeng·terr·naa·syo·*now*
mail	*correspondência* f	ko·hes·pong·*deng*·syaa
mailbox	*caixa* f *postal*	*kai*·sha pos·*tow*
postcode	*CEP* m	*se*·pee
registered	*registrado/ registrada* m/f	he·zhees·*traa*·do/ he·zhees·*traa*·daa
surface mail	*via terrestre*	*vee·aa te·hes·tre*

communications

71

Please send it by air/surface mail to (Australia).
Por favor envie via aérea/terrestre para a (Austrália).
porr faa·vorr eng·vee·e vee·aa aa·e·re·aa/te·hes·tre paa·raa aa (ows·traa·lya)

It contains (souvenirs).
Contém (souvenirs).
kong·teng (soo·ve·neers)

Where's the poste restante section?
Onde fica a seção de Poste Restante?
ong·de fee·kaa a se·sowng de pos·te hes·tang·te

Is there any mail for me?
Tem alguma correspondência para mim?
teng ow·goo·maa ko·hes·pong·deng·syaa paa·raa meeng

phone

What's your phone number?
Qual é o número do teu telefone?
kwow e o noo·me·ro do te·oo te·le·fo·ne

Where's the nearest public phone?
Onde fica o telefône público mais perto?
ong·de fee·kaa o te·le·fo·ne poo·blee·ko mais perr·to

Do you have a phonebook I can look at?
Posso dar uma olhada no catálogo telefônico?
po·so daarr oo·maa o·lyaa·daa no kaa·taa·lo·go te·le·fo·nee·ko

How much does … cost?	*Quanto custa …?*	kwang·to koos·taa …
a (three)-minute call	*uma ligação de (três) minutos*	oo·maa lee·gaa·sowng de (tres) mee·noo·tos
each extra minute	*cada minuto extra*	kaa·daa mee·noo·to es·traa

want to ...	Quero ...	ke·ro ...
buy a phone card	comprar um cartão telefônico	kong·praarr oom kaar·towng te·le·fo·nee·ko
call (Singapore)	telefonar (para Cingapura)	te·le·fo·naarr (paa·raa seen·gaa·poo·raa)
make a local call	fazer uma chamada local	faa·zerr oo·maa shaa·maa·daa lo·kow
reverse the charges	fazer uma chamada a cobrar	faa·zerr oo·maa shaa·maa·daa aa ko·braarr
speak for (three) minutes	falar por (três) minutos	faa·laarr por (tres) mee·noo·tos

The number is ...
O número é ...   o noo·me·ro e ...

What's the area code for (Recife)?
Qual é o código de   kwow e o ko·dee·go de
discagem para (Recife)?   dees·ka·zheng paa·raa (he·see·fe)

What's the country code for (New Zealand)?
Qual é o código de   kwow e o ko·dee·go de
discagem para   dees·ka·zheng paa·raa
(Nova Zelândia)?   (no·vaa ze·lang·dee·aa)

It's engaged.
Está ocupado.   es·taa o·koo·paa·do

I've been cut off.
A ligação caiu.   aa lee·gaa·sowng kaa·ee·oo

The connection's bad.
A conexão está ruim.   aa ko·nek·sowng es·taa hoo·eeng

communications

73

Hello.	*Alô.*	aa·*lo*
Can I speak to …?	*Posso falar com …?*	po·so faa·*laarr* kong ..
It's …	*Aqui é …*	a·*kee* e …
Is … there?	*O/A … está?* m/f	o/aa … es·*taa*

listen for …

e·le/e·laa nowng es·*taa*
Ele/Ela não está.
He/She is not here.

es·*pe*·raa oom mee·noo·tee·nyo
Espera um minutinho.
One moment.

keng es·*taa* faa·*lang*·do
Quem está falando?
Who's calling?

kong keng vo·*se* kerr faa·*laarr*
*Com quem você quer
falar?*
**Who do you want
to speak to?**

kwow o se·oo noo·me·ro paa·raa kong·*taa*·to
*Qual o seu número para
contato?*
**What's your
contact number?**

vo·*se* dees·ko o noo·me·ro e·*haa*·do
Você discou o número errado.
Wrong number.

Can I leave a message?
Posso deixar um recado? po·so day·*shaarr* oom he·*kaa*·do

Please tell him/her I called.
*Por favor diga a
ele/ela que eu liguei.* por faa·*vorr* dee·gaa a
e·le/e·laa ke e·oo lee·*gay*

I'll call back later.
Eu vou ligar mais tarde. e·oo vo lee·*gaarr* mais *taarr*·de

My number is …
Meu telefone é … me·oo te·le·fo·ne e …

mobile/cell phone

I'd like a …	Eu gostaria de …	e·oo gos·taa·*ree*·aa de …
charger for	comprar uma	kong·*praarr* oo·maa
my phone	bateria para o	baa·te·*ree*·aa paa·raa
o		
	meu telephone	me·oo te·le·*fo*·ne
mobile/cell	alugar um	aa·loo·*gaarr* oom
phone for hire	cellular	se·loo·*laarr*
prepaid mobile/	comprar um	kong·*praarr* oom
cell phone	cellular	se·loo·*laarr*
	pré-pago	pre·*paa*·go
SIM card for	comprar um	kong·*praarr* oom
your network	cartão SIM	kaarr·*towng* seeng
	para sua rede	paa·raa soo·aa he·de

What are the rates?

Qual é o valor cobrado?   kwow e o vaa·*lorr* ko·*braa*·do

(30c) per (30) seconds.

(Trinta centavos) por   (*treeng*·taa seng·*taa*·vos) porr
(trinta) segundos.   (*treeng*·taa) se·*goong*·dos

internetese

The word *Internetês* (Internetese) has been coined to describe the confusing mixture of English and Portuguese terms in Brazilian cyberspace. New words such as *surfar* (surf) and *scâner* (scanner) have been adapted from English but sometimes there are Portuguese alternatives for common internet terms:

bate-papo m	internet chat
ciberespaço m	cyberspace
endereço m *de email*	email address
hiperligação m	hyperlink
internauta f	net nerd
página f *inicial*	homepage
utilizador m&f	user

the internet

Where's the local Internet cafe?
Onde tem um internet	ong·de teng oom eeng·terr·ne·tee
café na redondeza?	kaa·fe naa he·dong·de·zaa

I'd like to …   *Gostaria de …*   gos·taa·ree·aa de …

check my email	*checar meu*	she·kaarr me·oo
	e-mail	e·mail
get Internet	*ter acesso à*	terr aa·se·so aa
access	*internet*	eeng·terr·ne·tee
use a printer	*usar a*	oo·zaarr aa
	impressora	eeng·pre·so·raa
use a scanner	*usar o*	oo·zaarr o
	escaner	ees·ka·nerr

Do you have …?   *Vocês tem …?*   vo·ses teng …

a Zip drive	*um zip drIve*	oom zeep drai·vee
Macs	*Apple Mac*	e·pel mak
PCs	*PC*	pe·se

How much   *Quanto custa*   kwang·to koos·taa
per …?   *por …?*   por …

hour	*hora*	aw·raa
(five) minutes	*(cinco) minutes*	(seeng·ko) mee·noo·to
page	*página*	paa·zhee·naa

How do I log on?
Como é que eu entro?	ko·mo e ke e·oo eng·tro

Please change it to the English-language setting.
Troca para inglês,	tro·kaa paa·raa eeng·gles
por favor.	porr faa·vorr

It's crashed.
Deu crash.	de·o krash

Where can I …?	*Onde posso …?*	*ong·de po·so …*
I'd like to …	*Gostaria de …*	*gos·taa·ree·aa de …*
cash a cheque	*descontar um cheque*	*des·kong·taarr oom she·kee*
change a travellers cheque	*trocar traveller cheques*	*tro·kaarr traa·ve·ler she·kes*
change money	*trocar dinheiro*	*tro·kaar dee·nyay·ro*
get a cash advance	*fazer um saque adiantado*	*fa·zerr oom saa·ke aa·dee·ang·taa·do*
withdraw money	*retirar dinheiro*	*he·tee·raarr dee·nyay·ro*
Where's …?	*Onde tem …?*	*ong·de teng …*
a foreign exchange office	*uma loja de câmbio*	*oo·maa lo·zhaa de kang·byo*
an automatic teller machine	*um caixa automático*	*oom kai·shaa ow·to·maa·tee·ko*

hat time does the bank open?

A que horas abre o banco?	*aa ke aw·raas aa·bre o bang·ko*

n I use my credit card to withdraw money?

Posso usar o meu cartão de crédito para retirar dinheiro?	*po·so oo·zaarr o me·oo kaar·towng de kre·dee·to paa·raa he·tee·raarr dee·nyay·ro*

What's the ...?	Qual ...?	kwow ...
exchange rate	o câmbio do dia	o *kang*·byo do *dee*·aa
charge for that	a taxa cobrada	aa *taa*·shaa ko·*braa*·daa

Has my money arrived yet?

O meu dinheiro já chegou? o *me*·oo dee·*nyay*·ro zhaa she·*go*

How long will it take to arrive?

Quanto tempo vai levar para chegar? *kwang*·to *teng*·po *vaa*·ee le·*vaarr paa*·raa she·*gaarr*

The automatic teller machine took my card.

O caixa eletrônico engoliu meu cartão. o *kai*·shaa e·le·*tro*·nee·ko eng·go·*lee*·oo *mee*·oo kaar·*towng*

I've forgotten my PIN.

Esqueci a minha senha. es·ke·*see* aa *mee*·nyaa *se*·nyaa

listen for ...

aa·*see*·ne aa·*kee* *Assine aqui.*	**Sign here.**
nowng po·*de*·mos faa·*zerr ee*·so *Não podemos fazer isso.*	**We can't do that.**
te·mos oom pro·*ble*·maa *Temos um problema.*	**There's a problem.**
ee·deng·tee·*daa*·de *identidade*	**identification**
paa·saa·*porr*·te *passaporte*	**passport**

sightseeing

passeando

I'd like a/an ...	Gostaria de um ...	gos·taa·*ree*·aa de oom ...
audio set	aparelho de audio	aa·paa·*re*·lyo de *ow*·dee·o
catalogue	catálogo	kaa·*taa*·lo·go
guide (person)	guia	*gee*·aa
guidebook in English	guia em Inglês	*gee*·aa eng eeng·*gles*
(local) map	mapa (local)	*maa*·paa (lo·*kow*)
Do you have information on ... sights?	Vocês tem informações sobre passeios ...?	vo·*ses* teng eeng·forr·maa·*soyngs so*·bre paa·*se*·os ...
cultural	culturais	kool·too·*rais*
historical	históricos	ees·*to*·ree·kos
religious	religiosos	he·lee·zhee·*o*·zos

I'd like to see ...
Gostaria de ver ...
gos·ta·*ree*·a de ver ...

What's that?
O que é isso?
o ke e *ee*·so

Who made it?
Quem fez isso?
keng fes *ee*·so

How old is it?
Quantos anos tem?
kwang·tos *a*·nos teng

Could you take a photograph of me?
Você poderia tirar minha foto, por favor?
vo·*se* po·de·*ree*·aa tee·*raarr mee*·nyaa *fo*·to porr faa·*vor*

Can I take a photograph?
Posso tirar uma foto?   po·so tee·*raarr* oo·ma *fo*·to

Can I take a photograph of you?
Posso tirar uma foto   po·so tee·*raarr* oo·ma *fo*·to
de você(s)? sg/pl   de vo·*se(s)*

I'll send you the photograph.
Eu te envio a foto.   e·oo te eng·*vee*·o a *fo*·to

getting in

What time does it open/close?
A que horas abre/fecha?   a ke *aw*·raas *aa*·bre/*fe*·shaa

What's the admission charge?
Qual o preço da entrada?   kwow o *pre*·so daa eng·*traa*·daa

Is there a discount for …?	Tem desconto para …?	teng des·*kong*·to pau·raa …
children	crianças	kree·*ang*·saas
families	famílias	faa·*mee*·lyaas
groups	grupos	*groo*·pos
older people	pessoas idosas	pe·*so*·aas ee·*do*·zaas
pensioners	pensionistas	peng·see·o·*nees*·taa
students	estudantes	es·too·*dang*·tes

galleries & museums

When's the gallery open?
Quando abre a galeria?   kwang·do *aa*·bre aa gaa·le·*ree*·aa

What kind of art are you interested in?
Você se interessa por   vo·*se* se eeng·te·*re*·saa porr
que tipo de arte?   ke *tee*·po de *aarr*·te

What's in the collection?
O que tem na coleção?   o ke teng naa ko·le·*sowng*

What do you think of (Renaissance art)?
O que você acha (arte Renascença)? — o ke vo·se aa·shaa (aarr·te he·naas·seng·saa)

It's a (Volpi) exhibition.
É uma (Volpi) exposição. — e oo·maa (vol·pee) es·po·zee·sowng

I'm interested in …
Estou interessado/ interessada em … m/f — es·to eeng·te·re·saa·do/ eeng·te·re·saa·daa eng …

I like the works of …
Eu gosto do trabalho do/da … m/f — e·oo gos·to do traa·baa·lyo do/daa …

It reminds me of …
Lembra o/a … m/f — leng·braa o/aa …

… art	arte … f	aarr·te …
graphic	gráfica	graa·fee·kaa
impressionist	impressionista	eeng·pre·syo·nees·taa
indigenous	indígena	eeng·dee·zhe·naa
modern	moderna	mo·derr·naa
performance	performance	perr·forr·mang·se
popular	popular	aarr·te po·poo·laarr

tours

Can you recommend a ...?	Vocês podem recomendar um ...?	vo·*ses* po·deng he·ko·meng·*daarr* oom ...
When's the next ...?	Quando sai o próximo ...?	*kwang*·do sai o pro·see·mo ...
boat-trip	barco	*baar*·ko
day trip	passeio do dia	paa·*se*·yo do *dee*·aa
tour	tour	toor
Is ... included?	Inclui ...?	eeng·*kloo*·ee ...
accommodation	ospedagem	os·pe·*daa*·zheng
food	comida	ko·*mee*·daa
transport	transporte	trans·*porr*·te

The guide will pay.
O guia vai pagar.   o *gee*·aa vai paa·*gaarr*

The guide has paid.
O guia pagou.   o *gee*·aa paa·*go*

How long is the tour?
Quanto tempo dura o   *kwang*·to *teng*·po *doo*·raa o
passeio?   paa·*say*·o

What time should we be back?
A que horas estaremos de   a ke *aw*·raas es·taa·*re*·mos de
volta?   *vol*·taa

I'm with them.
Estou com eles.   es·*to* kong e·les

I've lost my group.
Perdi o meu grupo.   perr·*dee* o me·oo *groo*·po

I'm attending a ...	Estou participando de ...	es·to paar·tee·see·pang·do de ...
conference	uma conferência	oo·maa kong·fe·reng·syaa
course	um curso	oom koor·so
meeting	uma reunião	oo·maa he·oo·nee·owng
trade fair	uma feira de negócios	oo·maa fay·raa de ne·go·see·os

I'm with ...	Estou com ...	es·to kong ...
my colleagues	meus/minhas colegas de trabalho m/f	me·oos/mee·nyaas ko·le·gaas de traa·baa·lyo
(the UN)	(a ONU)	(aa o·noo)
(two) others	outros (dois)	o·tros (doys)

I'm alone.
Estou sozinho.   es·to so·zee·nyo

I have an appointment with ...
Tenho uma hora   teng·nyo oo·maa aw·raa
marcada com ...   maarr·kaa·daa kong ...

I'm staying at ..., room ...
Estou no ..., quarto ...   es·to no ... kwaarr·to ...

I'm here for ...	Ficarei aqui por ...	fee·kaa·ray aa·kee porr ...
(two) days	(dois) dias	(doys) dee·aas
(two) weeks	(duas) semanas	(doo·aas) se·ma·naas

Here's my ...	Aqui está ...	a·kee es·taa ...
What's your ...?	Qual o seu ...?	kwow o se·oo ...
address	endereço	eng·de·re·so
business card	cartão de visitas	kaar·towng de vee·zee·taas
email address	endereço de e-mail	eng·de·re·so de e-mail
fax number	número de fax	noo·me·ro de faks
mobile number	número do celular	noo·me·ro do se·loo·laarr
pager number	número do pager	noo·me·ro do pa·zher
work number	telefone do trabalho	te·le·fo·ne do traa·baa·lyo

Where's the ...?	Onde é ...?	ong·de e ...
business centre	o centro de negócios	o seng·tro de ne·go·syos
conference	a conferência	aa kong·fe·reng·syaa
meeting	a reunião	a he·oo·nee·owng

I'd like to ...	Gostaria de ...	gos·taa·ree·aa de ...
check my email	checar meu e-mail	she·kaarr me·oo e-mail
send a fax	enviar um fax	eng·vee·aarr oom faks

That went very well.
Correu tudo muito bem.   ko·he·oo too·do mweeng·to beng

Thank you for your time.
Obrigado/Obrigada   o·bree·gaa·do/o·bree·gaa·daa
pela atenção. m/f   pe·laa aa·teng·sowng

Shall we go for a ...?	Vocês gostariam de ...?	vo·ses gos·taa·ree·ang de ...
drink	beber alguma coisa	be·berr ow·goo·maa koy·zaa
meal	jantar	zhang·taarr

| It's on me. | Eu convido. | e·oo kong·vee·do |

disabled travellers
viajantes com deficiência física

I have a disability.
*Eu tenho uma
deficiência física.*
e·oo te·nyo oo·ma
de·fee·see·eng·syaa fee·zee·kaa

I'm deaf.
Sou surdo.
so soorr·do

I have a hearing aid.
*Uso aparelho para
surdez.*
oo·zo aa·paa·re·lyo paa·raa
soor·des

I need assistance.
Preciso de ajuda.
pre·see·zo de a·zhoo·daa

What services do you have for people with a disability?
*Quais os serviços que
vocês oferecem para
pessoas com
deficiência física?*
kwais os serr·vee·sos ke
vo·ses o·fe·re·seng paa·raa
pe·so·aas kong
de·fee·see·eng·syaa fee·zee·kaa

Are there disabled toilets?
*Tem banheiro para
deficientes físicos?*
teng ba·nyay·ro paa·raa
de·fee·see·eng·tes fee·zee·kos

Are there rails in the bathroom?
*Tem corrimão no
banheiro?*
teng ko·hee·mowng no
ba·nyay·ro

Are there disabled parking spaces?
*Tem vaga para
deficientes físicos?*
teng vaa·gaa paa·raa
de·fee·see·eng·tes fee·zee·kos

85

Is there wheelchair access?
Tem acesso para   teng aa·*se*·so *paa*·raa
cadeira de rodas?   kaa·*day*·raa de *ho*·daas

How wide is the entrance?
Qual a largura da   kwow aa laarr·*goo*·raa daa
entrada?   eng·*traa*·daa

Is there a lift?
Tem elavador?   teng e·le·vaa·*dor*

How many steps are there?
Quantos degraus tem?   *kwang*·tos de·*grows* teng

Are guide dogs permitted?
É permitida a   e perr·mee·*tee*·daa aa
entrada de cães-guia?   eng·*traa*·daa de ka·*eengs*·*gee*·aa

Could you call me a disabled taxi?
Você poderia me   vo·*se* po·de·*ree*·aa me
chamar um taxi para   shaa·*maarr* oom *taak*·see *paa*·raa
deficientes físicos?   de·fee·see·*eng*·tes *fee*·zee·kos

Could you help me cross the street safely?
Você poderia me   vo·*se* po·de·*ree*·aa me
atravessar com   aa·traa·ve·*saarr* kong
segurança?   se·goo·*rang*·saa

Is there somewhere I can sit down?
Tem algum lugar onde   teng ow·*goom* loo·*gaarr* ong·de
eu posso sentar?   e·oo po·so seng·*taarr*

disabled person	*pessoa com deficiência física*	pe·*so*·aa kong de·fee·see·*eng*·syaa *fee*·zee·kaa
guide dog	*cães-guia* m	ka·*eengs*·*gee*·aa
older person	*pessoa idosa*	pe·*so*·aa ee·*do*·zaa
ramp	*rampa* f	*hang*·paa
walking frame	*andador* m	ang·daa·*dorr*
walking stick	*bengala* f	beng·*gaa*·laa
wheelchair	*cadeira* f *de rodas*	kaa·*day*·raa de *ho*·daas

travelling with children

viajando com crianças

Is there a ...?	Aqui tem ...?	aa·kee teng ...
baby change room	uma sala para trocar bebê	oo·maa saa·laa paa·raa tro·kaarr be·be
child discount	desconto para criança	des·kong·to paa·raa kree·ang·saa
child-minding service	serviço de babá	serr·vee·so de baa·baa
child-sized portion	porção para criança	porr·sowng paa·raa kree·ang·saa
children's menu	cardápio para criança	kaar·daa·pyo paa·raa kree·an·saa
creche	creche	kre·she
family ticket	passagem para familia	paa·saa·zheng paa·raa faa·mee·lyaa

Where's the nearest ...?	Qual ... mais perto?	kwow ... mais perr·to
drinking fountain	o bebedouro	o be·be·do·ro
park	o parque	o paarr·ke
playground	o playground	o play·grownd
swimming pool	a piscina	aa pee·see·naa
tap	a torneira	aa torr·nay·raa
theme park	o parque de diversões	o paarr·ke de dee·ver·soyngs
toyshop	a loja de brinquedos	aa lo·zhaa de breeng·ke·dos

I need a/an ...	Preciso de ...	pre·see·zo de ...
baby seat	um assento de criança	oom aa·seng·to de kree·ang·saa
(English-speaking) babysitter	uma babá (que fale ingles)	oo·maa baa·baa (ke faa·le eeng·gles)
booster seat	assento de elevação	aa·seng·to de e·le·vaa·sowng
highchair	uma cadeira de criança	oo·maa kaa·day·raa de kree·ang·saa
plastic sheet	um lençol plástico	oom leng·sol plaas·tee·ko
plastic bag	um saco plástico	oom saa·ko plaas·tee·ko
potty	um troninho	oom tro·nee·nyo
pram/pusher	carrinho de bebê	kaa·hee·nyo de be·be
sick bag	saco de vomito	saa·ko de vo·mee·to

Do you sell ...?	Vocês vendem ...?	vo·ses veng·deng ...
baby pain killers	analgésico para bebê	aa·naal·zhe·zee·ko paa·raa be·be
baby wipes	toalha molhada de bebê	to·aa·lyaa mo·lyaa·daa de be·be
disposable nappies	fraldas descartáveis	frow·daas des·kaarr·taa·vays
tissues	lencinhos de papel	leng·see·nyos de paa·pel

Do you hire prams?

Vocês alugam carrinho de bebê?	vo·ses aa·loo·gang kaa·hee·nyo de be·be

Are there any good places to take children around here?

Tem algum lugar agradável para levar as crianças por aqui perto?	teng ow·goom loo·gaarr aa·graa·daa·vel paa·raa le·vaarr aas kree·ang·saas porr aa·kee perr·to

Is there space for a pram?

Tem espaço para o
carrinho de bebê?

teng es·*paa*·so *paa*·raa o
kaa·*hee*·nyo de be·*be*

Are children allowed?

É permitida a
entrada de crianças?

e perr·mee·*tee*·daa aa
eng·*traa*·daa de kree·*ang*·saas

Where can I change a nappy?

Onde posso trocar
a fralda?

ong·de po·so tro·*kaarr*
aa *frow*·daa

Do you mind if I breast-feed here?

Você se importa se
eu amamentar aqui?

vo·se se eeng·*porr*·taa se
e·oo aa·maa·meng·*taarr* aa·*kee*

Could I have some paper and pencils, please?

Pode me dar papel e
lapis, por favor?

po·de me daarr paa·*pel* e
laa·pees porr faa·*vorr*

Is this suitable for (five-)year-old children?

Isto é adequado para
crianças de (cinco)
anos de idade?

ees·to e aa·de·*kwaa*·do *paa*·raa
kree·*ang*·saas de (*seeng*·ko)
a·nos de ee·*daa*·de

Do you know a dentist/doctor who is good with children?

Voce conhece algum
médico/dentista bom
para crianças?

vo·*se* ko·*nye*·se ow·*goom*
me·dee·ko/deng·*tees*·taa bong
paa·raa kree·*ang*·saas

For children's sicknesses, see **health**, page 177.

---

brazilian family tree

Ancient Celtic myths refer to the mist-shrouded island of Hy Brazil – a stormless haven somewhere in the Atlantic. The island appeared on charts in the 14th century and was to remain on British maps as late as the 1870s. Some scholars have suggested that Portuguese explorers were familiar with the Celtic stories and named the South American country after Hy Brazil. A more accepted theory is that Brazil is derived from the name of a dye-producing East Indian tree. When a similar tree was discovered in the new land it became Brazil's first successful export and lent the country its present name.

children

talking with children

Do you like ...?	Você gosta ...?	vo·se gos·taa ...
school	da escola	daa es·ko·laa
sport	de esporte	de es·porr·te
your teacher	do seu professor m	do se·oo pro·fe·sorr
	da sua professora f	da soo·aa pro·fe·so·raa

When's your birthday?
Quando é o seu aniversário?
kwang·do e o se·oo aa·nee·ver·saa·ryo

Do you go to school?
Você vai para escola?
vo·se vai paa·raa es·ko·laa

What grade are you in?
Em que ano você está?
eng ke a·no vo·se es·taa

What do you do after school?
O que você faz depois da escola?
o ke vo·se faz de·poys daa es·ko·laa

Do you learn English?
Você aprende ingles?
vo·se aa·preng·de eeng·gles

I come from very far away.
Eu venho de muito longe.
e·oo veng·nyo de mweeng·to long·zhe

Are you lost?
Você está perdido/ perdida? m/f
vo·se es·taa perr·dee·do/ perr·dee·daa

PRACTICAL

basics

conhecimentos básicos

Yes.	*Sim.*	seeng
No.	*Não.*	nowng
Please.	*Por favor.*	por faa·*vorr*
Thank you (very much).	*(Muito) Obrigado/ Obrigada.* m/f	*(mweeng·*to) o·bree·*gaa*·do/ o·bree·*gaa*·daa
You're welcome.	*De nada.*	de *naa*·daa
Excuse me.	*Com licença.*	kong lee·*seng*·saa
Sorry.	*Desculpa.*	des·*kool*·paa

greetings & goodbyes

saudações & despedidas

A greeting kiss on the cheek is quite common between women, and also between members of the opposite sex, even on first encounters. The number of kisses ranges from one to three, depending on the region. Shaking hands is the normal greeting between men, though a hug between friends is not uncommon.

Hello.	*Olá.*	o·*laa*
Hi.	*Oi.*	oy
Good ...		
afternoon	*Boa tarde.*	bo·aa *taarr*·de
day	*Bom dia.*	bong *dee*·aa
evening	*Boa noite.*	bo·aa *noy*·te
morning	*Bom dia.*	bong *dee*·aa

How are you?
Como vai?   ko·mo vai

Fine, and you?
Bem, e você?   beng e vo·se

What's your name?
Qual é o seu nome?   kwow e o se·oo no·me

My name is …
Meu nome é …   me·oo no·me e …

I'd like to introduce you to …
Eu gostaria de te   e·oo gos·taa·ree·aa de te
apresentar ao/à … m/f   aa·pre·zeng·taarr aa·o/aa …

I'm pleased to meet you.
Prazer em conhecê-lo/la. m/f   praa·zerr eng ko·nye·se·lo/laa

This is my …	*Este é meu …* m	es·te e me·oo …
	Esta é minha … f	es·taa e mee·nyaa …
colleague	*colega* m&f	ko·le·gaa
daughter	*filha*	fee·lyaa
friend	*amigo/*	aa·mee·go/
	amiga m/f	aa·mee·gaa
husband	*marido*	maa·ree·do
partner	*companheiro/*	kong·pa·nyay·ro/
(intimate)	*companheira* m/f	kong·pa·nyay·raa
son	*filho*	fee·lyo
wife	*esposa*	es·po·zaa

For family members, see **family,** page 97.

| **See you later.** | *Até mais tarde.* | aa·te mais taarr·de |
| **Goodbye.** | *Tchau.* | tee·show |

---

many thanks

You'll notice that there are two words for 'thank you' in Brazilian Potuguese, *obrigado* and *obrigada*. Their use is determined by the gender of the person doing the thanking. A male uses *obrigado* and a female uses *obrigada*.

addressing people

It's always best to address older people using *Senhor* or *Senhora*. You'll notice that first names are used with titles, often more so than family names.

Mr/Sir	*Senhor*	se·*nyorr*
Mrs/Ms	*Senhora*	se·*nyo*·raa
Miss	*Senhorita*	se·nyo·*ree*·taa
Doctor	*Doutor/Doutora* m/f	do·*torr*/do·*to*·raa
Professor	*Professor/*	pro·fe·*sorr*/
	Professora m/f	pro·fe·*so*·raa
young man/woman	*moço/moça* m/f	*mo*·so/*mo*·sa
mate	*cara* m	*kaa*·raa

making conversation

How's everything?
Tudo bem? — *too*·do beng

Do you live here?
Você mora aqui? — vo·*se mo*·raa aa·*kee*

It's so hot/cold !
Que calor/frio ! — ke kaa·*lorr*/*free*·o

It's so quiet here.
Aqui é tão tranquilo. — a·*kee* e towng trang·*kwee*·lo

What a beautiful view.
Que vista linda. — ke *vees*·taa *leeng*·daa

This is great!
Isso é demais! — *ee*·so e de·*mais*

Where are you going?
Onde você está indo? — *ong*·de vo·*se* es·*taa eeng*·do

What are you doing?
O que você está fazendo? — o ke vo·*se* es·*taa* faa·*zeng*·do

Do you like it here?
Você gosta daqui? vo·*se gos*·taa daa·*kee*

I love it here.
Eu adoro. e·oo aa·*do*·ro

What's this called?
Como se chama isto? *ko*·mo se *sha*·maa ees·to

Can I take a photo (of you)?
Posso tirar uma foto *po*·so tee·*raarr* oo·maa *fo*·to
(de você)? (de vo·*se*)

That's (beautiful), isn't it!
Isto é (lindo) você ees·to e (*leeng*·do) vo·*se*
não acha? nowng aa·shaa

Just joking.
Estou brincando. es·to breeng·*kang*·do

Are you here on holiday?
Você está aqui em férias? vo·*se* es·*taa* a·*kee* eng *fe*·ree·aas

I'm here … Estou aqui … es·to a·*kee* …
  for a holiday em férias eng *fe*·ree·aas
  on business à negócios aa ne·*go*·syos
  to study à estudos aa es·*too*·dos

How long are you here for?
Quanto tempo você vai *kwang*·to *teng*·po vo·*se* vai
ficar aqui? fee·*kaarr* aa·*kee*

I'm here for (four) weeks/days.
Ficarei aqui (quatro) fee·kaa·*ray* aa·*kee* (*kwaa*·tro)
semanas/dias. se·*ma*·naas/*dee*·aas

SOCIAL

94

What a beautiful day!
Que lindo dia!   ke *leeng*·do *dee*·aa

Want to talk about the weather? See **outdoors**, page 138.

local talk		
Hey!	*Ei!*	ay
Great!	*Ótimo!*	o·tee·mo
Sure.	*É claro.*	e *klaa*·ro
Maybe.	*Talvez.*	taal·*vez*
No way!	*De jeito nenhum!*	de *zhay*·to ne·*yoom*
Just a minute.	*Só um minuto.*	so oom mee·*noo*·to
It's OK.	*Está bom.*	es·*taa* bong
Good luck!	*Boa sorte!*	bo·aa *sorr*·te
No problem.	*Não tem problema.*	nowng teng pro·*ble*·maa

nationalities

nacionalidades

Where are you from?
De onde você é?   de *ong*·de vo·*se* e

I'm from ...	*Eu sou ...*	e·oo so ...
Australia	*da Austrália*	daa ows·*traa*·lyaa
Canada	*do Canadá*	do kaa·naa·*daa*
Singapore	*de Cingapura*	de seeng·gaa·*poo*·raa

age

idade

How old ...?	*Quantos anos ...?*	*kwang*·tos *a*·nos ...
are you	*você tem*	vo·*se* teng
is he/she	*ele/ela tem* m/f	e·le/e·laa teng

meeting people

95

I'm ... years old.
  Tenho ... anos.   te·nyo ... a·nos

He/She is ... years old.
  Ele/Ela tem ... anos. m/f   e·le/e·laa teng ... a·nos

Too old!
  Muito velho/velha! m/f   mweeng·to ve·lyo/ve·lya

I'm younger than I look.
  Sou mais novo/nova do   so mais no·vo/no·vaa do
  que aparento. m/f   ke aa·paa·reng·to

For your age, see **numbers & amounts**, page 29.

occupations & studies

What's your occupation?
  Você trabalha em que?   vo·se traa·baa·lyaa eng ke

I'm a ...	*Eu sou ...*	e·oo so ...
chef	*chefe* m&f *de*	she·fe de
	cozinha	ko·zee·nyaa
computer	*programador/*	pro·gra·maa·dorr/
programmer	*programadora de*	pro·gra·maa·do·raa de
	computação m/f	kong·poo·ta·sowng
exporter	*exportador/*	es·porr·taa·dorr/
	exportadora m/f	es·porr·taa·do·raa
journalist	*jornalista* m&f	zhor·naa·lees·taa
teacher	*professor/*	pro·fe·sorr/
	professora m/f	pro·fe·so·raa

I work in ...	*Trabalho na*	traa·baa·lyo naa
	área de ...	aa·re·aa de ...
administration	*administração*	aad·mee·nees·
		traa·sowng
health	*saúde*	saa·oo·de
sales &	*vendas e*	veng·daas e
marketing	*marketing*	maarr·ke·teeng

I'm ...	Eu ...	e·oo ...
self-employed	sou autônomo/	so ow·to·no·mo/
	autônoma m/f	ow·to·no·maa
unemployed	estou	es·to
	desempregado/	de·zeng·pre·gaa·do/
	desempregada m/f	de·zeng·pre·gaa·daa

What are you studying?

O que você está		o ke vo·se es·taa
estudando?		es·too·dang·do

I'm studying ...	Estou estudando ...	es·to es·too·dang·do ...
humanities	ciências	see·eng·syaas
	humanas	oo·ma·naas
Portuguese	português	porr·too·ges
science	ciências	see·eng·syaas

For other occupations and areas of study, see the **dictionary**.

family

família

Do you have a ...?	Você tem ...?	vo·se teng ...
I (don't) have a ...	Eu (não) tenho ...	e·oo (nowng) te·nyo ...
brother	irmão	eerr·mowng
daughter	filha	fee·lyaa
family	família	fa·mee·lyaa
father	pai	pai
grandfather	avô	aa·vo
grandmother	avó	aa·vaw
granddaughter	neta	ne·taa
grandson	neto	ne·to
husband	marido	maa·ree·do
mother	mãe	maing
partner	companheiro/	kong·pa·nyay·ro/
(intimate)	companheira m/f	kong·pa·nyay·raa
sister	irmã	eer·mang
son	filho	fee·lyo
wife	esposa	es·po·zaa

Are you married?
Você é casado/casada? m/f   vo·se e kaa·zaa·do/ kaa·zaa·daa

I live with someone.
Moro com uma pessoa.   mo·ro kong oo·maa pe·so·aa

I'm ...	*Eu sou ...*	e·oo so ...
married	*casado/*	kaa·zaa·do/
	casada m/f	kaa·zaa·daa
separated	*separado/*	se·paa·raa·daa
	separada m/f	se·paa·raa·do/
single	*solteiro/*	sol·tay·ro/
	solteira m/f	sol·tay·raa

farewells

Tomorrow is my last day here.
Amanhã é o meu   a·ma·nyang e o me·oo
ultimo dia aqui.   ool·tee·mo dee·aa aa·kee

Here's my ...	*Aqui está meu ...*	a·kee es·taa me·oo ...
What's your ...?	*Qual o seu ...?*	kwow o se·oo ...
address	*endereço*	eng·de·re·so
email address	*endereço de*	eng·de·re·so de
	e-mail	e·mail
phone number	*número de*	noo·me·ro de
	telephone	te·le·fo·ne

If you come to (Scotland), you can stay with me.
Se você for à (Escócia)   se vo·se forr aa (es·ko·syaa)
pode ficar na minha   po·de fee·kaarr naa mee·nyaa
casa.   kaa·zaa

Keep in touch!
Mantenha contato!   mang·te·nyaa kong·taa·to

It's been great meeting you.
Foi ótimo te conhecer.   foy o·tee·mo te ko·nye·serr

common interests

interesses comuns

What do you do in your spare time?

O que você gosta de fazer nas horas livres?	o ke vo·*se gos*·taa de faa·*zerr* naas *aw*·raas *lee*·vres	

Do you like …?	*Você gosta de …?*	vo·*se gos*·taa de …
I (don't) like …	*Eu (não) gosto de …*	e·oo (nowng) *gos*·to de …
arts and crafts	*artesanato* m	aarr·te·zaa·*naa*·to
Brazilian music	*música* f *brasileira*	*moo*·zee·kaa braa·zee·*lay*·raa
capoeira	*capoeira* f	kaa·po·*ay*·raa
carnival	*carnaval* m	kaarr·naa·*vow*
cooking	*cozinhar*	ko·zee·*nyaarr*
dancing	*dançar*	dang·*saarr*
drawing	*desenhar*	de·ze·*nyaarr*
films	*cinema* f	see·*ne*·maa
gardening	*jardinagem* f	zhaarr·dee·*naa*·zheng
hiking	*fazer caminhadas*	faa·*zerr* kaa·mee·*nyaa*·daas
live shows	*show* m *ao vivo*	show ow *vee*·vo
music	*música* f	*moo*·zee·kaa
painting	*pintar*	peeng·*taarr*
photography	*fotografia* f	fo·to·graa·*fee*·aa
reading	*ler*	lerr
shopping	*fazer compras*	faa·*zerr kong*·praas
socialising	*socializar*	so·see·aa·lee·*zaarr*
sport	*esporte* m	es·*porr*·te
travelling	*viajar*	vee·aa·*zhaarr*

For sporting activities, see **sport**, page 125.

music

Do you ...?	Você ...?	vo·se ...
dance	dança	dang·saa
go to concerts	vai à shows	vai aa shows
listen to music	escuta	es·koo·taa
	música	moo·zee·kaa
play an instrument	toca algum instrumento	to·kaa ow·goom eengs·troo·meng·to
sing	canta	kang·taa

What ... do you like?	De que ... você gosta?	de ke ... vo·se gos·taa
bands	bandas de música	bang·daas de moo·zee·kaa
music	música	moo·zee·kaa
singers	cantores	kang·to·res

kung fu dancing

Capoeira originated as an African martial art developed by slaves to fight their masters. It was disguised with the introduction of musical accompaniment to make it seem like dance. In its modern form, it combines elements of dance and fighting and is known for its fluid and circular movements.

classical music	música f clássica	moo·zee·kaa klaa·see·kaa
blues	blues m	blooz
electronic music	música f eletrônica	moo·zee·kaa e·le·tro·nee·kaa
jazz	jazz m	zhez
pop	pop m	po·pee
rock	rock m	ho·kee
traditional music	música f tradicional	moo·zee·kaa traa·dee·syo·now
world music	world music m	wol·dee mee·oo·zeek

Planning to go to a concert? See **tickets**, page 38 and **going out**, page 109.

cinema & theatre

cinema & teatro

I feel like going to a ...	Estou com vontade de ir ...	es·to kong vong·taa·de de eer ...
Did you like the ...?	Você gostou ...?	vo·se gos·to ...
ballet	do balé	do baa·le
film	do filme	do feel·me
play	da peça	daa pe·saa
I thought it was ...	Eu achei ...	e·oo aa·shay ...
excellent	excelente	es·se·leng·te
long	longo	long·go
OK	bom	bong

What's showing at the cinema/theatre tonight?
O que está passando no cinema/teatro hoje à noite?
o ke es·taa paa·sang·do no see·ne·maa/te·aa·tro o·zhe aa noy·te

Is it in English?
É em ingles?
e eng eeng·gles

Does it have (English) subtitles?
Tem sub·título (em inglês?)
teng soo·bee·tee·too·lo (eng eeng·gles)

I want to sell this ticket.
Quero vender este ingresso.
ke·ro veng·derr es·te eeng·gre·so

Is this seat taken?
Este lugar está vago?
es·te loo·gaarr es·taa vaa·go

Have you seen ...?
Você viu ...?
vo·se vee·oo ...

Who's in it?
É com quem?
e kong keng

It stars ...
É com ...
e kong ...

I (don't)	Eu (não)	e·oo (nowng)
like ...	gosto de ...	gos·to de ...
action movies	filmes de ação	feel·mes de aa·sowng
animated films	filmes de animação	feel·mes de aa·nee·maa·sowng
Brazilian cinema	cinema (brasileiro)	see·ne·maa (braa·zee·lay·ro)
comedies	comédias	ko·me·dyaas
documentaries	documentários	do·koo·meng·taa·ree·os
drama	drama	dra·maa
film noir	filme noir	feel·me noir
horror movies	filme de terror	feel·me de te·horr
sci-fi	ficção científica	feek·sowng see·eng·tee·fee·kaa
thrillers	suspense	soos·peng·se
war movies	filme de guerra	feel·me de ge·haa

feelings

sentimentos

Some feelings (like those in the first list) are described using 'be', *estar*, while others (see the second list) use 'be with', *estar com*.

Are you …?	Você está …?	vo·*se* es·*taa* …
I'm (not) …	(Não) Estou …	(nowng) es·*to* …
annoyed	*irritado/*	ee·hee·*taa*·do/
	irritada m/f	ee·hee·*taa*·daa
happy	*feliz*	fe·*lees*
sad	*triste*	*trees*·te
surprised	*surpreso/*	soorr·*pre*·zo/
	supresa m/f	soorr·*pre*·zaa
tired	*cansado/*	kang·*saa*·do/
	cansada m/f	kang·*saa*·daa
worried	*preocupado/*	pre·o·koo·*paa*·do/
	preocupada m/f	pre·o·koo·*paa*·daa

Are you …?	Você está com …?	vo·*se* es·*taa* kong …
I'm (not) …	(Não) Estou com …	(nowng) es·*to* kong…
cold	*frio*	*free*·o
embarrassed	*vergonha*	verr·*go*·nyaa
hot	*calor*	kaa·*lorr*
hungry	*fome*	*fo*·me
in a hurry	*pressa*	*pre*·saa
thirsty	*sede*	*se*·de

If feeling unwell, see **health**, page 177.

feelings & opinions

intense feelings

a little	um pouco	oom po·ko
I'm a little sad.	Estou um pouco triste.	es·to oom po·ko trees·te
very	muito/ muita m/f	mweeng·to/ mweeng·taa
I feel very lucky.	Estou com muita sorte.	es·to kong mweeng·taa sorr·te
extremely	super	soo·perr
I'm extremely happy.	Estou super feliz.	es·to soo·perr fe·lees

opinions

opiniões

Did you like it?
   Você gostou?   vo·se gos·to

What do you think of it?
   O que você achou?   o ke vo·se aa·sho·oo

I thought it was ...	Achei ...	aa·shay ...
It's ...	É ...	e ...
awful	péssimo/ péssima m/f	pe·see·mo/ pe·see·ma
beautiful	lindo/ linda m/f	leeng·do/ leeng·daa
boring	chato	shaa·to
great	ótimo/ótima m/f	o·tee·mo/o·tee·ma
interesting	interessante	eeng·te·re·sang·te
OK	bom	bong
too expensive	muito caro/cara m/f	mweeng·to kaa·ro/kaa·raa

politics & social issues

Who do you vote for?
Em quem você vota?   eng keng vo·se *vo*·taa

I support the ... party.	*Eu voto para o partido ...*	e·oo *vo*·to paa·raa o paarr·*tee*·do ...
I'm a member of the ... party.	*Eu sou membro do partido ...*	e·oo so *meng*·bro do paarr·*tee*·do ...
communist	*comunista*	ko·moo·*nees*·taa
conservative	*conservador*	kong·serr·vaa·*dorr*
democratic	*democrata*	de·mo·*kraa*·taa
green	*verde*	*verr*·de
liberal	*liberal*	lee·be·*row*
social democratic	*democrata-social*	de·mo·*kraa*·taa·so·see·*ow*
socialist	*socialista*	so·see·aa·*lees*·taa
workers	*dos trabalhadores*	dos traa·baa·lyaa·*do*·res

Did you hear about ...?
Você ouviu falar ...?   vo·se o·*vee*·oo faa·*laarr* ...

Do you agree with it?
Você concorda com isto?   vo·se kong·*korr*·daa kong *ees*·to

I (don't) agree with ...
Eu (não) concordo com ...   e·oo (nowng) kong·*korr*·do kong ...

How do people feel about ...?
O que as pessoas acham ...?   o ke aas pe·*so*·aas *aa*·shang ...

How can we protest against ...?
Como podemos protestar contra ...?   *ko*·mo po·*de*·mos pro·tes·*taarr* kong·traa ...

How can we support ...?
Como podemos apoiar ...?   *ko*·mo po·*de*·mos aa·po·*yaarr* ...

feelings & opinions

105

abortion	*aborto* m	aa·*borr*·to
animal rights	*direitos* m *dos animais*	dee·*ray*·tos dos aa·nee·*mais*
crime	*crime* m	*kree*·me
discrimination	*descriminação* f	des·kree·mee·na·*sowng*
drugs	*drogas* f pl	*dro*·gaas
the economy	*a economia* f	aa e·ko·no·*mee*·aa
education	*educação* f	e·doo·kaa·*sowng*
the environment	*o meio ambiente* m	o *may*·o ang·bee·*eng*·te
equal opportunity	*direitos* m pl *iguais*	dee·*ray*·tos ee·*gwais*
euthanasia	*euthanasia* f	e·oo·taa·*naa*·zyaa
globalisation	*globalização* f	glo·baa·lee·zaa·*sowng*
human rights	*direitos* m pl *humanos*	dee·*ray*·tos oo·*ma*·nos
immigration	*imigração* f	ee·mee·graa·*sowng*
income distribution·	*distribuição* f *de renda*	dees·tree·boo·ee·*sowng* de *heng*·daa
inequality	*desigualdade* f	de·zee·gwow·*daa*·de
inflation	*inflação* f	eeng·flaa·*sowng*
party politics	*política* f *partidária*	po·*lee*·tee·kaa paarr·tee·*daa*·ree·aa
privatisation	*privatização* f	pree·vaa·tee·zaa·*sowng*
racism	*racismo* m	haa·*sees*·mo
sexism	*machismo* m	maa·*shees*·mo
slums	*favelas* f pl	faa·*ve*·laas
social disparity	*disparidade* f *social*	dees·paa·ree·*daa*·de so·see·*ow*
social welfare	*justiça* f *social*	zhoos·*tee*·sa so·see·*ow*
unemployment	*desemprego* m	de·*zeng*·pre·go
work safety	*segurança* f *no trabalho*	se·goo·*rang*·saa no traa·*baa*·lyo
workers rights	*direitos* m *dos trabalhadores*	dee·*ray*·tos dos traa·baa·lyaa·*do*·res

the environment

Is there a … problem here?
Aqui tem problema de …?   a·*kee* teng pro·*ble*·maa de …

What should be done about …?
O que deveria ser feito   o ke de·ve·*ree*·aa serr *fay*·to
sobre …?   *so*·bre …

conservation	*conservação* f	kong·ser·va·*sowng*
deforestation	*desflorestamento* m	des·flo·res·taa·*meng*·to
drought	*seca* f	*se*·kaa
ecosystem	*eco-sistema* f	e·ko·sees·*te*·maa
endangered species	*espécies* f pl *ameaçadas de extinção*	es·*pe*·syes aa·me·a·*saa*·daas de es·teeng·*sowng*
genetically modified food	*alimentos* m pl *geneticamente modificados*	aa·lee·*meng*·tos ge·ne·tee·kaa·*meng*·te mo·dee·fee·*kaa*·dos
hunting	*caça* f	*kaa*·saa
hydroelectricity	*energia* f *hidroelétrica*	e·nerr·*zhee*·aa ee·dro·e·*le*·tree·kaa
irrigation	*irrigação* f	ee·hee·gaa·*sowng*
nuclear energy	*energia* f *nuclear*	e·nerr·*zhee*·aa noo·kle·*aarr*
nuclear testing	*teste* m *nuclear*	*tes*·te noo·kle·*aarr*
ozone layer	*camada* f *de ozônio*	kaa·*maa*·daa de o·zo·nee·o
pesticides	*pesticidas* f pl	pes·tee·*see*·daas
pollution	*poluição* f	po·loo·ee·*sowng*
recycling programme	*programa* f *de reciclagem*	pro·*gra*·maa de he·see·*klaa*·zheng
toxic waste	*resíduos* m pl *tóxicos*	he·*zee*·dwos tok·*see*·kos
water supply	*abastecimento* m *de água*	aa·baas·te·see·*meng*·to de *aa*·gwaa

Is this a protected ...?	Esta é ...	es·taa e ...
forest	uma floresta protegida	oo·maa flo·res·taa pro·te·zhee·daa
species	uma espécie protegida	oo·maa es·pe·sye pro·te·zhee·daa

indigenous languages

During the early days of colonisation, many Portuguese missionaries and colonists learnt how to speak *Tupinambá*, an indigenous language spoken along the Brazilian coast. Use of the language became so widespread within the colony that it became known as *Língua Brasilica* (Brazilian language) and later *Língua Geral* (general language). *Tupinambá* has since become extinct although *Nheengatu*, a derivation of the *Língua Geral*, is still spoken in the Negro River basin. It wasn't until the mid-18th century that the Portuguese language truly began to predominate and hundreds of local languages were slowly wiped out by colonial expansion. Historians have estimated that, prior to the arrival of the Portuguese, there were probably 400 or 500 languages spoken within the present boundaries of Brazil. Today less than 200 remain. Most of these are facing extinction, although the *Guaraní* language, spoken by over 30,000 people, is showing little evidence of decline.

Indigenous languages, particularly *Tupinambá*, have had a significant influence on Brazilian Portuguese. The words *jabuti* (turtle), *jacaré* (alligator), *capim* (grass), *cipó* (vine) and *piranha* (piranha) all originate from *Tupinambá*. Other Brazilian Portuguese words derived from indigenous languages include *abacaxi* (pineapple), *mandioca* (manioc flour), *caju* (cashew) and *tatu* (armadillo).

where to go

para onde ir

What's there to do in the evenings?
O que se tem para   o ke se teng *paa*·raa
fazer à noite?   faa·*zerr* aa *noy*·te

What's on …?	*O que está acontecendo …?*	o ke es·*taa* aa·kong·te·*seng*·do …
locally	*aqui perto*	aa·*kee perr*·to
this weekend	*neste final de semana*	*nes*·te fee·*now* de se·*ma*·naa
today	*hoje*	*o*·zhe
tonight	*à noite*	aa *noy*·te
Where can I find …?	*Onde posso encontrar …?*	*ong*·de *po*·so eng·kong·*traar* …
clubs	*um lugar para dançar*	oom loo·*gaarr paa*·raa dang·*saarr*
gay venues	*lugares gays*	loo·*gaa*·res gays
places to eat	*lugares para comer*	loo·*gaa*·res *paa*·raa ko·*merr*
pubs	*um bar*	oom baarr
Is there a local … guide?	*Existe algum guia de … dessa área?*	e·*zees*·te ow·*goom gee*·aa de … *de*·saa *aa*·re·aa
entertainment	*entretenimento*	eng·tre·te·nee·*meng*·to
film	*cinema*	see·*ne*·maa
gay	*de lugares gays*	de loo·*gaa*·res gays
music	*música*	*moo*·zee·kaa

going out

109

I feel like going to a …	Estou com vontade de ir …	es·to kong vong·taa·de de eerr …
ballet	ao balé	ow baa·le
bar	a um bar	aa oom baarr
cafe	a um café	aa oom kaa·fe
concert	a um show	aa oom show
film	ao cinema	ow see·ne·maa
karaoke bar	a um karaoke	aa oom kaa·raa·o·ke
nightclub	a uma boate	aa oo·maa bo·aa·te
party	a uma festa	aa oo·maa fes·taa
performance	a uma performance	aa oo·maa perr·forr·mang·se
play	a uma obra	aa oo·maa o·braa
pub	a um bar	aa oom baarr
restaurant	a um restaurante	aa oom hes·tow·rang·te

For more on bars and drinks, see **eating out,** page 149.

invitations

convites

What are you doing …?	O que você está fazendo …?	o ke vo·se es·taa faa·zeng·do …
now	agora	aa·go·raa
this weekend	neste final de semana	nes·te fee·now de se·ma·naa
tonight	hoje à noite	o·zhe aa noy·te

Would you like to go (for a) …?	Você gostaria de ir …?	vo·se gos·taa·ree·aa de irr …
chat	bater um papo	baa·terr oom paa·po
somewhere	em algum lugar	eng ow·goom loo·gaarr
coffee	tomar um café	to·maarr oom kaa·fe
drink	beber alguma coisa	be·berr ow·goo·maa koy·zaa
meal	jantar	zhang·taarr
walk	caminhar	kaa·mee·nyaarr

I feel like	Eu gostaria de	e·oo gos·taa·ree·aa de
going ... dancing	dançar ...	dang·saarr ...
samba	samba	sang·ba
forró	forró	fo·ho
gafieira	gafieira	gaa·fee·ay·raa
lambada	lambada	lang·baa·daa

My round.
Minha vez. mee·nyaa vez

Do you know a good restaurant?
Você conhece um bom vo·se ko·nye·se oom bom
restaurante? hes·tow·rang·te

Do you want to come to the concert with me?
Você quer vir ao show vo·se kerr veerr ow show
comigo? ko·mee·go

We're having a party.
Estamos dando uma es·ta·mos dang·do oo·maa
festa. fes·taa

You should come.
Você deveria vir. vo·se de·ve·ree·aa veer

responding to invitations

Sure!
Claro! klaa·ro

Yes, I'd love to.
Sim, adoraria. seeng aa·do·raa·ree·aa

That's very kind of you.
É muito gentil e mweeng·to zheng·teel
de sua parte. de soo·aa paarr·te

Where shall we go?
Onde podemos ir? ong·de po·de·mos eerr

No, I'm afraid I can't.
Não, infelizmente nowng eeng·fe·lees·meng·te
não posso. nowng po·so

going out

111

Sorry, I can't sing/dance.
Desculpe, mas eu   des·*kool*·pe mas e·oo
não sei cantar/   nowng say kang·*taarr*/
dançar.   dang·*saarr*

What about tomorrow?
Que tal amanhã?   ke tow aa·ma·*nyang*

arranging to meet

What time will we meet?
A que horas nos   aa ke *aw*·raas nos
encontramos?   eng·kong·*tra*·mos

Where will we meet?
Onde vamos nos   *ong*·de *va*·mos nos
encontrar?   eng·kong·*traarr*

Let's meet	*Vamos nos*	*va*·mos nos
at …	*encontrar …*	eng·kong·*traarr* …
(eight) o'clock	*às (oito) horas*	aas (*oy*·to) *aw*·raas
the (entrance)	*na (entrada)*	naa (eng·*traa*·daa)

I'll pick you up.
Eu te pego.   e·oo te *pe*·go

Are you ready?
Você está pronto/   vo·*se* es·*taa prong*·to/
pronta? m/f   *prong*·taa

I'm ready.
Estou pronto/pronta. m/f   es·*to prong*·to/*prong*·taa

I'll be coming later.
Eu vou mais tarde.   e·oo vo mais *taarr*·de

Where will you be?
Onde você vai estar?   ong·de vo·se vai es·taarr

If I'm not there by (nine), don't wait for me.
Se eu não chegar   se e·oo nowng she·gaarr
até às (nove), não me   aa·te aas (no·ve) nowng me
espere mais.   es·pe·re mais

OK!
Tá bom!   taa bong

I'll see you then.
Te vejo depois.   te ve·zho de·poys

See you later/tomorrow.
Até mais tarde/   aa·te mais taarr·de/
amanhã.   aa·ma·nyang

I'm looking forward to it.
Vou aguardar   vo aa·gwaar·daarr
ansiosamente.   ang·see·o·zaa·meng·te

Sorry I'm late.
Desculpe o atraso.   des·kool·pe o aa·traa·zo

Never mind.
Não tem problema.   nowng teng pro·ble·ma

---

samba jamming

From the religious dances of *Candomblé* to the martial arts movements of *capoeira*, dancing finds its way into almost all aspects of the Brazilian lifestyle. No dance has achieved the same popularity as *samba*, a composite of diverse indigenous, African and European dancing styles.

The origins of *samba* lie in a fusion between the indigenous *lundu* dance and the *batuque*, a circular dance practised by African slaves. By the late-19th century, these styles adopted European characteristics to become *mesemba* and eventually modern *samba*. The percussive music of *samba* is equally rich in its origins and influences.

Spontaneous *samba* jam sessions called *batucadas* erupt in the streets on occasions of national celebration.

drugs

I don't take drugs.
Eu não uso drogas.   e·oo nowng oo·zo dro·gaas

Do you want to have a smoke?
Você quer fumar um   vo·se kerr foo·maarr oom
unzinho?   oom·zee·nyo

Do you have a light?
Você tem isqueiro?   vo·se teng ees·kay·ro

romance

asking someone out

convidando alguém para sair

Would you like to do something (tomorrow)?
Você quer fazer alguma coisa (amanhã)?
vo·se kerr faa·zerr ow·goo·maa koy·zaa (aa·ma·nyang)

Yes, I'd love to.
Sim, adoraria.
seeng aa·do·raa·ree·aa

No, I can't.
Não, não posso.
nowng nowng po·so

Where would you like to go (tonight)?
Onde você quer ir (hoje à noite)?
ong·de vo·se kerr eerr (o·zhe aa noy·te)

pick-up lines

cantadas

Would you like a drink?
Você quer beber alguma coisa?
vo·se kerr be·berr ow·goo·maa koy·zaa

You look like someone I know.
Você parece com alguém que eu conheço.
vo·se paa·re·se kong ow·geng ke e·oo ko·nye·so

You're a fantastic dancer.
Você dança super bem.
vo·se dang·saa soo·perr beng

You're so beautiful!
Você é lindo/linda! m/f
vo·se e leeng·do/leeng·daa

Can I ...?	Posso ...?	po·so ...
dance with you	dançar com você	dang·saarr kong vo·se
sit here	sentar aqui	seng·taarr aa·kee
take you home	levar você em casa	le·vaarr vo·se eng kaa·zaa

romance

115

He/She is ...	Ele/Ela é ...	e·le/e·laa e ...
great	demais	de·mais
hot	tesão	te·sowng
very nice	super legal	soo·perr le·gow

What a babe!
Que gato/gata! m/f   ke *gaa*·to/*gaa*·taa

He/She gets around.
Ele/Ela dá suas   e·le/e·laa daa soo·aas
voltas. m/f   *vawl*·taas

rejections

I'm here with my ...	Estou com minha/ meu ... m/f	es·to kong mee·nyaa me·oo ...
boyfriend	namorado m	naa·mo·raa·do
girlfriend	namorada f	naa·mo·raa·daa

Excuse me, I have to go now.
Me dá licença, eu   me daa lee·*seng*·saa e·oo
tenho que ir embora.   *te*·nyo ke eerr eng·*bo*·raa

I'd rather not.
Prefiro que não.   pre·*fee*·ro ke nowng

No, thank you.
Não, obrigado/   nowng o·bree·*gaa*·do/
obrigada. m/f   o·bree·*gaa*·daa

getting closer

I like you very much.
Gostei muito de você.   gos·*tay* mweeng·to de vo·se

You're great.
Você é muito legal.   vo·se e mweeng·to le·*gow*

Can I kiss you?
Posso te dar um beijo?   po·so te daarr oom *bay*·zho

Do you want to come inside for a while?
Você quer entrar   vo·se kerr eng·*traarr*
um pouco?   oom po·ko

Do you want a massage?
Você quer uma   vo·se kerr oo·maa
massagem?   maa·*saa*·zheng

I'm not interested.
Não estou   nowng es·*to*
interessado/   eeng·te·re·*saa*·do/
interessada. m/f   eeng·te·re·*saa*·daa

Leave me alone!
Me deixe em paz!   me *day*·she eng paas

Piss off!
Sai fora!   sai *fo*·raa

Give me a break!
Dá um tempo!   daa oom *teng*·po

romance

117

Kiss me.
Me beija.   me *bay*·zhaa

I want you.
Eu quero você.   e·oo ke·ro vo·se

I want to make love to you.
Eu quero fazer amor   e·oo ke·ro faa·zerr aa·morr
com você.   kong vo·se

Let's go to bed.
Vamos para a cama.   va·mos paa·raa aa ka·maa

Do you have a (condom)?
Você tem (camisinha)?   vo·se teng (kaa·mee·zee·nyaa)

Let's use a (condom).
Vamos usar   va·mos oo·zaarr
(camisinha).   (kaa·mee·zee·nyaa)

I won't do it without protection.
Não faço sem   nowng faa·so seng
proteção.   pro·te·sowng

Touch me here.
Me toca aqui.   me to·kaa aa·kee

Do you like this?
Você gosta disso?   vo·se gos·taa dee·so

I (don't) like that.
Eu (não) gosto disso.   e·oo (nowng) gos·to dee·so

I think we should stop now.
Acho que devemos parar   aa·sho ke de·ve·mos paa·raarr
agora.   aa·go·raa

It's my first time.
É a minha   e aa mee·nyaa
primeira vez.   pree·may·raa vez

It helps to have a sense of humour.
É bom ter senso   e bong terr seng·so
de humor.   de oo·morr

Oh yeah!	*Uau!*	oo·ow
Oh my god!	*Ai meu Deus!*	ai *me*·oo *de*·oos
That's great.	*Que delícia.*	ke de·*lee*·syaa
Easy tiger!	*Calma!*	*kaal*·maa

That was …	*Foi …*	foy …
amazing	*incrível*	eeng·*kree*·vel
weird	*estranho*	es·*tra*·nyo
wild	*uma loucura*	oo·maa lo·*koo*·raa

Can I …?	*Posso …?*	*po*·so …
call you	*te ligar*	te lee·*gaarr*
meet you	*te encontrar*	te eng·kong·*traarr*
tomorrow	*amanhã*	aa·ma·*nyang*
stay over	*dormir aqui*	dorr·*meerr* aa·*kee*

love

amor

I love you.
Eu te amo.   e·oo te *a*·mo

I think we're good together.
Eu acho que nós somos   e·oo *aa*·sho ke nos *so*·mos
ótimos juntos.   o·tee·mos *zhoong*·tos

Will you …?	*Você quer …*	vo·*se* kerr …
	comigo?	ko·*mee*·go
go out with me	*sair*	saa·*eerr*
live with me	*morar*	mo·*raarr*
marry me	*casar*	kaa·*zaarr*

problems

Are you seeing someone else?
Você está saindo com
outra pessoa?
vo·se es·*taa* saa·*eeng*·do kong
o·traa pe·*so*·aa

We're just friends.
Somos só amigos.
so·mos so aa·*mee*·gos

You're just using me for sex.
Você está só me usando
para sexo.
vo·se es·*ta* so me oo·*zang*·do
paa·raa sek·so

I don't think it's working out.
Acho que não está
dando certo.
aa·sho ke nowng es·*taa*
dang·do serr·to

We'll work it out.
Vamos tentar resolver.
va·mos teng·*taarr* he·sol·*verr*

leaving

I have to leave tomorrow.
Eu tenho que ir
embora amanhã.
e·oo te·nyo ke eerr
eng·*bo*·raa aa·ma·*nyang*

I'll …	*Eu vou …*	e·oo vo …
keep in touch	*manter* *contato*	vo mang·*terr* kong·*taa*·to
miss you	*sentir* *sua falta*	seng·*teerr* soo·aa fow·taa

terms of endearment		
amorzão	aa·morr·*zowng*	big love
coração	ko·raa·*sowng*	heart
meu bem	me·oo beng	my good
meu amor	me·oo aa·*morr*	my love
querido/	ke·*ree*·do/	dear
querida m/f	ke·*ree*·daa	

SOCIAL

120

religion

religião

What's your religion?
Qual é a sua
religião?

kwow e aa *soo*·aa
he·lee·zhee·*owng*

I'm not religious.
Não sou religioso/
religiosa. m/f

nowng so he·lee·zhee·o·zo/
he·lee·zhee·o·zaa

I'm ...	Sou ...	so ...
agnostic	*agnóstico/*	aag·*nos*·tee·ko/
	agnóstica m/f	aag·*nos*·tee·kaa
Buddhist	*Budista*	boo·*dees*·taa
Catholic	*Católico/*	kaa·*to*·lee·ko/
	Católica m/f	kaa·*to*·lee·kaa
Christian	*Cristão/*	krees·*towng*/
	Cristã m/f	krees·*tang*
Hindu	*Hindu*	eeng·*doo*
Jewish	*Judeu/*	zhoo·*de*·oo/
	Judia m/f	zhoo·*dee*·aa
Muslim	*Muçulmano/*	moo·sool·*ma*·no/
	Muçulmana m/f	moo·sool·*ma*·naa
spiritist	*Espírita*	es·*pee*·ree·taa

gender bending

Remember, gender is indicated on nouns and adjectives. A
useful and almost guaranteed way to tell the gender: if it
ends in -*a*, it's femine, in -*o*, it's masculine.

out of africa

In addition to being home to various world religions, Brazil accommodates a number of unique faiths, often blends of indigenous beliefs, African cults and mainstream religions that have been introduced to the country. Two of the more common cults that you might come across are *Candomblé* and *Umbanda*.

Candomblé, an African word denoting a dance in honour of the gods, is a general term for the cult in Bahia, which was brought by the Nago, Yoruba and Jeje peoples. Elsewhere in Brazil the cult is known by different names and it has been adapted to include elements from other belief systems, including Christianity and indigenous faiths: in Rio it's *Macumba*; in Amazonas and Pará it's *Babassuê*; in Pernambuco and Alagoas it's *Xangô*; in Rio Grande do Sul it's either *Pará* or *Batuque*; and the term *Tambor* is used in Maranhão.

Umbanda, or white magic, is a mixture of *Candomblé* and spiritism. It traces its origins from various sources, including Bantu culture.

I (don't)	Eu (não)	e·oo (nowng)
believe in ...	acredito em ...	aa·kre·dee·to eng ...
astrology	astrologia	aas·tro·lo·zhee·aa
fate	destino	des·tee·no
God	Deus	de·oos

Can I ... here?	Posso ... aqui?	po·so ... aa·kee
Where can I ...?	Onde posso ...?	ong·de po·so ...
attend	assistir	aa·sees·teerr
mass	uma missa	oo·maa mee·saa
pray	rezar	he·zaarr
worship	venerar	ve·ne·haarr

SOCIAL

122

cultural differences

Is this a local or national custom?
Este é um costume   es·te e oom kos·*too*·me
local ou nacional?   lo·*kow* o·oo naa·see·o·*now*

I don't want to offend you.
Não quero ofendê-lo/   nowng *ke*·ro o·feng·*de*·lo/
ofendê-la. m/f   o·feng·*de*·laa

I'm not used to this.
Não estou   nowng es·*to*
acostumado/   aa·kos·too·*maa*·do/
acostumada com isso. m/f   aa·kos·too·*maa*·daa kong *ee*·so

I'd rather not join in.
Prefiro não fazer
parte.
pre·*fee*·ro nowng faa·*zerr*
paarr·te

I'll try it.
Vou experimentar.
vo es·pe·ree·meng·*taarr*

I didn't mean to do/say anything wrong.
Não tive intenção
de fazer/dizer qualquer
coisa errada.
nowng *tee*·ve eeng·teng·*sowng*
de faa·*zerr*/dee·*zerr* kwow·*kerr*
koy·zaa e·*haa*·daa

I'm sorry, it's	*Me desculpe, mas é*	me des·*kool*·pe maas e
against my ...	*contra minha ...*	*kong*·traa mee·*nyaa* ...
beliefs	*crença*	*kreng*·saa
religion	*religião*	he·lee·zhee·*owng*

This is ...	*Isto é ...*	*ees*·to e ...
different	*diferente*	dee·fe·*reng*·te
fun	*divertido*	dee·verr·*tee*·do
interesting	*interessante*	eeng·te·re·*sang*·te

sporting interests

interesses esportivos

What sport do you ...?	Que esporte você ...?	ke es·*porr*·te vo·*se* ...
follow	acompanha	aa·kong·*pa*·nyaa
play	pratica	praa·*tee*·kaa
I play ...	Eu jogo ...	e·oo zho·go ...
basketball	basquete	baas·*ke*·te
tennis	tênis	te·nees
volleyball	vôlei	vo·lay
I do ...	Eu faço ...	e·oo faa·so ...
athletics	atletismo	aat·le·*tees*·mo
karate	karatê	kaa·raa·*te*
scuba diving	mergulho	merr·*goo*·lyo

I follow ...	Eu acompanho ...	e·oo aa·kong·*pa*·nyo ...
football (soccer)	futebol de campo	foo·te·*bol* de *kang*·po
motor racing	corrida de carros	ko·*hee*·daa de *kaa*·hos
surfing	surfe	soorr·fe
I ...	Eu ...	e·oo ...
cycle	ando de bicicleta	*ang*·do de bee·see·*kle*·taa
run	corro	*ko*·ho
walk	caminho	ka·*mee*·nyo

For more sports, see the **dictionary**.

Do you like (cricket)?
Você gosta (de cricket)?   vo·se gos·taa (de kree·ke·tee)

Yes, very much.
Sim, gosto muito.   seeng gos·to mweeng·to

Not really.
Não muito.   nowng mweeng·to

I like watching it.
Eu gosto de assistir.   e·oo gos·to de aa·sees·teerr

Who's your   *Qual é o seu ...*   kwow e o se·oo ...
favourite ...?   *favorito?*   faa·vo·ree·to
   sportsperson   *esportista*   es·porr·tees·taa
   team   *time*   tee·me

scoring

What's the score?
Quanto está o jogo?   kwang·to es·taa o zho·go

draw/even   *empate*   eng·paa·te
love   *zero*   ze·ro
match-point   *match point*   me·tee po·eeng·tee
nil   *zero*   ze·ro

going to a game

indo a um jogo

Would you like to go to a game?
Você gostaria de ir   vo·se gos·taa·ree·aa de eerr
a um jogo?   aa oom zho·go

Who are you supporting?
Para quem você torce?   paa·raa keng vo·se torr·se

Who's ...?	Quem está ...?	keng es·*taa* ...
playing	jogando	zho·*gang*·do
winning	ganhando	ga·*nyang*·do
That was a ... game!	Foi um jogo ...!	foy oom *zho*·go ...
bad	ruim	hoo·*eeng*
boring	chato	*shaa*·to
great	ótimo	o·tee·mo

playing sport

praticando esporte

Do you want to play?
Você quer jogar?
vo·*se* kerr zho·*gaarr*

Can I join in?
Posso jogar com vocês?
po·so zho·*gaarr* kong vo·*ses*

That would be great.
Seria ótimo.
se·*ree*·aa o·tee·mo

I can't.
Não posso.
nowng *po*·so

I have an injury.
*Estou machucado/
machucado.* m/f
es·*to* maa·shoo·*kaa*·do
maa·shoo·*kaa*·daa

Your/My point.
Teu/Meu ponto.
te·oo/me·oo pong·to

Kick/Pass it to me!
*Chuta/Passa para
mim!*
shoo·taa/*paa*·saa *paa*·raa
meeng

You're a good player.
Você é um bom jogador.
vo·*se* e oom bong zho·gaa·*dorr*

Thanks for the game.
*Obrigado/obrigada
pelo jogo.* m/f
o·bree·*gaa*·do/o·bree·*gaa*·daa
pe·lo *zho*·go

sport

Where's a good place to ...?	Onde tem um bom lugar para ...?	ong·de teng oom bong loo·gaarr paa·raa ...
fish	pescar	pes·kaarr
go horse riding	andar à cavalo	ang·daar aa kaa·vaa·lo
run	correr	ko·herr
ski	esquiar	es·kee·aarr
snorkel	fazer snorkel	faa·zerr ees·norr·kel
surf	surfar	soor·faarr

Where's the nearest ...?	Onde fica ... mais perto?	ong·de fee·kaa ... mais perr·to
golf course	o campo de golfe	o kang·po de gol·fe
gym	a ginástica	aa zhee·naas·tee·kaa
swimming pool	a piscina	aa pee·see·naa
tennis court	a quadra de tênis	aa kwaa·draa de te·nees

What's the charge per ...?	Quanto custa por ...?	kwang·to koos·taa porr ...
day	dia	dee·aa
game	jogo	zho·go
hour	hora	aw·raa
visit	visita	vee·zee·taa

Can I hire a ...?	Posso alugar uma ...?	po·so aa·loo·gaarr oo·maa ...
ball	bola	bo·laa
bicycle	bicicleta	bee·see·kle·taa
court	quadra	kwaa·draa
racquet	raquete	haa·ke·te

Do I have to be a member to attend?

*Tem que ser membro
para entrar?*

teng ke ser *meng*·bro
paa·raa eng·traarr

Is there a women-only session?

*Tem uma seção só
para mulheres?*

teng oo·maa se·*sowng* so
paa·raa moo·*lye*·res

Where are the changing rooms?

*Onde ficam os
vestiários?*

ong·de *fee*·kang os
ves·tee·*aa*·ree·os

diving

Where's a good diving site?

*Onde tem um lugar
bom para mergulho?*

ong·de teng oom loo·*gaarr*
bong paa·raa merr·*goo*·lyo

Is the visibility good?

A visibilidade é boa?

aa vee·zee·bee·lee·*daa*·de e *bo*·aa

How deep is the dive?

Qual a profundidade?

kwow aa pro·foong·dee·*daa*·de

I need an air fill.

*Preciso encher o
tanque de ar.*

pre·*see*·zo eng·*sherr* o
tang·ke de aarr

Is it a …	*Este é um*	es·te e oom
dive?	*mergulho …?*	merr·*goo*·lyo …
boat	*a partir de
um barco*	aa paarr·*teerr* de
oom *baar*·ko
shore	*litorâneo*	lee·to·*ra*·ne·o

Are there …?	*Tem …?*	teng …
currents	*corrente*	ko·*heng*·te
sharks	*tubarão*	too·ba·*rowng*
whales	*baleia*	baa·*le*·yaa

I want to hire (a) ...	Quero alugar ...	ke·ro aa·loo·gaarr ...
buoyancy vest	colete	ko·le·te
diving equipment	equipamento de mergulho	e·kee·paa·meng·to de merr·goo·lyo
flippers	nadadeiras	na·da·dei·ras
mask	máscara	maas·kaa·raa
regulator	regulador	he·goo·laa·dorr
snorkel	snorkel	ees·norr·kel
tank	tanque	tang·ke
weight belt	cinto com peso	seeng·to kong pe·zo
wetsuit	roupa de borracha	ho·paa de bo·haa·shaa

I'd like to ...	Gostaria de ...	gos·taa·ree·aa de ...
explore caves	explorar cavernas	es·plo·raar kaa·verr·naas
explore wrecks	explorar navios naufragados	es·plo·raar naa·vee·os now·fraa·gaa·dos
go night diving	fazer um mergulho noturno	faa·zerr oom merr·goo·lyo no·toor·no
go scuba diving	mergulhar com tanque	merr·goo·lyaarr kong tang·ke
go snorkelling	fazer snorkel	faa·zerr ees·norr·kel
join a diving tour	fazer parte de um grupo de mergulho	faa·zerr paarr·te de oom groo·po de merr·goo·lyo
learn to dive	aprender a mergulhar	aa·preng·derr aa merr·goo·lyaarr

buddy	companheiro m	kong·pa·*nyay*·ro
cave	caverna f	kaa·*verr*·naa
a dive	mergulho m	merr·*goo*·lyo
to dive	mergulhar	merr·goo·*lyaarr*
diving boat	barco m para	baar·ko paa·raa
	mergulho	merr·*goo*·lyo
diving course	curso m de	*koor*·so de
	mergulho	merr·*goo*·lyo
night dive	mergulho m	merr·*goo*·lyo
	noturno	no·*toorr*·no
wreck	navio m	naa·*vee*·o
	naufragado	now·fraa·*gaa*·do

See also **watersports**, page 134.

See also **watersports**, page 134.

extreme sports

esportes radicais

I'd like to go ...	Eu queria fazer ...	e·oo ke·*ree*·aa faa·*zerr* ...
abseiling	rapel	haa·*pel*
caving	exploração de	es·plo·raa·*sowng* de
	cavernas	kaa·*verr*·naas
canyoning	canyoning	*kang*·nyo·neeng
hang-gliding	vôo livre	*vo*·o *lee*·vre
mountain	mountain	*maa*·oong·tayng
biking	bike	*bai*·kee
paragliding	parapente	paa·raa·*peng*·te
parasailing	parasailing	paa·raa·*say*·leeng
rock-climbing	escalada	es·kaa·*laa*·daa
skydiving	skydiving	ees·kai·*dai*·veeng
white-water rafting	rafting	haa·fee·teeng

Is the equipment secure?
Este equipamento é seguro? es·te e·kee·paa·*meng*·to e se·*goo*·ro

This is insane.
Isto é loucura. ees·to e lo·*koo*·raa

horse riding

How much is a (one) hour ride?
Quanto é o passeio de   *kwang*·to e o paa·*se*·yo de
(uma) hora?   (*oo*·maa) *aw*·raa

How long is the ride?
Quanto tempo é   *kwang*·to *teng*·po e
o passeio?   o paa·*se*·yo

I'm (not) an experienced rider.
Eu (não) sou experiente.   *e*·oo (nowng) so es·pe·ree·*eng*·te

Can I rent a hat and boots?
Posso alugar um   *po*·so aa·loo·*gaarr* oom
chapéu e botas?   shaa·*pe*·oo e *bo*·taas

bit	*freio* m	*fre*·yo
bridle	*rédea* f	*he*·dyaa
canter	*galope* m	gaa·*lo*·pe
crop	*chicote* m	shee·*ko*·te
gallop	*galope* m	gaa·*lo*·pe
groom	*tratar*	tra·*taarr*
horse	*cavalo* m	kaa·*vaa*·lo
pony	*pônei* m	*po*·nay
reins	*rédeas* f pl	*he*·dyaas
saddle	*sela* f	*se*·laa
stable	*estábulo* m	es·*taa*·boo·lo
stirrup	*estribo* m	es·*tree*·bo
trot	*trote* m	*tro*·te
walk	*andar*	ang·*daar*

soccer

Who plays for (Flamengo)?
   Quem joga no   keng *zho*·gaa no
   (Flamengo)?   (flaa·*meng*·go)

He's a great (player).
   Ele é um ótimo   *e*·le e oom o·tee·mo
   (jogador).   (zho·gaa·*dorr*)

He played brilliantly in the match against (Argentina).
   Ele jogou muito bem   *e*·le *zho*·goo mweeng·to beng
   no jogo contra   no *zho*·go kong·traa
   (a Argentina).   (aa aarr·zheng·*tee*·naa)

Which team is at the top of the league?
   Que time está na frente ke *tee*·me es·*taa* naa *freng*·te
   da liga?   daa *lee*·gaa

What a great/terrible team!
   Que time ótimo/horrível! ke *tee*·me o·tee·mo/o·*hee*·vel

ball	*bola* f	*bo*·laa
coach	*técnico* m	*tek*·nee·ko
corner (kick)	*escanteio* m	es·kang·*te*·yo
fan	*fã* m&f	fang
foul	*falta* f	*fow*·taa
free kick	*bater a falta*	baa·*terr* aa *fow*·taa
goal	*gol* m	gol
goal (place)	*trave* f	*tra*·ve
goalkeeper	*goleiro* m	go·*lay*·ro
offside	*lateral*	laa·te·*row*
penalty	*pênalti* m	pe·now·tee
player	*jogador* m	zho·gaa·*dorr*
red card	*cartão* m *vermelho*	kaarr·*towng* verr·*me*·lyo
referee	*juiz* m	joo·*ees*
striker	*atacante* m	aa·taa·*kang*·te
team	*time* m	*tee*·me
throw in	*bater a lateral*	baa·*terr* aa laa·te·*row*
yellow card	*cartão* m *amarelo*	kaarr·*towng* aa·maa·*re*·lo

water sports

Can I book a lesson?
Posso marcar uma   po·so maarr·*kaarr* oo·maa
aula?   ow·laa

Can I hire (a) ...	*Posso alugar ...*	po·so aa·loo·*gaarr* ...
boat	*um barco*	oom *baar*·ko
canoe	*uma canoa*	oo·maa ka·*no*·aa
kayak	*um caiaque*	oom kai·*aa*·ke
life jacket	*um colete*	oom ko·*le*·te
	salva-vidas	sow·vaa·*vee*·daas
snorkelling	*equipamento*	e·kee·paa·*meng*·to
gear	*para fazer*	paa·raa faa·*zerr*
	snorkel	ees·*norr*·kel
water-skis	*esqui*	es·*kee*
	aquático	aa·*kwaa*·tee·ko
wetsuit	*roupa de*	ho·paa de
	borracha	bo·*haa*·shaa

Are there any ...?	*Tem ...?*	teng ...
reefs	*recifes*	he·*see*·fes
rips	*corredeira*	ko·he·*day*·raa
water hazards	*algum risco*	ow·*goom hees*·ko
	na água	naa *aa*·gwaa
waves	*ondas*	ong·daas

boogie board	*morey* m *boogie*	*mo*·ray boo·gee
motorboat	*barco* m *a motor*	*baarr*·ko aa mo·*torr*
oars	*remos* m pl	*he*·mos
sailing boat	*barco* m *a vela*	*baarr*·ko aa ve·laa
surfboard	*prancha* f *de surfe*	*prang*·shaa de *soor*·fee
surfing	*surfe* m	*soorr*·fee
wave	*onda* f	*ong*·daa
wind	*vento* f	*veng*·to
windsurfing	*windsurf* m	weeng·dee·*soor*·fee

See also **diving,** page 129.

hiking

caminhada

Where can I ...?	*Onde posso ...?*	ong·de po·so ...
buy supplies	*comprar*	kong·praarr
	mantimentos	mang·tee·meng·tos
find someone	*encontrar*	eng·kong·traarr
who knows	*alguém que*	ow·geng ke
this area	*conheça esta*	ko·nye·saa es·taa
	area	aa·re·aa
get a map	*pegar um*	pe·gaarr oom
	mapa	maa·paa
hire hiking gear	*alugar*	aa·loo·gaarr
	equipamento	e·kee·paa·meng·to
	de caminhada	de kaa·mee·nyaa·daa
How ...?	*Qual é a ...?*	kwow e aa ...
high is the	*altura*	ow·too·raa
climb	*da subida?*	daa soo·bee·daa
long is the trail	*distância*	dees·tang·syaa
	do caminho	do ka·mee·nyo

Do we need a guide?
Precisamos de um guia?   pre·see·za·mos de oom gee·aa

Are there guided treks?
Tem caminhadas   teng ka·mee·nyaa·daas
com guia?   kong gee·aa

Is it safe?
É seguro?   e se·goo·ro

Is there a hut?
Tem abrigo?   teng aa·bree·go

When does it get dark?
Quando escurece?   kwang·do es·koo·re·se

Do we need to take …?	Precisamos levar …?	pre·see·za·mos le·vaarr …
bedding	roupa de cama	ho·paa de ka·maa
food	comida	ko·mee·daa
water	água	aa·gwaa

Is the track …?	O caminho …?	o ka·mee·nyo …
(well-)marked	é (bem) marcado	e (beng) maarr·kaa·do
open	esta aberto	es·taa aa·berr·to
scenic	é pitoresco	e pee·to·res·ko

Which is the … route?	Qual é a rota mais …?	kwow e aa ho·taa mais …
easiest	fácil	faa·seel
most interesting	interessante	eeng·te·re·sang·te
shortest	curta	koorr·taa

Where can I find a/the …?	Onde posso encontrar …?	ong·de po·so eng·kong·traarr …
camping ground	a área de camping	aa aa·re·aa de kang·peeng
nearest village	cidade mais perto	see·daa·de mais perr·to
showers	um chuveiro	oom shoo·vay·ro
toilets	um banheiro	oom ba·nyay·ro

Where have you come from?
De onde você veio?   de ong·de vo·se vay·o

How long did it take?
Quanto tempo leva?   kwang·to teng·po le·vaa

Does this path go to …?
| Este caminho | es·te ka·*mee*·nyo |
| leva para …? | le·vaa paa·raa … |

Can I go through here?
| Posso ir por aqui? | po·so eerr porr aa·*kee* |

Is the water OK to drink?
| A água é boa para | a *aa*·gwaa e bo·aa paa·raa |
| beber? | be·*berr* |

I'm lost.
| Estou perdido/perdida. **m/f** | es·to perr·*dee*·do/perr·*dee*·daa |

beach

a praia

Where's the … beach?	*Onde fica a …?*	ong·de *fee*·kaa aa …
best	melhor praia	me·*lyorr* prai·aa
nearest	praia	*praa*·yaa
	mais perto	mais *perr*·to
nudist	praia de	*praa*·yaa de
	nudismo	noo·*dees*·mo
public	praia	*praa*·yaa
	pública	poo·blee·kaa

Proibido Mergulhar	pro·ee·*bee*·do mer·goo·*lyaarr*	**No Diving**
Proibido Nadar	pro·ee·*bee*·do naa·*daarr*	**No Swimming**

How much for a/an …?	*Quanto custa …?*	kwang·to koos·taa …
chair	*uma cadeira*	oo·maa kaa·*day*·raa
hut	*um abrigo*	oom aa·*bree*·go
umbrella	*um guarda sol*	oom *gwaarr*·daa so

weather

tempo

What's the weather like?
Como está o tempo? ko·mo es·*taa* o *teng*·po

What will the weather be like tomorrow?
Como estará o tempo amanhã? ko·mo es·taa·*raa* o *teng*·po aa·ma·*nyang*

It's …	*Está …*	es·*taa* …
cloudy	*nublado*	noo·*blaa*·do
cold	*frio*	*free*·o
fine	*bom*	bong
freezing	*um gelo*	oom *zhe*·lo
hot	*quente*	*keng*·te
raining	*chovendo*	sho·*veng*·do
snowing	*nevando*	ne·*vang*·do
sunny	*ensolarado*	eng·so·laa·*raa*·do
warm	*ameno*	aa·*me*·no
windy	*ventando*	veng·*tang*·do

Where can I buy ...?	Onde posso comprar um ...?	ong·de po·so kong·praarr oom ...
a rain jacket	casaco de chuva	kaa·zaa·ko de shoo·vaa
an umbrella	guarda-chuva	gwaarr·daa·shoo·vaa
dry season	época f de seca	e·po·kaa de se·kaa
wet season	época f de chuvas	e·po·kaa de shoo·vaas

flora & fauna

What ... is that?	O que é ...?	o ke e ...
animal	aquele animal	aa·ke·le aa·nee·mow
flower	aquela flor	aa·ke·laa florr
plant	aquela planta	aa·ke·laa plang·taa
tree	aquela árvore	aa·ke·laa aarr·vo·re

local plants & animals

arara (macaw)	arara f	aa·raa·raa
golden lion	mico leão m	mee·ko le·owng
parrot	papagaio m	paa·paa·gaa·yo
toucan	tucano m	too·ka·no

jacaranda (flowering Brazilian tree)

jacarandá f		zhaa·kaa·rang·daa

Victoria Amazonica (the national flower, a water lily)

vitória-régia f		vee·to·ree·a·he·gee·aa

What's it used for?
Para que serve?   *paa·raa ke serr·ve*

Can you eat the fruit?
Pode-se comer a fruta?   *po·de·se ko·merr aa froo·taa*

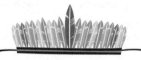

Is it …?	*Isto …?*	*ees·to …*
common	*é comum*	e ko·*moom*
dangerous	*é perigoso*	e pe·ree·*go*·zo
endangered	*está ameaçado/ ameaçada de extinção* m/f	es·*taa* aa·me·aa·*saa*·do/ aa·me·aa·*saa*·daa de es·teeng·*sowng*
poisonous	*é venenoso*	e ve·ne·*no*·zo
protected	*está protegido/ protegida* m/f	es·*taa* pro·te·*zhee*·do/ pro·te·*zhee*·daa

A typical breakfast consists of coffee, milk, juice, bread, jam, cheese, ham and fruit. Lunch is usually rice, beans (black or white depending on the region), vegetables and meat of some kind. Dinner is similar to lunch, though a lighter style of dinner, more akin to breakfast, is increasing in popularity.

key language

linguagem chave

breakfast	café m da manhã	kaa·*fe* daa ma·*nyang*
lunch	almoço m	ow·*mo*·so
dinner	jantar m	zhang·*taarr*
snack	lanche m	*lang*·she
eat	comer	ko·*merr*
drink	beber	be·*berr*
I'd like ...	Gostaria de ...	gos·taa·*ree*·aa de ...
Please.	Por favor.	porr faa·*vorr*
Thank you.	Obrigado/	o·bree·*gaa*·do/
	Obrigada. m/f	o·bree·*gaa*·daa
I'm starving!	Estou faminto/	es·*to* faa·*meeng*·to/
	faminta! m/f	faa·*meeng*·taa

finding a place to eat

encontrando um lugar para comer

Can you	Você pode	vo·*se po*·de
recommend a ...	recomendar	he·ko·*meng*·daarr
	um ...	oom ...
bar	bar	baarr
cafe	café	kaa·*fe*
restaurant	restaurante	hes·tow·*rang*·te

Where would you go for …?	Onde você iria para …?	ong·de vo·se ee·ree·aa paa·raa …
a celebration	uma comemoração	oo·maa ko·me·mo·ra·sowng
a cheap meal	uma refeição barata	oo·maa he·fay·sowng baa·raa·taa
local specialities	especialidades locais	es·pe·see·aa·lee·daa·des lo·kais

I'd like to reserve a table for …	Eu gostaria de reservar uma mesa para …	e·oo gos·taa·ree·aa de he·zer·vaarr oo·maa me·zaa paa·raa …
(two) people	(duas) pessoas	(doo·aas) pe·so·aas
(eight) o'clock	(às oito) horas	(aas oy·to) aw·raas

I'd like …, please.	Eu queria …, por favor.	e·oo ke·ree·aa … porr faa·vorr
a children's menu	o cardápio de crianças	o kaar·da·pyo de kree·ang·saas
a half portion	meia porção	me·yaa porr·sowng
a menu in English	o cardápio em inglês	o kaar·daa·pyo eng eeng·gles
a table for (five)	uma mesa para (cinco)	oo·maa me·zaa paa·raa (seeng·ko)
the drink list	a lista de bebidas	aa lees·taa de be·bee·daas
the menu	o cardápio	o kaar·daa·pyo
the (non-) smoking section	(não-) fumantes	(nowng·) foo·mang·tes

Are you still serving food?

Vocês ainda estão servindo comida?   vo·ses aa·eeng·daa es·towng serr·veeng·do ko·mee·daa

How long is the wait?

A espera é de quanto tempo?   aa es·pe·raa e de kwang·to teng·p

going nuts

There's no single word to translate 'nuts'. You have to say which kind of nut you mean, for example noz (walnut), amendoin (peanut), and amêndoas (almond).

FOOD

142

aa·*kee* es·*taa*
  Aqui está!   **Here you go!**

es·*ta*·mos fe·*shaa*·dos
  Estamos fechados.   **We're closed.**

es·*ta*·mos lo·*taa*·dos
  Estamos lotados.   **We're full.**

o ke *po*·so serr·*vee*·los
  O que posso serví-los?   **What can I get for you?**

ong·de vo·*ses* gos·taa·*ree*·ang de seng·*taarr*
  Onde vocês gostariam   **Where would you**
  de sentar?   **like to sit?**

oom mo·*meng*·to
  Um momento.   **One moment.**

restaurant

restaurante

At a restaurant, use *senhor* or *senhora* when addressing the
waiter or waitress.

What would you recommend?
  O que você recomenda?   o ke vo·*se* he·ko·*meng*·daa

What's in that dish?
  O que tem neste prato?   o ke teng *nes*·te *praa*·to

I'll have that.
  Eu quero isto.   e·oo *ke*·ro *ees*·to

Does it take long to prepare?
  Leva muito tempo   *le*·vaa *mweeng*·to *teng*·po
  para preparar?   *paa*·raa pre·paa·*raar*

Is it self-serve?
  Nós mesmos nos servimos?   nos *mes*·mos nos serr·*vee*·mos

Is service included in the bill?
  O serviço está   o serr·*vee*·so es·*taa*
  incluído na conta?   eeng·kloo·*ee*·do naa *kong*·taa

Are these complimentary?
  É cortesia da casa?   e kor·te·*zee*·aa daa *kaa*·zaa

I'd like ...	Eu quero ...	e·oo ke·ro ...
a local speciality	a especialidade local	aa es·pe·see·aa·lee·daa· lo·kow
a meal fit for a king	uma refeição suntuosa	oo·maa he·fay·sowng soom·too·o·zaa
the chicken	o frango	o frang·go
I'd like it with/ without ...	Eu queria com/ sem ...	e·oo ke·ree·aa kong/ seng ...
chilli	pimenta	pee·meng·taa
garlic	alho	aa·lyo
oil	óleo	o·lyo

listen for ...

e·oo soo·zhee·ro ...
Eu sugiro ...   **I suggest ...**

ko·mo vo·se gos·taa·ree·aa ke fo·se ko·zee·do
Como você gostaria que   **How would you like**
fosse cozido?   **that cooked?**

vo·se gos·taa de ...
Você gosta de ...?   **Do you like ...?**

at the table

à mesa

Please bring ...	Por favor traga ...	porr faa·vorr traa·gaa ...
a cloth	uma toalha	oo·maa to·aa·lyaa
a serviette	um guardanapo	oom gwaar·daa·naa·po
a wineglass	uma taça de vinho	oo·maa taa·saa de vee·nyo
the bill	a conta	aa kong·taa

FOOD

144

talking food

falando sobre comida

I love this dish.
Adorei este prato.
aa·do·*ray es*·te *praa*·to

I love the local cuisine.
Adorei a cozinha local.
aa·do·*ray* aa ko·*zee*·nyaa lo·*kow*

That was delicious!
Estava delicioso!
es·*taa*·vaa de·lee·see·o·zo

My compliments to the chef.
Meus cumprimentos ao chefe.
me·oos koom·pree·*meng*·tos ow *she*·fe

I'm full.
Estou satisfeito/ satisfeita. m/f
es·*to* saa·tees·*fay*·to/ saa·tees·*fay*·taa

This is …
  (too) cold
  spicy
  superb

Está …
  (demais) frio
  apimentado
  excelente

es·*taa* …
  (*zhee*·mais) *free*·o
  aa·pee·meng·*taa*·do
  e·se·*leng*·te

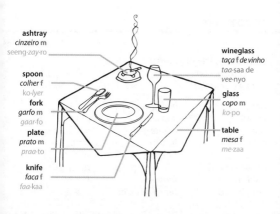

ashtray
cinzeiro m
seeng·*zay*·ro

spoon
colher f
ko·*lyer*

fork
garfo m
gaar·fo

plate
prato m
praa·to

knife
faca f
faa·kaa

wineglass
taça de vinho
taa·saa de *vee*·nyo

glass
copo m
ko·po

table
mesa f
me·zaa

eating out

145

aperitivos	aa·pe·ree·*tee*·vos	appetisers
sopas	*so*·paas	soups
entradas	eng·*traa*·daas	entrees
saladas	saa·*laa*·daas	salads
pratos	*praa*·tos	main courses
principais	preeng·see·*pais*	
sobremesas	so·bre·*me*·zaas	desserts
aperitivos	aa·pe·ree·*tee*·vos	aperitifs
refrigerantes	he·free·zhe·*rang*·tes	soft drinks
bebidas	be·*bee*·daas	spirits
destiladas	des·tee·*laa*·daas	
cervejas	serr·*ve*·zhaas	beers
vinhos	*vee*·nyos	sparkling wines
espumantes	es·poo·*mang*·tes	
vinhos brancos	*vee*·nyos *brang*·kos	white wines
vinhos tintos	*vee*·nyos *teeng*·tos	red wines
vinhos de	*vee*·nyos de	dessert wines
sobremesa	so·bre·*me*·zaa	
digestivos	dee·zhes·*tee*·vos	digestifs

breakfast

café da manhã

What's a typical breakfast?

Como é um típico	*ko*·mo e oom *tee*·pee·ko	
café da manhã?	kaa·*fe* daa ma·*nyang*	

bacon	*bacon* m	*bay*·kon
bread	*pão* m	powng
butter	*manteiga* f	mang·*tay*·gaa
cake	*bolo* m	*bo*·lo
cereal	*cereal* m	se·re·*ow*
cheese bread	*pão* m *de queijo*	powng de *kay*·zho
cold cuts	*frios* m	*free*·os
corn bread	*broa* f *de milho*	*bro*·aa de *mee*·lyo

FOOD

146

... eggs	ovos ... m	o·vos ...
boiled	quentes	keng·tes
fried	fritos	free·tos
hard-boiled	cozidos duros	ko·zee·dos doo·ros
poached	pochés	po·shes
scrambled	mexidos	me·shee·dos

fruit juice	suco m de frutas	soo·ko de froo·taas
jam	geléia f	zhe·le·yaa
milk	leite m	lay·te
muesli	muesli m	moos·lee
omelette	omelete f	o·me·le·te
(oat/maize)	mingau m	meeng·gow
porridge	(de aveia/maizena)	(de aa·ve·yaa/mai·ze·naa)
toast	torrada f	to·haa·daa

For other breakfast items and related language, see self-catering, page 153, and the menu decoder, page 159.

light meals

refeições leves

What's that called?
Como se chama isso?   ko·mo se sha·maa ee·so

I'd like ...,	Eu queria ...,	e·oo ke·ree·aa ...
please.	por favor.	porr faa·vorr
a piece	um pedaço	oom pe·daa·so
a sandwich	um sanduiche	oom sang·doo·ee·she
one slice	uma fatia	oo·maa faa·tee·aa
that one	aquele	aa·ke·le
two	dois	doys

condiments

Do you have …?	Tem …?	teng …
chilli sauce	molho de pimenta	mo·lyo de pee·meng·taa
ketchup	ketchup	ket·shoo·pee
pepper	pimenta	pee·meng·taa
salt	sal	sow
tomato sauce	molho de tomate	mo·lyo de to·maa·te
vinegar	vinagre	vee·naa·gre

For additional items, see the **menu decoder**, page 159.

methods of preparation

métodos de preparo

I'd like it …	Eu queria …	e·oo ke·ree·aa …
I don't want it …	Eu não queria …	e·oo nowng ke·ree·aa …
boiled	cozido/ cozido m/f	ko·zee·do/ ko·zee·daa
broiled	na brasa	naa braa·zaa
deep-fried	frito/frita em recipiente m/f	free·to/free·taa eng he·see·pyeng·te
fried	frito/frita m/f	free·to/free·taa
grilled	grelhado/ grelhada m/f	gre·lyaa·do/ gre·lyaa·daa
medium	ao ponto	ow pong·to
rare	mal passado/ passada m/f	mow paa·saa·do/ paa·saa·daa
re-heated	requentado/ requentada m/f	he·keng·taa·do/ he·keng·taa·daa
steamed	ao vapor	ow vaa·porr
well-done	bem passado/ passado m/f	beng paa·saa·do/ paa·saa·daa
with the dressing on the side	com o molho separado	kong o mo·lyo se·paa·raa·do
without …	sem …	seng …

Everywhere you go, you'll find places selling the famous *pastel* and *caldo de cana*, a must. The *pastel* is a deep-fried pastry with chicken, mince or cheese filling. Don't be intimidated by their size (usually huge!) – there's a lot of air inside the pastry. It's generally washed down with *caldo de cana*, sugar cane juice. Other local snacks include:

coxinha f *de galinha*	ko·*shee*·nyaa de gaa·*lee*·nyaa	chicken-filled croquette
empada f *de frango/camarão*	eng·paa·*daa* de fran·go/kaa·maa·*rowng*	chicken/prawn pastry
quibe m	*kee*·be	deep-fried meatballs

in the bar

Excuse me!
Com licença! kong lee·*seng*·saa

I'll have …
Eu queria … e·oo ke·*ree*·aa …

I'm next.
Eu sou o próximo/ próxima. m/f e·oo so o *pro*·see·mo/ *pro*·see·maa

Same again, please.
O mesmo, por favor. o *mes*·mo porr faa·*vorr*

No ice, thanks.
Sem gelo, obrigado/ obrigada. m/f seng *zhe*·lo o·bree·*gaa*·do/ o·bree·*gaa*·daa

I'll buy you a drink.
Eu te pago uma bebida. e·oo te *paa*·go *oo*·maa be·*bee*·daa

What would you like?
O que você quer? o ke vo·*se* kerr

It's my round.
  É minha vez. e *mee*·nyaa ves

How much is that?
  Quanto é? kwang·to e

Do you serve meals here?
  Vocês servem refeições vo·ses serr·veng he·fay·soyngs
  aqui? aa·kee

listen for ...

a·sho ke ja *she*·gaa *paa*·raa vo·*se*
  Acho que já chega para   **I think you've had**
  você.   **enough.**

o ke vo·*se* es·*taa* be·*bang*·do
  O que você está bebando?   **What are you having?**

ool·tee·mos pe·*dee*·dos
  Últimos pedidos.   **Last orders.**

nonalcoholic drinks

bebidas sem álcool

... mineral water	*água mineral ...*	aa·gwaa mee·ne·*row* ...
sparkling	*com gás*	kong gaas
still	*sem gás*	seng gaas
orange juice	*suco de laranja*	soo·ko de laa·*rang*·zhaa
soft drink	*refrigerante*	he·free·zhe·*rang*·te
(hot) water	*água (quente)*	aa·gwaa (keng·te)
(cup of) tea	*(xícara) de chá*	(shee·kaa·raa) de shaa
(cup of) coffee	*(xícara) de café*	(shee·kaa·raa) de kaa·fe
... with (milk)	*... com (leite)*	... kong (lay·te)
... without (sugar)	*... sem (açúcar)*	... seng (aa·soo·kaarr)

alcoholic drinks

beer	cerveja f	serr·ve·zhaa
brandy	brandy m	brang·dee
champagne	champagne f	shang·pa·nye
cocktail	coquetel m	ko·ke·tel

a shot of ...	uma dose de ...	oo·maa do·ze de ...
gin	gin	zheeng
rum	rum	hoom
tequila	tequila	te·kee·laa
vodka	vodka	vo·dee·kaa
whisky	whisky	oo·ees·kee
cachaça	cachaça	kaa·shaa·saa

a bottle/glass	uma garrafa/	oo·maa gaa·haa·faa/
of ... wine	taça de vinho ...	taa·saa de vee·nyo ...
dessert	de sobremesa	de so·bre·me·zaa
red	tinto	teeng·to
rosé	rosé	ho·ze
sparkling	espumante	es·poo·mang·te
white	branco	brang·ko

a ... of beer	... de cerveja	... de serr·ve·jaa
glass	um copo	oom ko·po
jug	uma jarra	oo·maa zhaa·haa
large bottle	uma garrafa	oo·maa gaa·haa·faa
	grande	grang·de
pint	um choppe	oom sho·pee
small bottle	uma garrafa	oo·maa gaa·haa·faa
	pequena	pe·ke·naa

drinking up

Cheers!
Saúde! sa·*oo*·de

This is hitting the spot.
Caiu bem. kaa·*ee*·oo beng

Pull my finger!
Puxe meu dedo! poo·*she* me·oo *de*·do

I think I've had one too many.
Acho que bebi mais do que a·sho ke be·*bee* mais do ke
deveria. de·ve·*ree*·aa

I'm feeling drunk.
Estou me sentindo es·*to* me seng·*teeng*·do
bêbado/bêbada. m/f *be*·baa·do/*be*·baa·daa

I feel ill.
Estou me sentindo mal. es·*to* me seng·*teeng*·do mow

Where's the toilet?
Onde é o banheiro? *ong*·de e o ba·*nyay*·ro

Can you call a taxi for me?
Você pode chamar um vo·*se po*·de shaa·*maarr* oom
táxi para mim? *taak*·see *paa*·raa meeng

local drinks

água f de côco	aa·gwaa de ko·ko	coconut water
batida f	baa·*tee*·daa	pureed fruit and *cachaça* cocktail
cachaça f	kaa·*shaa*·saa	white spirit made from sugar cane
caipirinha f	kai·pee·*ree*·nyaa	lime and *cachaça* cocktail
caldo m de cana	kow·do de ka·naa	sugar cane juice
mate m	maa·te	iced tea

buying food

comprando alimentos

What's the local speciality?
Qual é a especialidade local?
kwow e a es·pe·see·aa·lee·*daa*·de lo·*kow*

What's that?
O que é aquilo?
o ke e aa·*kee*·lo

Can I taste it?
Posso experimentar?
po·so es·pe·ree·meng·*taarr*

Can I have a bag, please?
Pode me dar uma bolsa, por favor?
po·de me daarr oo·ma *bol*·sa porr faa·*vorr*

How much is (a kilo of cheese)?
Quanto é (o kilo do queijo)?
kwang·to e (o *kee*·lo do *kay*·zho)

How much is it?
Quanto custa?
kwang·to *koos*·taa

food stuff

cooked	*cozido/cozida* m/f	ko·*zee*·do/ko·*zee*·daa
cured	*curado/curada* m/f	koo·*raa*·do/koo·*raa*·daa
dried	*seco/seca* m/f	*se*·ko
fresh	*fresco/fresca* m/f	*fres*·ko/*fres*·kaa
frozen	*congelado/ congelada* m/f	kong·zhe·*laa*·do kong·zhe·*laa*·daa
smoked	*defumado/ defumada* m/f	de·foo·*maa*·do de·foo·*maa*·daa
raw	*cru/crua* m/f	kroo/*kroo*·a

I'd like ...	*Eu gostaria de ...*	*e·oo gos·taa·ree·aa de*
(200) grams	*(duzentas) gramas*	*(doo·zeng·taas) gra·maas*
half a kilo	*meio kilo*	*me·yo kee·lo*
a kilo	*um kilo*	*oom kee·lo*
(two) kilos	*(dois) kilos*	*(doys) kee·los*
a bottle	*uma garrafa*	*oo·maa gaa·haa·faa*
a dozen	*uma dúzia*	*oo·maa doo·zyaa*
half a dozen	*meia dúzia*	*me·yaa doo·zee·aa*
a jar	*um vidro*	*oom vee·dro*
a packet	*um pacote*	*oom paa·ko·te*
a piece	*um pedaço*	*oom pe·daa·so*
(three) pieces	*(três) pedaços*	*(tres) pe·daa·sos*
a slice	*uma fatia*	*oo·maa faa·tee·aa*
(six) slices	*(seis) fatias*	*(says) faa·tee·aas*
a tin	*uma lata*	*oo·maa laa·taa*
(just) a little	*(só) um pouco*	*(so) oom po·ko*
more	*mais*	*mais*
some ...	*um pouco ...*	*oom po·ko ...*
that one	*aquele*	*aa·ke·le*
this one	*este*	*es·te*

mais ow·goo·maa koy·zaa	
Mais alguma coisa?	**Anything else?**
o ke vo·se gos·taa·ree·aa	
O que você gostaria?	**What would you like?**
po·so aa·zhoo·daa·lo/aa·zhoo·daa·laa	
Posso ajudá-lo/ajudá-la? m/f	**Can I help you?**
sowng (seeng·ko he·ais)	
São (cinco Reais).	**That's (five reals).**

Less.	Menos.	me·nos
A bit more.	Um pouco mais.	oom po·ko mais
Enough.	Chega.	she·gaa

Do you have ...?	Vocês tem ...?	vo·ses teng ...
anything cheaper	algo mais barato	ow·go mais baa·raa·to
other kinds	outros tipos	o·tros tee·pos

Where can I find the ... section?	Onde posso encontrar a seção de ...?	ong·de po·so eng·kong·traarr aa se·sowng de ...
dairy	laticínios	laa·tee·see·nyos
fish	peixe	pay·she
frozen goods	congelados	kong·zhe·laa·dos
fruit and vegetable	frutas e legumes	froo·taas e le·goo·mes
meat	carne	kaar·ne
poultry	frango	frang·go

cooking utensils

Could I please borrow a/an ...?
Posso pegar um/uma ...   po·so pe·*gaarr* oom/*oo*·maa ...
emprestado/   eng·pres·*taa*·do/
emprestada? m/f   eng·pres·*taa*·daa

I need a/an ...
Preciso de um/uma ... m/f   pre·*see*·zo de oom/*oo*·maa ...

bottle opener	*abridor* m	aa·bree·*dor*
	de garrafas	de gaa·*haa*·faas
bowl	*tigela* f	tee·*zhe*·laa
can opener	*abridor* m	aa·bree·*dorr*
	de latas	de *laa*·taas
chopping board	*tábua* f *de*	*taa*·bwaa de
	cortar	korr·*taarr*
corkscrew	*abridor* m	aa·bree·*dorr*
cup	*xícara* f	*shee*·kaa·raa
fork	*garfo* m	*gaarr*·fo
fridge	*geladeira* f	zhe·laa·*day*·raa
frying pan	*frigideira* f	free·zhee·*day*·raa
glass	*copo* m	*ko*·po
knife	*faca* f	*faa*·kaa
microwave	*microondas* m	mee·kro·*ong*·daas
oven	*forno* m	*forr*·no
plate	*prato* m	*praa*·to
saucepan	*panela* f	paa·*ne*·laa
spoon	*colher* f	ko·*lyerr*
toaster	*torradeira* f	to·haa·*day*·raa

vegetarian & special meals
comida vegetariana & especial

ordering food

Is there a (vegetarian) restaurant near here?

Tem um restaurante (vegetariana) aqui por perto?	teng oom hes·tow·*rang*·te (ve·zhe·taa·ree·*a*·naa) aa·*kee* porr *perr*·to

Do you have … food?	*Você tem comida …?*	vo·*se* teng ko·*mee*·daa …
halal	*halal*	a·*low*
kosher	*kosher*	ko·sherr
vegetarian	*vegetariana*	ve·zhe·taa·ree·*a*·naa

I don't eat …	*Eu não como …*	e·oo nowng *ko*·mo …
fish	*peixe*	*pay*·she
poultry	*frango*	*frang*·go
(red) meat	*carne (vermelha)*	*kaar*·ne (verr·*me*·lyaa)

Is it cooked in/with …?	*Isto é feito em/ com …?*	*ees*·to e *fay*·to eng/ kong …
butter	*manteiga*	mang·*te*·gaa
fish stock	*caldo de peixe*	*kow*·do de *pay*·she
meat stock	*caldo de carne*	*kow*·do de *kaarr*·ne

Could you prepare a meal without …?	*Você poderia preparar uma refeição sem …?*	vo·*se* po·de·ree·aa pre·paa·*raarr* oo·maa he·fay·*sowng* seng …
eggs	*ovos*	*o*·vos
pork	*porco*	*porr*·ko
seafood	*frutos do mar*	*froo*·tos do maarr

Is this …?	*Isto é …?*	*ees*·to ee …
free of animal produce	*sem derivados de animais*	seng de·ree·*vaa*·dos de aa·nee·*mais*
free-range	*de caipira*	kai·pee·raa
genetically modified	*transgênico*	trans·*zhe*·nee·ko

decaffeinated	descafeinado	des·kaa·fe·ee·*naa*·do
gluten-free	sem glúten	seng *gloo*·teng
halal	halal	a·*low*
kosher	kosher	ko·sherr
low-fat	de baixo teor	de *bai*·sho te·*orr*
	de gordura	de gorr·*doo*·raa
low in sugar	de baixo teor	de *bai*·sho te·*orr*
	de açúcar	de aa·*soo*·kaarr
organic	orgânico	orr·*ga*·nee·ko
salt-free	sem sal	seng sow

special diets & allergies

I'm on a special diet.
Estou numa dieta   es·to *noo*·maa dee·e·taa
especial.   es·pe·see·*ow*

I'm (a) ...	Eu sou ...	e·oo so ...
Buddhist	Budista	boo·*dees*·taa
Hindu	Hindu	*eeng*·doo
Jewish	Judeu/Judia m/f	zhoo·*de*·o/zhoo·*dee*·aa
Muslim	Muçulmano/	moo·sool·*ma*·no/
	Muçulmana m/f	moo·sool·*ma*·naa
vegan	vegitalista m&f	ve·zhee·ta·*lees*·taa
vegetarian	vegetariano/	ve·zhe·taa·ree·*a*·no/
	vegetariana m/f	ve·zhe·taa·ree·*a*·naa

I'm allergic to ...	Eu sou alérgico/	e·oo so aa·*lerr*·zhee·ko/
	alérgica à ... m/f	aa·*lerr*·zhee·kaa aa ...
dairy produce	laticínios	laa·tee·*see*·nyos
eggs	ovos	o·vos
gelatin	gelatina	zhe·laa·*tee*·naa
gluten	glúten	*gloo*·teng
honey	mel	mel
MSG	monoglutamato	mo·no·gloo·taa·*maa*·to
	de sódio	de *so*·dyo
peanuts	amendoims	aa·meng·do·*eengs*
seafood	frutos do mar	*froo*·tos do maarr

A

abacate ⓜ a-baa-*kaa*-te *avocado*

abacaxí ⓜ aa-baa-kaa-*shee* *pineapple*

abóbora ⓕ aa-*bo*-bo-raa *pumpkin*

açafrão ⓜ aa-saa-*frowng saffron*

açaí ⓜ aa-saa-*ee deep purple fruit of a palm tree – it has a gritty taste*

acarajé ⓜ aa-kaa-raa-*zhe a Bahian street food made from mashed brown beans formed into balls & stuffed with* **vatapá***, then fried in* **dendê** *oil*

acebolado/acebolada ⓜ/ⓕ aa-se-bo-*laa*-do/aa-se-bo-*laa*-daa *saute of onion, garlic, olive oil & sometimes a bay leaf served with steak*

acompanhamento ⓜ aa-kong-pa-nyaa-*meng*-to *accompaniment*

açúcar ⓜ aa-*soo*-kaarr *sugar*
   — **mascavo** maas-*kaa*-vo *brown sugar*
   — **refinado** he-fee-*naa*-do/he-fee-*naa*-daa *refined sugar*

adoçante ⓜ aa-do-*sang*-te *sugar substitute*

agrião ⓜ aa-gree-*owng watercress*

água ⓕ *aa*-gwaa *water*
   — **da nascente** daa naa-*seng*-te *spring water*
   — **da torneira** daa torr-*nay*-raa *tap water*
   — **mineral (com/sem gás)** mee-ne-*row* (kong/seng gas) *mineral water (still/sparkling)*

aguardente ⓜ aa-gwaarr-*deng*-te *strong sugar cane alcohol drunk throughout the country, also known as* **cachaça**

aipo ⓜ *ai*-po *celery*

alcachofra ⓕ ow-kaa-*sho*-fraa *artichoke*

alecrim ⓜ aa-le-*kreeng rosemary*

alface ⓕ ow-*faa*-se *lettuce*

alho ⓜ **porro** *aa*-lyo po-*ho garlic leek*

almoço ⓜ ow-*mo*-so *lunch*

almôndegas ⓕ pl ow-*mong*-de-gaas *meatballs, usually beef or pork, served in a tomato-based sauce*

ambrosia ⓕ ang-bro-*zee*-aa *sweetened egg yolks thickened to a soft creamy texture, eaten as a dessert*

amêijoa ⓕ aa-*may*-zho-aa *cockle*

ameixa ⓕ aa-*may*-shaa *plum*

amêndoa ⓕ aa-*meng*-dwaa *almond*

amendoim ⓜ aa-meng-doo-*eeng peanut*

amora ⓕ aa-*mo*-raa *blackberry*

angú ⓜ ang-*goo runny polenta (corn meal porridge)*

cordeiro ⓜ korr-*day*-ro *lamb*

arroz ⓜ aa-*hoz rice*
   — **cozido** ko-*zee*-do *cooked rice*
   — **de carreteiro** de kaa-he-*tay*-ro *rice mixed with fried salted beef, served with fried manioc*
   — **de marisco** de maa-*rees*-ko *casserole of seafood & rice in tomato sauce*
   — **integral** eeng-te-*grow brown rice*

asa ① *aa*-zaa *wing*
— **assada** aa-*saa*-daa *roasted wing*
— **de frango** de *fraug*-go
chicken wing
— **frita** *free*-taa *fried wing*
aspargo ⓜ aas-*paar*-go *asparagus*
atum ⓜ aa-*toong* *tuna*
avelã ① aa-ve-*lang* *hazelnut*
aves ① pl *aa*-ves *poultry*
avestruz ⓜ aa-ves-*troos* *ostrich*
azeite ⓜ aa-*zay*-te *olive oil*
azeitonas ① pl aa-*zay*-to-naas *olives*
— **pretas** *pre*-taas *black olives*
— **recheadas** re-she-*aa*-daas
stuffed olives
— **sem caroço** seng kaa-*ro*-so
pitted olives
— **verdes** *verr*-des *green olives*

B

bacaba ① baa-*kaa*-baa *Amazonian
fruit used in wines & syrups*
bacalhau ⓜ baa-kaa-*lyow*
dried salted cod
banha ① *ba*-nyaa *lard*
batata ① baa-*taa*-taa *do*-se
sweet potato
batatas ① pl baa-*taa*-taas *potatoes*
— **cozidas** ko-*zee*-daas
boiled potatoes
— **fritas** *free*-taas *potato chips
or crisps*
baunilha ① bow-*nee*-lyaa *vanilla*
bavaroise ① baa-vaa-hoo-*waa*-ze
*whipped gelatinous dessert made
with cream & pieces of fruit such as
strawberries or pineapple*
bebida ① be-*bee*-daa *beverage*
— **(sem) álcool** (seng) *ow*-kol *(non)
alcoholic beverage*
— **destilada** des-tee-*laa*-daa *spirits*
— **gelada** zhe-*laa*-daa *cold beverage*
— **quente** *keng*-te *hot beverage*

beringela ① be-reeng-*zhe*-laa
aubergine • eggplant
beterraba ① be-te-*haa*-baa *beetroot*
bicarbonato ⓜ **de sódio**
bee-kaa-borr-*naa*-to de *so*-dyo
baking soda • bicarbonate of soda
bife ⓜ *bee*-fe *steak of beef, other meats,
poultry or fish • fillet*
— **ao ponto** ow *pong*-to *steak that's
medium cooked*
— **bem passado** beng paa-*saa*-do
well-done steak
— **de alcatra** de ow-*kaa*-traa
rump steak
— **de atum** de aa-*toong* *tuna steak*
— **de filé** de fee-*le* *sirloin steak*
— **de lombinho** de long-*bee*-nyo
pork fillet steak
— **de vaca** de *vaa*-kaa *beef steak*
biscoitos ⓜ pl bees-*koy*-tos
biscuits • cookies
bobó ⓜ **de camarão** bo-*bo* de
kaa-maa-*rowng* *thick stew of fresh
prawns, coconut milk,* **dendê** *oil,
coriander & pureed manioc*
bolachas ① pl as bo-*laa*-shaas
crackers • biscuits
bolo ⓜ *bo*-lo *cake*
— **de aniversário**
de aa-nee-verr-*saa*-ryo *birthday cake*
— **de carne** de *kaar*-ne *meatloaf*
— **de casamento**
de kaa-zaa-*meng*-to *wedding cake*
— **de chocolate** de sho-ko-*laa*-te
chocolate cake
— **de laranja** de laa-*rang*-zhaa
orange cake
— **de nozes** de *no*-zes *walnut cake*
— **rei** hay *a Christmas bread in the
shape of a large ring, studded with
walnuts, pine nuts, almonds & raisins &
decorated with glazed fruit*
bombons ⓜ pl bong-*bongs* *bonbons*
brasa *braa*-zaa *see* **na brasa**
brócolis ⓜ pl *bro*-ko-lees *broccoli*

FOOD

160

ucho ⊛ *boo*·sho tripe

ufet ⊛ **de saladas frias** boo·*fe* de
saa·*laa*·daas *free*·aas *cold salad buffet
with vegetable, pasta & bean salads*

uriti ⊛ boo·ree·*tee* *a palm-tree fruit
with a mealy texture & a hint of peach*

C

cabidela, à kaa·bee·*de*·la, aa *any dish
made with blood & giblets of poultry*

cabrito ⊛ kaa·*bree*·to *kid (goat)*

cacau ⊛ ka·*kow* *cocoa • pulp from
cocoa pod*

— **chocolate quente** sho·ko·*laa*·te
keng·te *hot cocoa (beverage)*

caça ① *kaa*·saa *game*

cação ⊛ kaa·*sowng* *shark meat*

cachaça ① kaa·*shaa*·saa *strong
sugar cane spirit produced & drunk
throughout the country*

café ⊛ kaa·*fe* *coffee • cafe*

— **com leite** kong *lay*·te *medium-
sized cup of half milk & half filter
coffee*

— **descafeinado**
des·kaa·fe·ee·*naa*·do
decaffeinated coffee

— **em grão** eng growng
coffee beans

— **instantâneo** eengs·tang·*ta*·nyo
instant coffee

— **moído** mo·ee·do *ground coffee*

— **pingado** peen·*gaa*·do *short black •
espresso with a dash of cold milk*

cafeteria ① kaa·fe·te·*ree*·aa *coffee shop
or cafeteria*

cafezinho kaa·fe·zee·nyo *short black •
espresso topped with hot water*

caipirinha ① kai·pee·ree·nyaa *cocktail
of lime, sugar & cachaça on ice*

cajú ⊛ kaa·*zhoo* *cashew • tart fruit of
cashew (the nut is enclosed in the
fruit), usually used in juices*

caldeirada ① kow·day·*raa*·daa *soup-
like stew, usually made with fish*

caldo ⊛ *kow*·do *soup • broth*

— **de galinha** de gaa·lee·nyaa
chicken broth

— **verde** verr·de *potato-based soup
with* **couve** & **paio**

camarão ⊛ kaa·maa·*rowng* *prawn*

— **á paulista** aa pow·*lees*·taa
*unshelled fresh prawn fried in olive oil
with garlic & salt*

canela ① kaa·*ne*·la *cinnamon*

canja ① *kang*·zhaa *soup made with
chicken broth, often a meal in itself*

— **de galinha** de gaa·lee·nyaa
chicken soup

carambola ① kaa·rang·*bo*·laa *starfruit*

caramelo ⊛ kaa·raa·*me*·lo *caramel •
hard candy*

caranguejada ① kaa·rang·ge·*zhaa*·daa
*a feast of crab cooked whole on salt,
accompanied by chilli &* **farofa**

camarão ⊛ ka·ma·*rowng* *prawns*

— **frito com alho** *free*·to kong *aa*·lyo
*prawns sauteed in garlic, sometimes
with chilli*

carne ① *kaar*·ne *meat*

— **assada** aa·*saa*·daa *roast meat*

— **de porco** de porr·ko *pork*

— **de sol** de sol *a tasty, salted meat,
fried in oil*

— **de vaca** de vaa·kaa *beef*

— **picada** pee·*kaa*·daa
chopped meat

carneiro ⊛ kaarr·*nay*·ro *mutton*

cardápio ⊛ kaar·*daa*·pyo *menu*

— **de vinhos** de vee·nyos *wine list*

carvão, no ⊛&① kaar·*vowng*, no
char-grilled

caruru ⊛ kaa·roo·*roo* *one of the
most popular Brazilian dishes of
African origin, made with okra,
onions, salt, dried shrimp &* **dendê**
*oil. Traditionally, a sea fish such as
grouper is added.*

casa, à moda da ⓜ&ⓕ *kaa*-zaa, aa mo-daa daa *house-style*

casa ⓕ **de chá** *kaa*-zaa de shaa *teahouse selling pastries, sweets, coffee as well as herbal & black teas*

caseira/caseiro ⓜ/ⓕ kaa-*zay*-raa/kaa-*zay*-ro *home-style cooking*

castanhas ⓕ pl **de cajú** kas-*ta*-nyaas de kaa-*zhoo chestnuts*

castanhas ⓕ pl **portuguesas** kas-*ta*-nyaas porr-too-ge-zaas *chestnuts*

cavalas ⓕ pl kaa-*vaa*-laas *mackerel*

casquinha ⓕ **de siri** kaas-kee-nyaa de see-ree *stuffed crab*

cebola ⓕ se-*bo*-la *onion*

cenoura ⓕ se-*no*-raa *carrot*

cereal ⓜ se-re-ow *cereal, grains or breakfast cereal*

cereja ⓕ se-re-zhaa *(sweet) cherry*

cerveja ⓕ serr-*ve*-zhaa *beer*

cervejaria ⓕ serr-ve-zhaa-*ree*-aa *beer house (also serves food)*

chá ⓜ shaa *tea*
— **com limão** kong lee-*mowng black tea with thick strip of lemon peel*
— **de ervas** de err-vaas *herb tea*
— **de erva doce** de err-vaa *do*-se *aniseed tea (very commonly given to children)*
— **de limão** de lee-*mowng glass or cup of hot water with a twist of lemon rind*
— **preto** pre-to *black tea*
— **verde** verr-de *green tea*

champanhe ⓜ shang-*pa*-nye *champagne*

chef ⓜ&ⓕ she-fe *chef*

chocolate ⓜ sho-ko-*laa*-te *chocolate*
— **ao leite** ow lay-te *milk chocolate*
— **branco** brang-ko *white chocolate*
— **preto** pre-to *dark chocolate*

choppe ⓜ sho-pee *large glass of draught beer*
— **preto** pre-to *dark beer • stout*

chouriço ⓜ sho-ree-so *garlicky pork sausage flavoured with red pepper paste*
— **de sangue** de sang-ge *blood sausage*

churrasco ⓜ shoo-*haas*-ko *barbecue*

claras ⓕ pl **de ovos** klaa-raas de o-vos *egg whites*

côco ⓜ ko-ko *coconut*

codorna ⓕ ko-dorr-na *quail*

coelho ⓜ ko-e-lyo *rabbit*
— **à caçador** aa kaa-saa-dorr *'hunter's style rabbit' – rabbit stewed with red & white wine & tomato*
— **ao vinha d'alho** ow vee-nyaa daa-lyo *baked rabbit set atop slices of fried bread, covered with onion slices & drizzled with port or white wine*

coentro ⓜ ko-eng-tro *coriander*

cogumelos ⓜ pl ko-goo-me-los *mushrooms*

colorau ⓜ ko-lo-row *sweet paprika*

com tudo kong too-do *'with everything' – a dish with the lot*

compota ⓕ kong-po-taa *fruit preserve*

confeitaria ⓕ kong-fay-taa-ree-aa *patisserie*

congelado/congelada ⓜ/ⓕ kong-zhe-*laa*-do/kong-zhe-*laa*-daa *frozen*

conserva ⓕ kong-serr-vaa *tinned/canned goods*

consomé ⓜ kong-so-me *consomme*

corante ⓜ ko-rang-te *food colouring*

cordeiro ⓜ korr-day-ro *mutton*

costeleta ⓕ **de porco** kos-te-le-taa de porr-ko *pork chop*

couve ⓕ ko-ve *green edible leaf*
— **de Bruxelas** de broo-she-laas *Brussels sprout*
— **flor** florr *cauliflower*

coxinha ⓕ **de galinha** ko-shee-nyaa de gaa-lee-nyaa *fried, savoury chicken mixture in the form of a drumstick*

cozido ⓜ **(à brasileira)** ko-*zee*-do (aa bra-see-*le*-raa) *Brazilian stew, full of meat, vegetables, beans & rice*

cozido/cozida ⓜ/ⓕ ko-*zee*-do/ko-*zee*-daa *cooked*

cozinha ⓕ ko-*zee*-nyaa *kitchen*
— **tradicional** traa-dee-syo-*now traditional cooking*

cravo ⓜ *kraa*-vo *cloves*

creme ⓜ *kre*-me *whipped cream*
— **chantilly** shang-*tee*-lee *whipped cream*
— **de legumes** de le-*goo*-mes *cream of vegetable soup*
— **pasteleiro** paas-te-*lay*-ro *egg-based cream filling used in pastries*

croissant ⓜ krwaa-*sang croissant*
— **com chocolate** kong sho-ko-*laa*-te *chocolate-filled croissant*
— **com creme** kong *kre*-me *custard-filled croissant*
— **com presunto** kong pre-*zoong*-to *croissant with ham*
— **com queijo** kong *kay*-zho *croissant with cheese*
— **misto** *mees*-to *croissant with ham & cheese*

croquete ⓜ kro-*ke*-te *meat croquette*

cru/crua m/f kroo/*kroo*-a *raw*

curado/curada m/f koo-*raa*-do/koo-*raa*-daa *cured*

D

damasco ⓜ daa-*maas*-ko *apricot*

defumado/defumada ⓜ/ⓕ de-foo-*maa*-do/de-foo-*maa*-daa *smoked*

desossado/desossada ⓜ/ⓕ de-zo-*saa*-do/de-zo-*saa*-daa *boned*

digestivo ⓜ dee-zhes-*tee*-vo *after-dinner drink, usually a liqueur, brandy or port*

dobradinha ⓕ do-braa-*dee*-nyaa *tripe with white beans & rice*

doce ⓜ *do*-se *sweet • dessert • jam*
— **de abóbora com requeijão** de aa-*bo*-bo-raa kong he-kay-*zhowng pumpkin jam*
— **de goiaba** de go-*yaa*-baa *guava jam*
— **de ovos** de o-vos *egg yolk sweets*

doces ⓟ pl **regionais** *do*-ses he-zhyo-*nais regional sweets*

dourado ⓜ do-*raa*-do *freshwater fish found throughout Brazil*

E

empada ⓕ eng-*paa*-daa *miniature pot pie*
— **de carne** de *kaarr*-ne *with meat filling*
— **de camarão** dekaa-maa-*rowng* *with prawn filling*
— **de frango** de *fran*-go *with chicken filling*
— **de galinha** de gaa-*lee*-nyaa *with chicken filling*
— **de legumes** de le-*goo*-mes *with vegetable filling*

empadão ⓜ eng-paa-*downg* *a big empada*

enguia ⓕ eng-*gee*-aa *eel*

entrada ⓕ eng-*traa*-daa *entree*

erva-doce ⓕ err-vaa-*do*-se *aniseed*

ervas ⓕ pl err-vaas *herbs*
— **aromáticas** aa-ro-*maa*-tee-kaas *mixture of cooking herbs*

ervilhas ⓕ pl err-*vee*-lyaas *peas*

escabeche ⓜ es-kaa-*be*-she *tomato, onion, parsley & garlic fried with a dash of vinegar & poured over fried fish*

escalopinho ⓜ es-kaa-lo-*pee*-nyo *medallion-shaped, high quality cuts of boneless meat*

espada ⓕ es-*paa*-daa *swordfish*

espanhola, à es-pa-*nyo*-laa, aa *dish in tomato & onion sauce*

163

espaguete ⓜ es·paa·*ge*·te *spaghetti*
especialidade ⓕ **da casa**
es·pe·syaa·lee·*daa*·de daa *kaa*·zaa
house speciality
especiarias ⓕ pl es·pe·syaa·*ree*·aas
spices
espeto ⓜ es·*pe*·to *on a skewer*
 — de camarão de kaa·maa·*rowng*
 skewered prawn
 — de carne de *kaar*·ne *skewered beef*
 — de lula de *loo*·laa *skewered squid*
 — misto *mees*·to *mixed grill ·*
 skewered chunks of veal and/or pork,
 separated by bacon or sausage slices,
 green capsicum & onion
espinafre ⓜ es·pee·*naa*·fre *spinach*
espumante ⓜ&ⓕ es·poo·*mang*·te
 sparkling wine

F

faisão ⓜ fai·*sowng* *pheasant*
farinha ⓕ **de trigo** fa·*ree*·nyaa de
 tree·go *wheat flour*
farinha ⓕ **de mandioca** faa·*ree*·nyaa
 de mang·dee·o·kaa *manioc flour*
farofa ⓕ faa·ro·faa *manioc flour fried*
 with oil, garlic, salt & sometimes
 sausage & eggs
favas ⓕ pl *faa*·vaas *broad beans*
feijão ⓜ fay·*zhowng* *bean*
 — branco *brang*·ko *white bean*
 — fradinho fraa·*dee*·nyo
 black-eyed pea
 — manteiga mang·*tay*·gaa
 butter bean
 — preto *pre*·to *black bean*
feijoada ⓕ fay·zho·*aa*·daa *the national*
 dish of Brazil – pork & black bean stew
 served with rice
fígado ⓜ *fee*·gaa·do *liver*
figo ⓜ *fee*·go *fig*
filé ⓜ fee·*le* *fish fillet*
 — de pescada de pes·*kaa*·daa
 breaded & fried whiting fillet

folhado ⓜ **de carne** fo·*lyaa*·do de
 kaarr·ne *puff pastry with meat filling*
folhado ⓜ **de salsicha** fo·*lyaa*·do de
 sow·*see*·shaa *puff pastry with sausage*
 filling
forno, ao *forr*·no, ow *oven baked*
framboesa ⓕ frang·bo·e·zaa *raspberry*
frango ⓜ *frang*·go *chicken*
 — assado aa·*saa*·do *roast chicken*
 — na brasa naa *braa*·zaa *char-grilled*
 chicken seasoned with garlic, bay leaf,
 paprika & olive oil
fresco/fresca ⓜ/ⓕ *fres*·ko/*fres*·kaa
 fresh · cool · cold
frigideira ⓕ free·zhee·*day*·raa *frying*
 pan or skillet
frio/fria ⓜ/ⓕ *free*·o/*free*·aa *cold*
frito/frita ⓜ/ⓕ *free*·to/*free*·taa *fried*
frios ⓜ pl *free*·os *cold cuts of meat*
fruta ⓕ *froo*·taa *fruit*
 — cristalizada krees·taa·lee·*zaa*·daa
 candied/glazed fruit
 — da época daa *e*·po·kaa
 seasonal fruit
fruta-do-conde ⓕ froo·taa·do·*kong*·de
 custard apple
frutas secas ⓕ pl *froo*·taas *se*·kaas
 dried fruit & nuts
folha ⓜ **do funcho** fo·lyaa do
 foong·sho *dill*

G

galinha ⓕ gaa·*lee*·nyaa *chicken*
 — caipira kai·*pee*·raa *free-range*
 chicken
garrafa ⓕ gaa·*haa*·faa *bottle*
 — de meio litro de *me*·yo *lee*·tro
 half-litre bottle
 — de um litro de oom *lee*·tro
 litre bottle
 — pequena pe·*ke*·naa *small bottle*
gelatina ⓕ zhe·laa·*tee*·naa *gelatin*
geléia ⓕ zhe·*le*·yaa *jelly*
gelo ⓜ *zhe*·lo *ice*
gemas ⓕ pl zhe·maas *egg yolks*

engibre ⓜ zheng·*zhee*·bre *ginger*
goiaba ① go-*yaa*-baa *guava*
goiabada ① go-yaa-*baa*-daa *guava jam*
grão (de bico) ⓜ growng (de *bee*-ko) *chickpeas • garbanzo beans*
gratinado/gratinada ⓜ/①
graa-tee-*naa*-do/graa-tee-*naa*-daa *au gratin – topped with breadcrumbs & browned*
graviola ① graa-vee-o-laa *custard apple*
grelhado/grelhada ⓜ/①
gre-*lyaa*-do/gre-*lyaa*-daa *grilled*
groselha ① gro-ze-lyaa *gooseberry • gooseberry syrup*
guarnecido/guarnecida ⓜ/①
gwaar·ne·*see*·do/gwaar·ne·*see*·daa *garnished with pickled cauliflower, carrots, onion & sometimes olives*
guisado/guisada ⓜ/①
gee-*zaa*-do/gee-*zaa*-daa *braised*

H

hortaliça ① or·taa·*lee*·saa *green leafy vegetables*
— **cozida** ko·zee·daa *boiled green leafy vegetables*
— **refogada** he·fo·*gaa*·daa *sauteed green leafy vegetables*
hortelã ① or·te·*lang* *mint*

inhame ⓜ ee·*nyaa*·me *yam*
iogurte ⓜ ee·o·*goorr*·te *yogurt*
— **líquido** lee·kee·do *liquid yogurt*
iscas ① pl **de fígado** ees·kaas de *fee*·gaa·do *chopped liver*

J

jaca ① zhaa·kaa *jackfruit*
jambu ⓜ zham·*boo* *a Brazilian herb*
jantar ⓜ zhang·*taarr* *dinner*

jardineira ① zhaar·dee·*nay*·raa *hearty beef & vegetable stew*
javali ⓜ zhaa·vaa·*lee* *wild boar*

L

lagosta ① laa·*gos*·taa *lobster*
lagostim ⓜ laa·gos·teeng *crayfish*
lanche ⓜ lang·she *afternoon snack*
laranja ① laa·*rang*·zhaa *orange*
lata ① laa·taa *can*
lebre ① le·bre *hare*
legumes ⓜ pl le·*goo*·mes *vegetables*
leitão ⓜ lay·*towng* *suckling pig roasted in a wood-fired oven*
leite ⓜ lay·te *milk*
— **condensado** kong·deng·*saa*·do *condensed milk*
— **gordo** *gorr*·do *full cream milk*
— **desnatado** des·naa·taa·do *skim milk*
lesma ① les·maa *snails*
licor ⓜ lee·*korr* *liqueur*
limão ⓜ lee·*mowng* *lime*
— **galego** gaa·le·go *lemon*
língua ① *leeng*·gwaa *tongue*
linguado ⓜ leeng·*gwaa*·do *sole*
— **à (la) Meunière** aa (laa) mo·nee·*err* *lightly pan-fried sole sprinkled with parsley & lemon juice*
linguiça ① leen·*gwee*·saa *thin, long garlicky pork sausage*
lombinho ⓜ **de porco** long·*bee*·nyo de *porr*·ko *thinly sliced pork tenderloin*
lombo ⓜ **de porco assado** *long*·bo de *porr*·ko aa·*saa*·do *roast pork loin*
louro ⓜ lo·ro *bay leaf*
lula ① loo·laa *squid*
— **à Sevilhana** aa se·vee·*lya*·naa *fried squid rings served with mayonnaise*
— **recheada** he·she·*aa*·daa *small squid stuffed with rice, tomatoes & parsley*

menu decoder

165

M

maçã ① maa-*sang* apple

— **assada** a-*saa*-daa baked apple

maduro/madura ⑩/① maa-*doo*-ro/maa-*doo*-raa ripe (fruit) • mature (wine)

maionese ① maa-yo-*ne*-ze mayonnaise

mamão ⑩ maa-*mowng* papaya

mandioca ① mang-dee-o-kaa manioc • cassava

— **frita** *free*-taa deep-fried cassava – a common bar snack

moda, à mo-daa, aa in the manner of

manga ① mang-gaa mango

manjerona ① mang-zhe-*ro*-naa marjoram

manteiga ① mang-*tay*-gaa butter

maracujá ⑩ maa-raa-koo-*zhaa* passionfruit

margarina ① maarr-gaa-*ree*-naa margarine

marisco ⑩ maa-*rees*-ko shellfish

marmelada ① maarr-me-*laa*-daa firm quince paste

marisqueira ① maa-rees-*kay*-raa seafood restaurant

massa ① maa-saa pasta • dough

— **folhada** fo-*lyaa*-daa flaky pastry

medalhão ⑩ me-daa-*lyowng* medallion of meat or fish

mel ⑩ mel honey

melaço ⑩ me-*laa*-so molasses

melancia ① me-lang-*see*-aa watermelon

melão ⑩ me-*lowng* melon

— **com presunto** kong pre-*zoong*-to slices of honeydew melon topped with thin slices of ham

mercado ⑩ merr-*kaa*-do market

merenda ① me-*reng*-daa snack • light lunch • picnic lunch

merengue ⑩ me-*reng*-ge meringue

mexilhões ⑩ pl me-shee-*lyoyngs* mussels

mil folhas ⑩ pl meel fo-*lyaas* layers of flaky pastry with custard filling

milho ⑩ **doce** mee-lyo do-se sweet corn

minimercado ⑩ mee-nee-merr-*kaa*-do small convenience store

mini-prato ⑩ mee-nee-*praa*-to very small serving

miolos ⑩ pl mee-o-los brains

miudos ⑩ pl mee-oo-dos giblets

moda ① **da casa** mo-daa daa kaa-zaa house-style – usually describes a meat dish accompanied by rice, chips, salad & a fried egg

moelas ① pl as mo-e-laas chicken gizzards

molho ⑩ mo-lyo sauce • gravy • dressing

— **branco** brang-ko white sauce

— **de caramelo** de kaa-raa-*me*-lo caramel sauce

— **de cocktail** de ko-kee-*tel* sauce made from mayonnaise, tomato sauce & a dash of whisky

— **de manteiga** de mang-*tay*-gaa butter sauce

— **verde** verr-de sauce for fish or octopus made with chopped onion, garlic, red capsicum, parsley, vinegar & lots of olive oil

molusco ⑩ mo-*loos*-ko clam

moqueca ① mo-*ke*-kaa style of cooking from Bahia • a kind of sauce or stew made from **dendê** oil & coconut milk, cooked in a covered clay pot

moqueca ① **(de peixe) capixaba** mo-*ke*-kaa (de *pay*-she) kaa-pee-*shaa*-baa fish stew traditionally made in a clay pot

morangos ⑩ pl mo-*rang*-gos strawberries

morcela ① morr-*se*-laa blood sausage

moscatel ① mos-kaa-*tel* sweet dessert wine

mostarda ① mos-*taarr*-daa mustard

N

a brasa naa *braa*·zaa
  char-grilled
a chapa naa *shaa*·paa *cooked on
  a hot steel plate*
a pedra naa *pe*·draa *meat or fish
  grilled on a hot stone at the table*
abo ⑩ *naa*·bo *turnip*
êspera ① *nes*·pe·raa *loquat*
novilho ⑩ no·*vee*·lyo *veal*
noz ① *noz walnut*

O

óleo ⑩ *o*·lyo *oil*
  — de amendoim de
  aa·meng·do·*eeng peanut oil*
  — de cozinha de ko·*zee*·nyaa
  cooking oil
  — de girassol de zhee·raa·*sol
  sunflower seed oil*
  — de milho de *mee*·lyo *corn oil*
  — de soja de *so*·zhaa *soybean oil*
  — vegetal ve·zhe·*tow vegetable oil*
omelete ⑩ o·me·*le*·te *omelette*
orégano ⑩ o·*re*·ga·no *oregano*
ostra ① *os*·traa *oyster*
ovas ① pl **(de pescada)** o·vaas (de
  pes·*kaa*·daa) *fish eggs, usually hake*
ovo ⑩ *o*·vo *egg*
  — cozido ko·*zee*·do *boiled egg*
  — frito *free*·to *fried egg*
  — mexido me·*shee*·do
  scrambled egg
  — poché po·*she poached egg*

P

pá ① paa *beef cut*
padaria ① paa·daa·*ree*·aa *bakery*
paio ⑩ *paa*·yo *smoked pork tenderloin
  sausage*
palmier ⑩ pow·mee·*err flat, palm-
  shaped puff pastry*

panqueca ① pang·*ke*·kaa *crepe*
  — de galinha de gaa·*lee*·nyaa
  chicken crepe
  — de legumes de le·*goo*·mes
  vegetable crepe
pão ⑩ powng *bread*
  — com linguiça
  kong leeng·*gwee*·saa
  bread roll with sausage
  — da casa daa *kaa*·zaa *'house bread'*
  — de centeio de seng·*te*·yo
  light rye bread
  — de forma de *forr*·maa
  loaf of bread
  — de-ló de lo *collapsed sponge cake*
  — de milho de *mee*·lyo *corn bread*
  — de trigo integral de *tree*·go
  eeng·te·*grow wheat-flour bread*
  — doce *do*·se *sweetened bread roll
  with cream, icing or sugar*
  — integral eeng·te·*grow wholegrain
  bread*
papa ① **de milho** *paa*·paa de *mee*·lyo
  cornmeal porridge
papos-de-anjo ⑩ pl *paa*·pos·de·*ang*·zho
  little egg-based puffs in a sugar syrup
passas ① pl *paa*·saas *raisins*
pastéis ⑩ pl pas·*tays pastries • small
  savoury fritters or something that
  looks more like a pie*
  — de bacalhau de baa·kaa·*lyow
  deep-fried, oval-shaped savouries
  made of mashed potato, onion,
  parsley & salt cod*
pastel ⑩ paas·*tel pastry*
pastelaria ① paas·te·laa·*ree*·aa
  pastry shop • coffee shop • pastries
pato ⑩ *paa*·to *duck*
  — no tucupi no too·koo·*pee
  roast duck flavoured with garlic &
  cooked in* **tucupi**
pé ⑩ **de porco com feijão branco** pe
  de *porr*·ko kong fay·*zowng brang*·ko
  *stew made from pig's feet and white
  beans*

peito ⓜ **de frango** *pay*-to de *frang*-go chicken breast

peixada ⓕ *pay-shaa-daa fish cooked in broth with vegetables & tomatoes*

peixe ⓜ *pay*-she *fish*
— **assado no forno** *aa-saa*-do no *forr*-no *baked fish*
— **frito** *free*-to *fried fish*

pepino ⓜ pe-*pee*-no *cucumber*

pêra ⓕ *pe-raa pear*

peru ⓜ pe-*roo turkey*

pescada ⓕ pes-*kaa*-daa *whiting*

pescadinhas ⓕ pl pes-kaa-*dee*-nyaas *fried small whiting*

pêssego ⓜ *pe*-se-go *peach*

petiscos ⓜ pl pe-*tees*-kos *appetisers including sausages, cheese & olives, fried manioc, French fries*

picanha ⓕ pee-*ka*-nyaa *thin cut of rump steak*

picante pee-*kang*-te *describes any spicy or hot sauce*

pimenta ⓕ pee-*meng*-taa *pepper*
— **branca** *brang*-kaa *white pepper*
— **do reino** do *hay*-no *black pepper*

pimentão ⓜ pee-meng-*towng* *(sweet) pepper · capsicum*
— **assado** aa-*saa*-do *roast capsicum*
— **verde** *verr*-de *green capsicum*
— **vermelho** verr-*me*-lyo *red capsicum*

pinhão ⓜ pee-*nyowng pine nut*

pirarucu ⓜ pee-raa-hoo-*koo common Amazonian river fish*
— **ao forno** ow *forr*-no *oven-cooked pirarucu with lemon & other seasonings*

poché ⓜ po-*she poached*

polpa ⓕ *pol*-paa *fruit or vegetable pulp*
— **de fruta** de *froo*-taa *fruit pulp*
— **de tomate** de to-*maa*-te *tomato pulp*

polvo ⓜ *pol*-vo *octopus*

porco ⓜ *porr*-ko *pork*

posta ⓕ *pos*-taa *fish steak*

prato ⓜ *praa*-to *dish*
— **de verão** de ve-*rowng fruit salad common in Rio de Janeiro*
— **do dia** do *dee*-aa *the daily special*
— **feito (PF)** *fay*-to (pe-*e*-fe) *set meal*
— **principal** preeng-seee-*pow main dish*

presunto ⓜ pre-*zoong*-to *smoked ham*

pudim ⓜ poo-*deeng pudding*
— **de leite condensado** de *lay*-te kong-deng-*saa*-do *a desert similar to creme caramel*
— **de ovos** de o-vos *baked egg-custard pudding*

pupunha ⓕ poo-*poo*-nyaa *a fatty, vitamin-rich Amazonian fruit eaten with coffee*

Q

queijo ⓜ *kay*-zho *cheese*
— **de cabra** de *kaa*-braa *goat's milk cheese*
— **de ovelha** de o-*ve*-lyaa *sheep's milk cheese*
— **de vaca** de *vaa*-kaa *cow's milk cheese*
— **quente** *keng*-te *cheese melt*

quibe ⓜ *kee*-be *deep-fried meatballs*

R

recheado/recheada ⓜ/ⓕ he-she-*aa*-do/he-she-*aa*-daa *stuffed*

recheio ⓜ he-*shay*-o *stuffing or filling*

refeição ⓕ he-fay-*sowng meal*
— **rápida** *haa*-pee-daa *quick meal · fast food*

refogado ⓜ he-fo-*gaa*-do *quick fry*

refrigerante ⓜ he-free-zhe-*rang*-te *soft drink*

repolho ⓜ he-*po*-lyo *variety of cabbage with crinkly leaves*
— **roxo** ho-sho *purple cabbage*

rim ⓜ heeng *kidney*

FOOD

risole ⓜ hee-zo-le *rissole • fried pasty*
— **de camarão** de-kaa-maa-*rowng*
pasty or rissole with prawn filling
— **de carne** de *kaarr*-ne *pasty or
rissole with meat filling*
— **de frango** de *frang*-go *pasty or
rissole with chicken filling*
rodízio ⓜ ho-*dee*-zyo *Brazilian
barbecue featuring various grilled
meats on skewers and a cold salad
buffet*
rosbife ⓜ hos-*bee*-fe *roast beef*

S

sal ⓜ sow *salt*
salada ⓕ saa-*laa*-daa *salad*
— **de alface** de ow-*faa*-se
lettuce salad
— **de atum** de aa-*toong* *salad of
tuna, potato, peas, carrots, boiled
eggs with an olive oil & vinegar
dressing*
— **de bacalhau com feijão
fradinho** de baa-kaa-*lyow* kong
fay-*zhowng* fraa-dee-nyo *salad of
shredded, uncooked salt cod & black-
eyed peas with olive oil & vinegar
dressing*
— **de feijão fradinho** de fay-*zhowng*
fraa-*dee*-nyo *black-eyed pea salad
flavoured with onion, garlic, olive oil &
vinegar, sprinkled with chopped
boiled egg & parsley*
— **de tomate** de to-*maa*-te *tomato &
onion salad, often flavoured with
oregano*
— **mista** *mees*-taa *tomato, lettuce &
onion salad*
— **palmito** pow-*mee*-to
palm heart salad
— **russa** hoo-*saa* *potato salad with
peas, carrots mayonnaise*
salgadinho ⓜ sow-gaa-*dee*-nyos *small
savoury pastry*

salgado/salgada ⓜ/ⓕ sow-*gaa*-do/
sow-*gaa*-daa *small savoury pastry*
salmão ⓜ sow-*mowng* *salmon*
— **defumado** de-foo-*maa*-do
smoked salmon
salpicão ⓜ sow-pee-*kowng* *smoked
pork sausage flavoured with garlic,
bay leaf & sometimes wine*
salsa ⓕ sow-*saa* *parsley*
salsicha ⓕ sow-*see*-shaa *sausage*
sálvia ⓕ sow-*vyaa* *sage*
sanduíche ⓜ sang-doo-ee-she
sandwich
sardinha ⓕ saarr-*dee*-nyaa *sardine*
seco/seca ⓜ/ⓕ se-ko/se-kaa *dry • dried*
sobremesa ⓕ so-bre-*me*-zaa *sweet •
dessert • jam*
sonhos ⓜ pl so-nyos *doughnut-
like pastry sprinkled with sugar &
cinnamon*
sopa ⓕ so-*paa* *soup*
— **de feijão** de fay-*zhowng* *soup •
made from dried pulses or beans*
— **de feijão fradinho** de fay-*zwong*
fraa-*dee*-nyo *black-eyed pea soup
flavoured with sausages*
— **de legumes** de le-*goo*-mes
vegetable soup
— **de peixe** de *pay*-she *fish in a
tomato & onion broth, served over
chunks of bread*
— **do dia** do *dee*-aa *soup of the day*
— **juliana** zhoo-lee-*a*-naa *soup made
with mixed, julienned vegetables*
sorvete ⓜ sorr-*ve*-te *ice cream*
suco ⓜ soo-ko *juice*
— **de laranja natural** de
laa-*rang*-zhaa naa-*too*-row
freshly squeezed orange juice

T

tacacá ⓕ taa-kaa-*kaa* *an Indian dish
of dried shrimp cooked with pepper,
jambu & manioc*

tamboril ⓜ tang·bo·*reel* monkfish

tamarindo ⓜ taa·maa·*reeng*·do tamarind

torta ① **de amêndoaa** torr·taa de aa·*meng*·dwaa almond tart

torta ① **de maçã** torr·taa de maa·*sang* apple tart

tomate ⓜ to·*maa*·te tomato

tomilho ⓜ to·*mee*·lyo thyme

torrada ① to·*haa*·daa toast

torresmo ⓜ to·*hes*·mo pork cracklings served hot or cold as a snack

toucinho ⓜ too·*see*·nyo bacon
— **defumado** de·foo·*maa*·do smoked bacon
— **salgado** sow·*gaa*·do salt-cured bacon

trança ① trang·saa pastry topped with coconut mixture & chopped nuts

tremoços ⓜ pl tre·mo·sos salted, preserved yellow beans eaten as a snack

tripa ① *tree*·pa tripe

truta ① *troo*·taa trout

tucupi ⓜ too·koo·*pee* sauce made from the juice of the manioc plant & **jambu**

tutu ⓜ **á mineira** too·*too* aa mee·*nay*·raa a bean paste with toasted bacon & manioc flour, often served with cooked cabbage

U

uvas ① pl oo·*vaas* grapes

V

vatapá ⓜ vaa·taa·*paa* dried shrimp, cashew, fish, pepper & tomato sauce

veado ⓜ ve·*aa*·do venison

vinagre ⓜ vee·*naa*·gre vinegar

vinha ⓜ **d'alho** vee·nyaa daa·lyo meat marinated in wine or vinegar, olive oil, garlic & bay leaf

vinho ⓜ *vee*·nyo wine
— **branco** brang·ko white wine
— **da casa** daa kaa·zaa house wine
— **da região** daa he·zhee·owng local wine
— **quente** keng·te mulled wine
— **rosé** ho·ze rosé wine
— **tinto** teeng·to red wine
— **verde** verr·de 'green wine' – light sparkling red, white or rosé wine

vitamina ① vee·taa·mee·naa milk & fruit shake

vitela ① vee·te·laa veal

X

xerém chouriço ⓜ she·*reng* sho·*ree*·so cornmeal porridge served with shellfish, pork or other meat

xinxim de galinha ⓜ sheeng·*sheeng* de gaa·*lee*·nyaa chicken pieces flavoured with garlic, salt & lemon

emergencies

emergências

Help, I'm being robbed!
Socorro, estou sendo
assaltado/assaltada! m/f
so·*ko*·ho es·*to seng*·do
aa·sow·*taa*·do/aa·sow·*taa*·daa

Stop, thief!
Pega ladrão!
pe·gaa la·*drowng*

Can I use your phone?
Posso usar seu telefone?
po·so oo·*zaarr se*·oo te·le·*fo*·ne

It's an emergency.
É uma emergência.
e oo·maa e·merr·*zheng*·see·aa

Call the police!
Chame a polícia!
sha·me aa po·*lee*·syaa

Call a doctor!
Chame um médico!
sha·me oom *me*·dee·ko

Call an ambulance!
Chame uma
ambulância!
sha·me oo·maa
am·boo·*lang*·see·aa

Could you please help?
Você pode ajudar,
por favor?
vo·*se po*·de aa·zhoo·*daarr*
porr faa·*vorr*

I'm lost.
Estou perdido/
perdida. m/f
es·*to* perr·*dee*·do/
perr·*dee*·daa

Is it dangerous here?
Aqui é perigoso?
a·*kee* e pe·ree·*go*·zo

Where are the toilets?
Onde tem um banheiro?
on·de teng oom ba·*nyay*·ro

I'm ill.
Estou doente.   es·*to* do·*eng*·te

She's having a baby.
Ela está tendo um bebê   e·laa es·*taa teng*·do oom be·*be*

My … is ill.	*… está doente.*	… es·*taa* do·*eng*·te
daughter	*Minha filha*	mee·nyaa *fee*·lyaa
friend (female)	*Minha amiga*	mee·nyaa aa·*mee*·gaa
friend (male)	*Meu amigo*	me·oo aa·*mee*·go
son	*Meu filho*	me·oo *fee*·lyo

He/She is having a/an …	*Ele/Ela está tendo …*	e·le/e·laa es·*taa teng*·do …
allergic reaction	*uma reação alérgica*	*oo*·maa he·aa·*sowng* aa·*lerr*·zhee·kaa
asthma attack	*um ataque de asma*	oom aa·*taa*·ke de *aas*·maa
epileptic fit	*um ataque epilético*	oom aa·*taa*·ke e·pee·*le*·tee·ko
heart attack	*um ataque cardíaco*	oom aa·*taa*·ke kaarr·*dee*·aa·ko

signs

Delegacia de Polícia	de·le·gaa·*see*·aa de po·*lee*·syaa	Police Station
Hospital	os·pee·*tow*	Hospital
Polícia	po·*lee*·syaa	Police
Pronto Socorro	*prong*·to so·ko·ho	Emergency Department

police

Where's the police station?
Onde é a delegacia
de polícia?
ong·de e aa de·le·gaa·*see*·aa
de po·*lee*·syaa

Please telephone the Tourist Police.
Por favor telefone para
a Polícia de Turistas.
porr faa·*vorr* te·le·*fo*·ne *paa*·raa
aa po·*lee*·syaa de too·*rees*·taas

I want to report an offence.
Eu quero fazer uma
queixa.
e·oo *ke*·ro faa·*zerr* oo·maa
kay·shaa

He/She tried to ... me.	*Ele/Ela tentou me ...*	e·le/e·laa teng·*to* me ...
rape	*estrupar*	es·troo·*paarr*
rob	*roubar*	ho·*baarr*

I've been ... He/She has been ...	*Eu fui ...* *Ele/Ela foi ...*	e·oo foo·ee ... e·le/e·laa foy ...
assaulted	*agredido/* *agredida* m/f	aa·gre·*dee*·do/ aa·gre·*dee*·daa
raped	*estrupado/* *estrupada* m/f	es·troo·*paa*·do/ es·troo·*paa*·daa
robbed	*assaltado/* *assaltada* m/f	aa·sow·*taa*·do/ aa·sow·*taa*·daa

My ... was stolen.	*... foi roubado/* *roubada.* m/f	... foy ho·*baa*·do/ ho·*baa*·daa
credit card	*Meu cartão* m *de crédito*	me·oo kaarr·*towng* de kre·dee·to
money	*Meu dinheiro* m	me·oo dee·*nyay*·ro
wallet	*Minha* *carteira* f	*mee*·nyaa kaar·*tay*·raa

My … were stolen.	… foram roubados/ roubadas. m/f pl	… fo·rang ho·baa·dos/ ho·baa·daas
bags	Minhas bolsas f pl	mee·nyaas bol·saas
papers	Meus papéis m pl	me·oos paa·peys
travellers cheques	Meus travellers cheques m pl	me·oos traa·ve·ler she·kes

---

the police may say …

You're charged with …
Você está sendo acusado/ acusada de … m/f	vo·se es·taa seng·do aa·koo·zaa·do/ aa·koo·zaa·daa de …

He/She is charged with …
Ele/Ela está sendo acusado/ acusada de … m/f	e·le/e·laa es·taa seng·do aa·koo·zaa·do/ aa·koo·zaa·daa de …

assault	agressão	aa·gre·sowng
disturbing the peace	perturbar a paz	perr·toor·baarr aa pas
not having a visa	não ter visto	nowng terr vees·to
overstaying your visa	ter ultrapassado o seu visto	terr ool·traa·paa·saa·do o se·oo vees·to
possession (of illegal substances)	posse (de substâncias ilegais)	po·se (de soo·bees·tang·syaas ee·le·gais)
shoplifting	furto	foor·to
theft	roubo	ho·bo
It's a … fine.	É uma multa de …	e oo·maa mool·taa de …
parking	estacionamento	es·taa·see·o· naa·meng·to
speeding	velocidade	ve·lo·see·daa·de

SAFE TRAVEL

174

I've lost my …	Perdi …	perr·dee …
backpack	minha mochila	mee·nyaa mo·shee·laa
handbag	minha bolsa	mee·nyaa bol·saa
	de mão	de mowng
passport	meu passaporte	me·oo paa·saa·porr·te

It was him/her.
Foi ele/ela.   foy e·le/e·laa

I have insurance.
Eu tenho seguro.   e·oo te·nyo se·goo·ro

What am I accused of?
Do que estou sendo   do ke es·to seng·do
acusado/acusada? m/f   aa·koo·zaa·do/aa·koo·zaa·daa

I'm sorry.
Desculpe.   des·kool·pe

I didn't realise I was doing anything wrong.
Eu não sabia que   e·oo nowng saa·bee·aa ke
estava fazendo algo   es·taa·vaa faa·zeng·do ow·go
errado.   e·haa·do

I didn't do it.
Eu não fiz isso.   e·oo nowng fees ee·so

Can I pay an on-the-spot fine?
Posso pagar a multa   po·so paa·gaarr aa mool·taa
na hora?   naa aw·raa

Can I make a phone call?
Posso fazer uma   po·so faa·zerr oo·maa
ligação?   lee·gaa·sowng

Can I have a lawyer (who speaks English?)
Posso ter um advogado   po·so terr oom ad·vo·gaa·do
(que fale inglês?)   (ke faa·le eeng·gles)

This medication is for personal use.

Esta medicação é	es·taa me·dee·ka·*sowng* e
para uso pessoal.	paa·raa oo·zo pe·so·ow

I have a prescription for this drug.

Eu tenho receita médica	e·oo te·nyo he·*say*·taa me·dee·kaa
para esta droga.	paa·raa es·taa dro·gaa

I (don't) understand.

Eu (não) entendo.	e·oo (nowng) eng·*teng*·do

I want to	*Eu quero entrar em*	e·oo *ke*·ro eng·*traarr* eng
contact my ...	*contato com a ...*	kong·*taa*·to kong aa ...
consulate	*meu*	me·oo
	consulado	kong·soo·*laa*·do
embassy	*minha*	*mee*·nyaa
	embaixada	eng·bai·*shaa*·daa

---

as the saying goes ...

A mentira tem pernas curtas.
aa meng·*tee*·ra perr·naas   A lie has short legs.
koor·taas

Mais vale um pássaro na mâo que dois voando.
mais vaa·le oom paa·saa·ro na   A bird in the hand
mowng ke doys vwang·do   is worth two in the bush.

doctor

o médico

Where's the nearest ...?	Onde fica ... mais perto?	ong·de fee·kaa ... mais perr·to
(night) chemist	a farmácia (noturna)	aa faarr·maa·syaa (no·toor·naa)
dentist	o dentista	o deng·tees·taa
doctor	o médico	o me·dee·ko
emergency department	o pronto socorro	o prong·to so·ko·ho
hospital	o hospital	o os·pee·tow
medical centre	a clínica médica	aa klee·nee·kaa me·dee·kaa
optometrist	o optometrista	o op·to·me·trees·taa

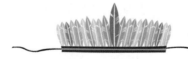

I need a doctor (who speaks English).
Eu preciso de um — e·oo pre·see·zo de oom
médico (que fale inglês). — me·dee·ko (ke faa·le eeng·gles)

Could I see a female doctor?
Posso ver uma médica? — po·so verr oo·maa me·dee·kaa

Could the doctor come here?
O médico pode vir aqui? — o me·dee·ko po·de veerr aa·kee

Is there an after-hours emergency number?
Tem um número para — teng oom noo·me·ro paa·raa
emergência? — e·merr·zheng·syaa

the doctor may say ...

What's the problem?
Qual é o problema?   kwow e o pro·*ble*·maa

Where does it hurt?
Onde dói?   ong·de doy

Do you have a temperature?
Você tem febre?   vo·se teng *fe*·bre

How long have you been like this?
Há quanto tempo você   aa *kwang*·to *teng*·po vo·se
está assim?   es·*taa* aa·*seeng*

Have you had this before?
Você já teve isso antes?   vo·se jaa *te*·ve *ee*·so ang·tes

Are you sexually active?
Você está sexualmente   vo·se es·*taa* sek·soo·ow·*meng*·te
ativo/ativa? **m/f**   aa·*tee*·vo/aa·*tee*·vaa

Have you had unprotected sex?
Você fez sexo sem   vo·se fes *sek*·so seng
proteção?   pro·te·*sowng*

Do you ...?	*Você ...?*	vo·se ...
drink	*bebe*	*be*·be
smoke	*fuma*	*foo*·maa
take drugs	*usa drogas*	oo·zaa *dro*·gaas

Are you ...?	*Você ...?*	vo·se ...
allergic to	*é alérgico/*	e aa·*lerr*·zhee·ko/
anything	*alérgica*	aa·*lerr*·zhee·kaa
	à alguma	aa ow·*goo*·maa
	coisa **m/f**	*koy*·zaa
on medication	*está tomando*	es·*taa* to·*mang*·do
	remédio	he·*me*·dyo

How long are you travelling for?
Quanto tempo você   *kwang*·to *teng*·po vo·se
vai viajar?   vai vee·aa·*zhaarr*

You need to be admitted to hospital.
Você precisa ser   vo·se pre·*see*·zaa serr
internado/internada   eeng·terr·*naa*·do/eeng·terr·*naa*·daa
num hospital. **m/f**   noom os·pee·*tow*

You should have it checked when you go home.
Você deverá checar   vo·*se* de·ve·*raa* she·*kaarr*
isto quando voltar   ees·to *kwang*·do vol·*taarr*
para casa.   paa·raa *kaa*·zaa

You should return home for treatment.
Você deveria voltar   vo·*se* de·ve·*ree*·aa vol·*taarr*
para casa para   paa·raa *kaa*·zaa paa·raa
tratamento.   traa·taa·*meng*·to

You're a hypochondriac.
Você é hipocondríaco/   vo·*se* e ee·po·kong·*dree*·aa·ko/
hipocondríaca. **m/f**   ee·po·kong·*dree*·aa·kaa

I've run out of my medication.
Estou sem remédio.   es·to seng he·*me*·dee·yo

This is my usual medicine.
Este é meu remédio   es·te e *me*·oo he·*me*·dyo
habitual.   aa·bee·too·*ow*

My son weighs (20 kilos).
Meu filho pesa   me·oo *fee*·lyo pe·zaa
(vinte kilos).   (*veeng*·te *kee*·los)

My daughter weighs (20 kilos).
Minha filha pesa   mee·nyaa *fee*·lyaa pe·zaa
(vinte kilos).   (*veeng*·te *kee*·los)

What's the correct dosage?
Qual é a dosagem   kwow e aa do·zaa·*zheng*
correta?   ko·*he*·taa

I don't want a blood transfusion.
Eu não quero uma   e·oo nowng *ke*·ro oo·maa
transfusão de sangue.   trans·foo·*zowng* de *sang*·ge

Please use a new syringe.
Por favor use uma   porr faa·*vorr* oo·ze oo·maa
seringa nova.   se·*reeng*·gaa *no*·vaa

I have my own syringe.
Eu tenho minha   e·oo te·nyo mee·nyaa
própria seringa.   pro·pree·ya se·*reeng*·gaa

I've been vaccinated against ...	Eu fui vacinado/ vacinada contra ... m/f	e·oo foo·ee vaa·see·naa·do/ vaa·see·naa·daa kong·traa ...
hepatitis A/B/C	hepatite A/B/C	e·paa·tee·te aa/be/se
yellow fever	febre amarela	fe·bre aa·maa·re·laa
He/She has been vaccinated against ...	Ele/Ela foi vacinado/ vacinada contra ...	e·le/e·laa foy vaa·see·naa·do/ vaa·see·naa·daa kong·traa ...
tetanus	tétano	te·ta·no
typhoid	tifo	tee·fo
I need new ...	Eu preciso de ...	e·oo pre·see·zo de ...
contact lenses	novas lentes de contato	no·vaas leng·tes de kong·taa·to
glasses	novos óculos	no·vos o·koo·los

My prescription is ...

Minha receita médica é ...

mee·nyaa he·say·taa me·dee·kaa e ...

How much will it cost?

Quanto vai custar?

kwang·to vai koos·tarr

Can I have a receipt for my insurance?

Posso pegar um recibo para meu seguro?

po·so pe·gaarr oom he·see·bo paa·ra me·oo se·goo·ro

symptoms & conditions

I'm ill.
Estou doente.
es·to do·eng·te

My friend is ill.
Meu amigo está
doente. m
me·oo aa·mee·go es·taa
do·eng·te

Minha amiga está
doente. f
mee·nyaa aa·mee·gaa es·taa
do·eng·te

My son is ill.
Meu filho está doente.
me·oo fee·lyo es·taa do·eng·te

My daughter is ill.
Minha filha está
doente.
mee·nyaa fee·lyaa es·taa
do·eng·te

It hurts here.
Aqui dói.
aa·kee doy

I'm dehydrated.
Estou desidratado/
desidratada. m/f
es·to de·zee·draa·taa·do/
de·zee·draa·taa·daa

I can't sleep.
Eu não consigo
dormir.
e·oo nowng kong·see·go
dorr·meerr

I've been ...	Fui ...	foo·ee ...
He/She has been ...	Ele/Ela está ...	e·le/e·laa es·taa ...
injured	machucado/	.maa·shoo·kaa·do/
	machucada m/f	maa·shoo·kaa·daa
vomiting	vomitando	vo·mee·tang·do

I feel ...	Estou me sentindo ...	es·to me seng·teeng·do ...
anxious	ansioso/ ansiosa m/f	ang·see·o·zo/ ang·see·o·zaa
better	melhor	me·lyorr
depressed	deprimido/ deprimida m/f	de·pree·mee·do/ de·pree·mee·daa
dizzy	tonto/tonta m/f	tong·to/tong·taa
hot and cold	com calor e com frio	kong kaa·lorr e kong free·o
nauseous	enjoado/ enjoada m/f	eng·zho·aa·do/ en·zho·aa·daa
shivery	com tremedeira	kong tre·me·day·raa
strange	estranho/ estranha m/f	es·tra·nyo/ es·tra·nyaa
weak	fraco/fraca m/f	fraa·ko/fraa·kaa
worse	pior	pee·orr

I think it's the medication I'm on.
Acho que é este remédio que estou tomando.
a·sho ke e es·te he·me·dyo ke es·to to·mang·do

I'm on medication for ...
Estou tomando remédio para ...
es·to to·mang·do he·me·dyo paa·raa ...

He/She is on medication for ...
Ele/Ela está tomando remédio para ...
e·le/e·laa es·taa to·mang·do he·me·dyo paa·raa ...

I have ...
Tenho ...
te·nyo ...

He/She has ...
Ele/Ela tem ...
e·le/e·laa teng ...

I've (recently) had ...
(Recentemente) Tive ...
(he·seng·te·meng·te) tee·ve ...

He/She has (recently) had ...
Ele/Ela (recentemente) teve ...
e·le/e·laa (he·seng·te·meng·te) te·ve ...

asthma	asma f	aas·maa
cold	resfriado f	hes·free·aa·do
headache	dor f de cabeça	dorr de kaa·be·saa
diabetes	diabete f	dee·aa·be·te
diarrhoea	diarréia f	dee·aa·he·yaa
fever	febre f	fe·bre
nausea	náusea f	now·ze·aa
pain	dor f	dorr
sore throat	dor f de garganta	dorr de gaar·gang·taa

women's health

saúde da mulher

(I think) I'm pregnant.
(Acho que) Estou grávida.   (aa·sho ke) es·to graa·vee·daa

I'm on the Pill.
Estou tomando a pílula.   es·to to·mang·do a pee·loo·laa

I haven't had my period for (six) days/weeks.
Não fico menstruada   nowng fee·ko mengs·troo·aa·daa
há (seis) dias/semanas.   aa (says) dee·aas/se·ma·naas

I've noticed a lump here.
Notei um caroço aqui.   no·tay oom kaa·ro·so aa·kee

the doctor may say ...

Are you using contraception?
Você está usando   vo·se es·taa oo·zang·do
algum método   ow·goom me·to·do
anticoncepcional?   an·tee·kong·sep·syo·now

Are you menstruating?
Você está   vo·se es·taa
menstruando?   mengs·troo·ang·do

Are you pregnant?
Você está grávida?   vo·se es·taa graa·vee·daa

When did you last have your period?
Quando foi sua   kwang·do foy soo·aa
última menstruação?   ool·tee·maa mengs·troo·aa·sowng

You're pregnant.
Você está grávida.   vo·se es·taa graa·vee·daa

I need ...	Eu preciso ...	e·oo pre·see·zo ...
a pregnancy test	fazer um teste de gravidez	faa·zerr oom tes·te de graa·vee·dez
contraception	de anticoncepcional	de ang·tee·kong·sep·syo·now
the morning-after pill	a pílula do dia seguinte	aa pee·loo·laa do dee·aa se·geeng·te

allergies

For food-related allergies, see **vegetarian & special meals**, page 158.

I have a skin allergy.
Eu tenho alergia de pele.   e·oo te·nyo aa·lerr·zhee·aa de pe·le

I'm allergic to ...	Tenho alergia à ...	te·nyo aa·lerr·zhee·aa aa ...
He/She is allergic to ...	Ele/Ela é alérgico/ alérgica à ... m/f	e·le/e·laa e aa·lerr·zhee·ko/ aa·lerr·zhee·kaa aa ...
antibiotics	antibióticos	ang·tee·bee·o·tee·kos
anti-inflammatories	anti-inflamatórios	ang·tee·eeng·fla·ma·to·ree·os
aspirin	aspirina	aas·pee·ree·naa
bees	abelhas	aa·be·lyaas
codeine	codeína	ko·de·ee·naa
penicillin	penicilina	pe·nee·see·lee·naa
pollen	pólem	po·leng
sulphur-based drugs	drogas à base de súlfura	dro·gaas aa baa·ze de sool·foo·raa
inhaler	respirador m	hes·pee·raa·dorr
injection	injeção f	eeng·zhe·sowng
antihistamines	antiestamínico m	ang·tee·es·ta·mee·nee·ko

parts of the body

My ... hurts.
Meu/Minha ... dói. m/f   me·oo/mee·nyaa ... doy

I can't move my ...
Não consigo mover   nowng kong·see·go mo·verr
meu/minha ... m/f   me·oo/mee·nyaa ...

My ... is swollen.
Meu ... está inchado. m   me·oo ... es·taa eeng·shaa·do
Minha ... está inchada. f   mee·nyaa ... es·taa
eeng·shaa·daa

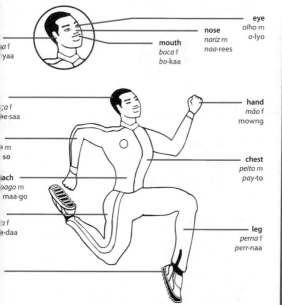

eye
olho m
o·lyo

nose
nariz m
naa·rees

mouth
boca f
bo·kaa

a f
yaa

ça f
·e·saa

· m
so

ach
·ago m
·maa·go

a f
·daa

hand
mão f
mowng

chest
peito m
pay·to

leg
perna f
perr·naa

alternative treatments

I don't use (Western medicine).
Eu não uso   e·oo nowng oo·zo
(medicina ocidental).   (me·dee·*see*·naa o·see·deng·*tow*)

I prefer ...   *Eu prefiro ...*   e·oo pre·*fee*·ro ...
Can I see   *Posso ver alguém*   *po*·so verr ow·*geng*
someone who   *que pratica ...*   ke pra·*tee*·kaa ...
practices ...?
    acupuncture   *acupuntura*   aa·koo·poom·*too*·raa
    naturopathy   *naturapatia*   naa·too·ro·paa·*tee*·aa
    reflexology   *reflexologia*   he·flek·so·lo·*zhee*·aa

chemist

I need something for ...
Preciso de alguma   pre·*see*·zo de ow·*goo*·maa
coisa para ...   koy·zaa *paa*·raa ...

Do I need a prescription for ...?
Preciso de receita   pre·*see*·zo de he·*say*·taa
médica para ...?   me·dee·kaa *paa*·raa ...

I have a prescription.
Eu tenho receita médica.   e·oo te·nyo he·*say*·taa me·dee·ka

How many times a day?
Quantas vezes ao dia?   kwang·taas *ve*·zes ow *dee*·aa

Will it make me drowsy?
Isto vai me deixar   *ees*·to vai me day·*shaarr*
tonto/tonta? m/f   *tong*·to/*tong*·taa

antiseptic	*anti-séptico* m	ang·tee·*sep*·tee·ko
contraceptive	*anti-*	ang·tee·
	concepcional m	kong·*sep*·syo·now
painkillers	*analgésicos* m pl	aa·now·*zhe*·zee·kos
thermometer	*termômetro* m	terr·*mo*·me·tro
rehydration salts	*sais* m pl *de*	sais de
	hidratação	ee·draa·taa·*sowng*

listen for ...

doo·aas *ve*·zes porr *dee*·aa (aas he·fay·*soyngs*)
  Duas vezes por dia
  (às refeições).

**Twice a day
(with food).**

vo·*se* zhaa to·*mo* ee·so *ang*·tes
  Você já tomou isso antes?

**Have you taken this
before?**

vo·*se* teng ke to·*maarr* too·do
  Você tem que tomar tudo.

**You must complete
the course.**

dentist

dentista

I have a ...	*Eu tenho ...*	e·oo te·nyo ...
broken tooth	*um dente*	oom *deng*·te
	quebrado	ke·*braa*·do
cavity	*uma cárie*	oo·maa *kaa*·ree·e
toothache	*dor de dente*	dorr de *deng*·te

I've lost a filling.
  Perdi uma obturação.   perr·*dee* oo·maa ob·too·raa·*sowng*

My dentures are broken.
  Minha dentadura   mee·nyaa deng·taa·*doo*·raa
  está quebrada.   es·taa ke·*braa*·daa

health

187

My gums hurt.
  Minha gengivas dói.   mee·nyaa zheng·*zhee*·vaas doy

I don't want it extracted.
  Eu não quero extrair.   e·oo nowng *ke*·ro es·traa·*eerr*

Ouch!
  Au!   ow

I need …	*Preciso …*	pre·*see*·zo …
an anaesthetic	*de analgésico*	de aa·now·*zhe*·zee·ko
a filling	*de uma*	de *oo*·maa
	obturação	ob·too·ra·*sowng*

---

listen for …

aa·bre beng
  Abra bem.   **Open wide.**

eng·*shaa*·gwe
  Enxágue.   **Rinse.**

morr·de
  Morde.   **Bite down on this.**

nowng se *me*·shaa
  Não se mexa.   **Don't move.**

nowng vai do·*err naa*·daa
  Não vai doer nada.   **This won't hurt a bit.**

SUSTAINABLE TRAVEL

As the climate change debate heats up, the matter of sustainability becomes an important part of the travel vernacular. In practical terms, this means assessing our impact on the environment and local cultures and economies – and acting to make that impact as positive as possible. Here are some basic phrases to get you on your way …

communication & cultural differences

I'd like to learn some of your local dialects.

Eu gostaria de	e·oo gos·taa·ree·aa de
aprender algo do seu	aa·preng·derr ow·go do se·oo
dialeto local.	dee·aa·le·to lo·kow

Would you like me to teach you some English?

Você gostaria que eu te	vo·se gos·taa·ree·aa ke e·oo te
ensine algo em inglês?	en·see·ne ow·go eng eeng·gles

I respect your customs.

Eu respeito os seus	e·oo hes·pay·to os se·oos
costumes.	kos·too·mes

community benefit & involvement

What sorts of issues is this community facing?

Que tipo de problemas	ke tee·po de pro·ble·mas
a comunidade está	aa ko·moo·nee·da·de es·taa
enfrentando?	eng·freng·tang·do

literacy	analfabetismo m	aa·nal·fa·be·tees·mo
poverty	pobreza f	po·bre·zaa
tree-logging	desmatamento m	des·ma·ta·meng·to

Are there any volunteer programs available in the area?

Tem algum programa voluntário a disposição na redondeza?

teng ow·*goong* pro·*gra*·maa vo·loong·*taa*·ryo aa dees·po·zee·*sowng* naa he·downg·*de*·zaa

I'd like to volunteer my skills.

Eu gostaria de voluntariar com minha especialização.

e·oo gos·taa·*ree*·aa de vo·loong·taa·ree·*aarr* kong *meen*·ya es·pe·syaa·lee·zaa·*sowng*

environment

Does your company have a green policy?

A sua empresa tem algum acordo de preservação do meio-ambiente?

aa *soo*·aa eng·*pre*·zaa teng ow·*goong* aa·*korr*·do de pre·zerr·vaa·*sowng* do *may*·o ang·bee·*eng*·te

Where can I recycle this?

Onde posso reciclar isto? ong·de po·so he·see·*klaarr* ees·to

transport

Can we get there by public transport?

Podemos chegar lá de transporte público?

po·*de*·mos she·*gaarr* laa de trans·*porr*·te poob·lee·ko

Can we get there by bicycle?

Podemos ir até lá de bicicleta?

po·*de*·mos eerr aa·*te* laa de bee·see·*kle*·taa

I'd prefer to walk there.

Eu prefiro caminhar até lá.

e·oo pre·*fee*·ro ka·meeng·*nyarr* aa·*te* laa

accommodation

Are there any ecolodges here?

Tem algum hospedagem ecológica por aqui?

teng ow·*goong* os·pe·*daa*·zheng e·ko·*lo*·zhee·ka porr aa·*kee*

I'd like to stay at a locally run hotel.

Eu gostaria de me	e·oo gos·taa·ree·aa de me
hospedar em um hotel	os·pe·daarr eng oong o·tel
de proprietários locais.	de pro·pree·e·taa·ryos lo·kais

Can I turn the air conditioning off and open the window?

Posso desligar o	po·so des·lee·garr o
ar condicionado	aarr kong·dee·syo·naa·do
e abrir a janela?	e aa·breerr aa zhaa·ne·laa

There's no need to change my sheets, they're still clean.

Não prescisa trocar	nowng pre·see·zaa tro·kaarr
os meus lençóis,	os me·oos len·soys
ainda estão limpos.	aa·eeng·da es·towng leeng·pos

shopping

Where can I buy locally produced goods/souvenirs?

Onde posso comprar	ong·de po·so kong·praarr
produtos/souvenirs	pro·doo·tos/soo·ve·neers
produzidos localmente?	pro·doo·zee·dos lo·kow·meng·te

Do you sell Fair Trade products?

Você vende produtos	vo·se veng·de pro·doo·tos
de comércio justo?	de ko·merr·syo zhoos·to

s this made	Isto é feito	ee·sto e fay·to
from ...?	com ...?	kong ...
coral	coral	ko·row
local wood	madeira	maa·day·raa
products	local	lo·kow

food

Can you tell me what traditional foods I should try?

Você pode me dizer	vo·se po·de me dee·zherr
quais comidas	kwais ko·mee·das
tradicionais eu devo	traa·dee·syo·nais e·oo de·vo
esperimentar?	es·pe·ree·meng·taarr

Do you sell ...?	Você vende ...?	vo·se veng·de ...
locally	alimentos	a·lee·meng·tos
produced	produzidos	pro·doo·zee·dos
food	localmente	lo·kow·meng·te
organic	produtos	pro·doo·tos
produce	orgânicos	orr·ga·nee·kos

sightseeing

Does your	A sua	aa soo·aa
company ...?	empresa ...?	eng·pre·zaa ...
donate money	doa dinheiro	do·aa dee·nyay·ro
to charity	para a	paa·raa aa
	comunidade	ko·moo·nee·daa·de
hire local	tem guias	teng gee·aas
guides	turisticos	too·rees·tee·kos
	locais	lo·kais
visit local	leva a estabele-	le·va aa es·ta·be·le·
businesses	cimentos de	see·meng·tos de
	proprietarios	pro·pree·e·taa·ryos
	locais	lo·kais

Does the guide	O guia fala ...?	o gee·aa faa·la ...
speak ...?		
Apalai	Apalai	aa·pa·lai
Arara	Arara	aa·raa·ra
Bororo	Bororó	bo·ro·ro
Canela	Canela	ka·ne·la
Caraja	Carajá	ka·raa·zhaa
Guarani	Guaraní	gwaa·ra·nee
Terena	Terena	te·re·naa
Tucano	Tucano	too·ka·no

I'd like to hire a local guide.

Eu gostaria de	e·oo gos·taa·ree·aa de
contratar um	kong·traa·taarr oong
guia local.	gee·aa lo·kow

Are cultural tours available?

Tem excursões	teng es·koorr·soyngs
culturais?	kool·too·rais

Nouns in the dictionary have their gender indicated by ⓜ or ⓕ. If it's a plural noun, you'll also see pl. Where a word that could be either a noun or a verb has no gender indicated, it's the verb. For all words relating to local food, see the **menu decoder**, page 159.

A

aboard *a bordo* aa borr-do
abortion *aborto* ⓜ aa-borr-to
about *sobre* so-bre
above *sobre* so-bre
abroad *exterior* es-te-ree-orr
accident *acidente* ⓜ aa-see-*deng*-te
accommodation *hospedagem* ⓕ
   os-pe-*daa*-zheng
across *através* aa-traa-*ves*
activist *ativista* ⓜ&ⓕ aa-tee-*vees*-taa
acupuncture *acupuntura* ⓕ
   aa-koo-poom-*too*-raa
adaptor *adaptador* ⓜ aa-daa-pee-taa-*dorr*
addiction *vício* ⓜ *vee*-syo
address *endereço* ⓜ eng-de-*re*-so
administration *administração* ⓕ
   aa-dee-mee-nees-traa-*sowng*
admission price *preço* ⓜ *da entrada*
   pre-so daa eng-*traa*-daa
admit (acknowledge) *admitir*
   aa-dee-mee-*teerr*
adult *adulto/adulta* ⓜ/ⓕ
   aa-*dool*-to/aa-*dool*-taa
advertisement *anúncio* ⓜ aa-*noom*-see-o
advice *conselho* ⓜ kong-*se*-lyo
aerobics *aeróbica* ⓕ aa-e-ro-bee-kaa
aeroplane *aeroplano* ⓜ aa-e-ro-*pla*-no
Africa *África* ⓕ *aa*-free-kaa
after *depois* de-*poys*
(this) afternoon *(esta) tarde* ⓕ
   (es-taa) *taarr*-de
aftershave *pós barba* ⓜ pos *baarr*-baa
again *novamente* no-vaa-*meng*-te
age *idade* ⓕ ee-*daa*-de
(three days) ago *há (três dias)*
   aa (tres *dee*-aas)
agree *concordar* kong-korr-*daarr*

agriculture *agricultura* ⓕ
   aa-gree-kool-*too*-raa
ahead *em frente* eng *freng*-te
AIDS *Aids* ⓕ *ai*-dees
air *ar* ⓜ aarr
air-conditioning *ar* ⓜ *condicionado*
   aarr kong-dee-syo-*naa*-do
airline *linha aérea* ⓕ pl lee-nyaa aa-e-re-aa
airmail *via* ⓕ *aérea* vee-aa aa-e-re-aa
airplane *avião* ⓜ aa-vee-*owng*
airport *aeroporto* ⓜ aa-e-ro-*porr*-to
airport tax *taxa* ⓕ *de aeroporto*
   taa-shaa de aa-e-ro-porr-to
aisle *corredor* ⓜ ko-he-*dorr*
alarm clock *despertador* ⓜ
   des-perr-taa-*dorr*
alcohol *álcool* ⓜ *ow*-kol
all *tudo/tuda* ⓜ/ⓕ *too*-do/too-daa
allergy *alergia* ⓕ aa-lerr-*zhee*-aa
almond *amêndoa* ⓕ aa-*meng*-dwaa
almost *quase* *kwaa*-ze
alone *sozinho/sozinha* ⓜ/ⓕ so-zee-nyo/
   so-*zee*-nyaa
already *já* zhaa
also *também* tang-*beng*
altar *altar* ⓜ ow-*taarr*
altitude *altitude* ⓕ ow-tee-*too*-de
always *sempre* *seng*-pre
ambassador *embaixador/*
   embaixadora ⓜ/ⓕ
   eng-bai-shaa-*dorr*/eng-bai-shaa-*do*-raa
American football *futebol* ⓜ *americano*
   foo-te-*bol* aa-me-ree-*ka*-no
anaemia *anemia* ⓕ aa-ne-*mee*-aa
anarchist *anarquista* ⓜ&ⓕ
   aa-naarr-*kees*-taa
ancient *ancião/anciã* ⓜ/ⓕ
   ang-see-*owng*/ang-see-*ang*
and *e* e

angry *zangado/zangada* ⓜ/ⓕ
zang-*gaa*-do/zang-*gaa*-daa
animal *animal* ⓜ&ⓕ aa-nee-*mow*
ankle *tornozelo* ⓜ torr-no-ze-lo
answer *resposta* ⓕ hes-*pos*-taa
ant *formiga* ⓕ forr-*mee*-gaa
antibiotics *antibióticos* ⓜ pl
ang-tee-bee-o-te-kos
antinuclear *antinuclear* ⓜ
ang-tee-noo-kle-*aarr*
antique *antigo/antiga* ⓜ/ⓕ ang-*tee*-go/
ang-*tee*-gaa
antiseptic *anti-séptico* ⓜ
ang-tee-*sep*-tee-ko
any *qualquer* kwow-*kerr*
apartment *apartamento* ⓜ
aa-paarr-taa-*meng*-to
appendix (body) *apêndice* ⓜ
aa-*peng*-dee-se
apple *maçã* ⓕ maa-*sang*
appointment *consulta* ⓕ kong-*sool*-taa
apricot *damasco* ⓜ daa-*maas*-ko
April *abril* aa-*breel*
archaeological *arqueológico/
arqueulógica* ⓜ/ⓕ aarr-ke-o-lo-zhee-ko/
aarr-ke-o-lo-zhee-kaa
architect *arquiteto/arquiteta* ⓜ/ⓕ
aarr-kee-*te*-to/aarr-kee-*te*-taa
architecture *arquitetura* ⓕ
aar-kee-te-*too*-raa
argue *discutir* dees-koo-*teerr*
arm *braço* ⓜ *braa*-so
aromatherapy *aromaterapia* ⓕ aa
aa-ro-maa-te-raa-*pee*-aa
arrest *prender* preng-*derr*
arrival *chegada* ⓕ she-*gaa*-daa
arrivals *chegadas* ⓕ pl she-*gaa*-daas
arrive *chegar* she-*gaarr*
art *arte* ⓕ *aarr*-te
art gallery *galeria* ⓕ *de arte* gaa-le-*ree*-aa
de *aarr*-te
artist *artista* ⓜ&ⓕ aar-*tees*-taa
ashtray *cinzeiro* ⓜ seen-*zay*-ro
Asia *Ásia* ⓕ *aa*-zyaa
ask (a question) *perguntar*
perr-goong-*taarr*
ask (for something) *pedir* pe-*deerr*
asparagus *aspargo* ⓜ aas-*paarr*-go
aspirin *aspirina* ⓕ aas-pee-*ree*-naa

asthma *asma* ⓕ *aas*-maa
athletics *atletismo* ⓜ aat-le-*tees*-mo
atmosphere *atmosfera* ⓕ
aa-tee-mos-*fe*-raa
aubergine *beringela* ⓕ be-reeng-*zhe*-la
August *agosto* aa-*gos*-to
aunt *tia* ⓕ *tee*-aa
Australia *austrália* ⓕ ows-*traa*-lya
Australian Rules Football *Futebol* ⓜ
Australian Rules foo-te-*bol*
ows-*tra*-lee-ang roo-les
automatic teller machine (ATM) *caixa* ⓕ
automático kai-shaa ow-to-*maa*-tee-ko
autumn *outono* ⓜ o-*to*-no
avenue *avenida* ⓕ aa-ve-*nee*-daa
avocado *abacate* ⓜ aa-baa-*kaa*-te
awful *horrível* o-*hee*-vel

B

B&W (film) *preto e branco*
pre-to e *brang*-ko
baby *bebê* ⓜ&ⓕ be-*be*
baby food *comida* ⓕ *de bebê*
ko-*mee*-daa de be-*be*
baby powder *talco* ⓜ *tow*-ko
babysitter *babá* ⓕ baa-*baa*
back (position) *de costas de kos*-taas
back (body) *costas* ⓕ *kos*-taas
backpack *mochila* ⓕ mo-*shee*-la
bacon *bacon* ⓜ *bay*-kong
bad *ruim* hoo-*eeng*
bag *saco* ⓜ *saa*-ko
baggage *bagagem* ⓕ baa-*gaa*-zheng
baggage allowance *limité* ⓜ *de peso*
lee-*mee*-te de *pe*-zo
baggage claim *requerimento* ⓜ *de
bagagem* he-ke-ree-*meng*-to de
baa-*gaa*-zheng
bakery *padaria* ⓕ paa-daa-*ree*-aa
balance (account) *balanço* ⓜ baa-*lang*-so
balcony *varanda* ⓕ vaa-*rang*-daa
ball *bola* ⓕ bo-laa
ballet *balé* ⓜ ba-*le*
banana *banana* ⓕ baa-*na*-naa
band (music) *banda* ⓕ *(de música)*
bang-daa (de *moo*-zee-kaa)
bandage *curativo* ⓜ koo-raa-*tee*-vo
Band-Aid *band-aid* ⓜ bang-*day*-dee

bank *banco* ⓜ *bang*·ko
bank account *conta* ⓕ *bancária*
kong·taa bang·*kaa*·rya
banknote *nota* ⓕ *no*·taa
baptism *batismo* ⓜ baa·*tees*·mo
bar *bar* ⓜ baarr
bar work *trabalho* ⓜ *em bar*
traa·*ba*·lyo eng baarr
barber *barbeiro* ⓜ baar·*bay*·ro
baseball *baseball* ⓜ *bay*·ze·bol
basket *cesta* ⓕ *ses*·taa
basketball *basquete* ⓜ baas·*ke*·te
bath *banheira* ⓕ ba·*nyay*·raa
bathing suit *roupa* ⓕ *de banho*
ho·paa de ba·nyo
bathroom *banheiro* ⓜ ba·*nyay*·ro
battery *pilha* ⓕ *pee*·lyaa
be (temporary) *estar* es·*taarr*
be (ongoing) *ser* serr
beach *praia* ⓕ *prai*·aa
beach volleyball *vôlei* ⓜ *de praia*
vo·lay de praa·yaa
bean *feijão* fay·*zhowng*
beansprout *broto* ⓜ *de feijão*
bro·to de fay·*zhowng*
beautiful *bonito/bonita* ⓜ/ⓕ
bo·*nee*·to/bo·*nee*·taa
beauty salon *salão* ⓜ *de beleza*
saa·*lowng* de be·*le*·zaa
because *por que por*·ke
bed *cama* ⓕ *ka*·maa
bedding *roupa* ⓕ *de cama*
ho·paa de *ka*·maa
bedroom *quarto* ⓜ *kwaarr*·to
bee *abelha* ⓕ aa·*be*·lyaa
beef *bife* ⓜ *bee*·fe
beer *cerveja* ⓕ serr·*ve*·zhaa
beetroot *beterraba* ⓕ be·te·*haa*·baa
before *antes ang*·tes
beggar *pedinte* ⓜ&ⓕ pe·*deeng*·te
behind *atrás* aa·*traas*
below *abaixo* aa·*bai*·sho
best *melhor* me·*lyorr*
bet *aposta* ⓕ aa·*pos*·taa
better *melhor* me·*lyorr*
between *entre eng*·tre
bible *bíblia* ⓕ *bee*·blyaa
bicycle *bicicleta* ⓕ bee·see·*kle*·taa
big *grande grang*·de

bike *bicicleta* ⓕ bee·see·*kle*·taa
bike chain *corrente* ⓕ *de bicicleta*
ko·*heng*·te de bee·see·*kle*·taa
bike lock *tranca* ⓕ *de bicicleta* trang·kaa
de bee·see·*kle*·taa
bike path *rota* ⓕ *de bicicleta*
ho·ta de bee·see·*kle*·taa
bike shop *loja* ⓕ *de bicicleta*
lo·zhaa de bee·see·*kle*·taa
bill (account) *conta* ⓕ *kong*·taa
binoculars *binóculos* ⓜ pl bee·no·koo·los
bird *pássaro* ⓜ paa·saa·ro
birth certificate *certidão* ⓕ *de nascimento*
serr·tee·*downg* de naa·see·*meng*·to
birthday *aniversário* ⓜ aa·nee·verr·*saa*·ryo
biscuit *biscoito* ⓜ bees·*koy*·to
bite (dog) *mordida* ⓕ morr·*dee*·daa
bite (insect) *mordida* ⓕ morr·*dee*·daa
black *preto/preta* ⓜ/ⓕ *pre*·to/*pre*·taa
bladder *bexiga* ⓕ be·*shee*·gaa
blanket *cobertor* ⓜ ko·berr·*torr*
blind *cego/cega* ⓜ/ⓕ *se*·go/*se*·gaa
blister *bolha* ⓕ *bo*·lyaa
blocked *bloqueado/bloqueada* ⓜ/ⓕ
blo·ke·*aa*·do/blo·ke·*aa*·daa
blood *sangue* ⓜ *sang*·ge
blood group *grupo* ⓜ *sanguíneo*
groo·po sang·*gwee*·ne·o
blood pressure *pressão* ⓕ *arterial*
pre·*sowng* aar·te·ree·*ow*
blood test *exame* ⓜ *de sangue*
e·*za*·me de *sang*·ge
blue *azul* aa·*zool*
board (a plane, ship, etc) *subir a bordo*
soo·*beerr* aa borr·do
boarding house *casa* ⓕ *de cômodos* •
pensão ⓕ *kaa*·zaa de *ko*·mo·dos •
peng·*sowng*
boarding pass *boarding pass* ⓜ
borr·deeng paas
boat *barco* ⓜ *baar*·ko
body *corpo* ⓜ *korr*·po
bone *osso* ⓜ *o*·so
book *livro* ⓜ *lee*·vro
book (make a booking) *reservar*
he·zerr·*vaarr*
booked out *esgotado/esgotada* ⓜ/ⓕ
es·go·*taa*·do/es·go·*taa*·daa
book shop *livraria* ⓕ lee·vraa·*ree*·aa

boot (footwear) *bota* ① bo·taa
boots (footwear) *botas* ① pl bo·taas
border *borda* ① borr·daa
bored *entediado/entediada* ⓜ/①
    eng·te·dee·aa·do/eng·te·dee·aa·daa
boring *entediante* eng·te·dee·ang·te
borrow *emprestar* eng·pres·taarr
botanic garden *jardim* ⓜ *botânico*
    zharr·deeng bo·ta·nee·ko
both *ambos/ambas* ⓜ/①
    ang·bos/ang·baas
bottle *garrafa* ① gaa·haa·faa
bottle opener *abridor* ⓜ *de garrafas*
    aa·bree·dorr de gaa·haa·faas
bottle shop *loja* ① *de bebidas*
    lo·zhaa de be·bee·daas
bottom (position) *fundo* foong·do
bottom (body) *traseiro* ⓜ traa·zay·ro
bowl *tigela* ① tee·zhe·laa
box *caixa* ① kai·shaa
boxer shorts *ciroula* ① se·ro·laa
boxing *boxe* ⓜ bo·kee·see
boy *menino* ⓜ me·nee·no
boyfriend *namorado* ⓜ na·mo·raa·do
bra *sutiã* ⓜ soõ·tee·ang
brake *freio* ⓜ fray·o
brandy *brandy* ⓜ brang·dee
brave *corajoso/corajosa* ⓜ/①
    ko·raa·zho·zo/ko·raa·zho·zaa
bread *pão* ⓜ powng
bread rolls *pães* ⓜ pl payngs
break *quebrar* ke·braarr
break down *pifar* • *enguiçar*
    pee·faarr • eng·gee·saarr
breakfast *café* ⓜ *da manhã*
    ka·fe da ma·nyang
breast (body) *peito* ⓜ pay·to
breasts (body) *seios* ⓜ pl say·os
breathe *respirar* hes·pee·raarr
bribe *suborno* ⓜ soo·borr·no
bridge *ponte* ① pong·te
briefcase *pasta* ① pas·taa
brilliant *brilhante* bree·lyang·te
bring *trazer* traa·zerr
broccoli *brocolis* ⓜ pl bro·ko·lees
brochure *brochura* ① bro·shoo·raa
broken *quebrado/quebrada* ⓜ/①
    ke·braa·do/ke·braa·daa
bronchitis *bronquite* ① brong·kee·te

brother *irmão* ⓜ eerr·mowng
brown *marron* maa·hong
bruise *hematoma* ① e·maa·to·maa
brush (hair) *escova* ① es·ko·vaa
bucket *balde* ⓜ bow·de
Buddhist *Budista* boo·dees·taa
buffet *buffet* ⓜ boo·fe
bug *bicho* ⓜ bee·sho
build *construir* kongs·troo·eerr
builder *construtor* ⓜ kongs·troo·tor
building *prédio* ⓜ pre·dyo
bumbag *pochete* ① po·she·te
burn *queimadura* ① kay·maa·doo·raa
burnt *queimado/queimada* ⓜ/①
    kay·maa·do/kay·maa·daa
bus (city) *ônibus* ⓜ o·nee·boos
bus (intercity) *ônibus* ⓜ o·nee·boos
bus station *rodoviária* ①
    ho·do·vee·aa·ryaa
bus stop *ponto* ⓜ *de ônibus*
    pong·to de o·nee·boos
business *negócios* ⓜ pl ne·go·syos
business class *business class* ①
    bee·zee·nes klaas
business person *homem/mulher* ⓜ/①
    de negócios o·meng/moo·lyerr de
    ne·go·syos
business trip *viagem* ① *de negócios*
    vee·aa·zheng de ne·goo·syos
busker *artista* ⓜ&① *de rua*
    aar·tees·taa de hoo·aa
busy *ocupado/ocupada* ⓜ/①
    oo·koo·paa·do/o·koo·paa·daa
but *mas* maas
butcher *açougueiro/açougueira* ⓜ/①
    aa·so·gay·ro/aa·so·gay·raa
butcher's shop *açougue* ① aa·so·ge
butter *manteiga* ① man·tay·gaa
butterfly *borboleta* ① borr·bo·le·taa
buttons *botões* ⓜ pl bo·toyngs
buy *comprar* kong·praarr

C

cabbage *repolho* ⓜ he·po·lyo
cable car *bonde* ⓜ bong·de
cafe *café* ⓜ kaa·fe
cake *bolo* ⓜ bo·lo

cake shop *confeitaria* ①
  kong·fay·taa·*ree*·aa
calculator *calculadora* ①
  kow·koo·laa·*do*·raa
calendar *calendário* ⓜ kaa·leng·*daa*·ryo
camera *câmera* ① *ka*·me·raa
camera shop *loja* ① *de equipamentos fotográficos* lo·zhaa de
  e·kee·pa·*meng*·tos fo·to·*graa*·fee·kos
camp *acampar* aa·kang·*paarr*
camp site *local* ⓜ *para acampar* lo·kow
  paa·raa aa·kang·*paarr*
camping ground *acampamento* ⓜ
  aa·kang·paa·*meng*·to
camping store *loja* ⓜ *de acampamento*
  lo·zhaa de aa·kam·paa·*meng*·to
can (be able) *poder* po·*derr*
can (have permission) *poder* po·*derr*
can (tin) *lata* ① *laa*·taa
can opener *abridor* ⓜ *de lata* aa·bree·*dorr*
  de *laa*·taa
Canada *Canadá* ⓜ kaa·naa·*daa*
cancel *cancelar* kang·se·*laarr*
cancer *câncer* ⓜ *kang*·serr
candle *vela* ① *ve*·laa
candy *bala* ① *baa*·laa
cantaloupe *melão* ⓜ me·*lowng*
capsicum *pimentão* ⓜ pee·meng·*towng*
car *carro* ⓜ *kaa*·ho
car hire *aluguel* ⓜ *de carro*
  aa·loo·*gel* de *kaa*·ho
car registration *registro* ⓜ *de carro*
  he·*zhees*·tro de *kaa*·ho
caravan *caravan* ① kaa·raa·*vang*
cardiac arrest *parada* ① *cardíaca*
  paa·*raa*·daa kaarr·*dee*·aa·kaa
cards (playing) *cartas* ① pl kaarr·tas
care (for someone) *gostar (de alguém)*
  gos·*taarr* (de ow·*geng*)
car park *estacionamento* ⓜ
  es·taa·syo·naa·*meng*·to
carrot *cenoura* ① se·*no*·raa
carry *carregar* kaa·he·*gaarr*
carton *caixa* ① *de papelão*
  kai·shaa de paa·pe·*lowng*
cash *em espécie* eng es·*pe*·sye
cash (a cheque) *descontar (um cheque)*
  des·kong·*taarr* (oom *she*·ke)

cash register *caixa* ① *registradora*
  kai·shaa he·gees·traa·*do*·raa
cashew *castanha* ① *de cajú* kas·*ta*·nyaa
  de *kaa*·zhoo
cashier *caixa* ⓜ&① *kai*·sha
casino *casino* ⓜ kaa·*see*·no
cassette *fita* ① *cassete* fee·taa kaa·*se*·te
castle *castelo* ⓜ kaas·*te*·lo
casual work *trabalho* ⓜ *ocasional*
  traa·*baa*·lyo o·kaa·zee·o·*now*
cat *gato/gata* ⓜ/① *gaa*·to/*gaa*·taa
cathedral *catedral* ① kaa·te·*drow*
Catholic *Católico/Católica* ⓜ/①
  kaa·to·lee·ko/kaa·to·lee·kaa
cauliflower *couve flor* ① *ko*·ve florr
cave *caverna* ① kaa·*verr*·naa
CD *CD* ⓜ se·*de*
celebration *comemoração* ①
  ko·me·mo·raa·*sowng*
cent *centavos* ⓜ pl seng·*taa*·vos
centimetre *centímetro* ⓜ seng·*tee*·me·tro
centre *centro* ⓜ *seng*·tro
ceramics *cerâmica* ① se·*ra*·mee·kaa
cereal *cereal* ⓜ se·re·*ow*
certificate *certificado* ⓜ
  serr·tee·fee·*kaa*·do
chain *corrente* ① ko·*heng*·te
chair *cadeira* ① kaa·*day*·raa
chairlift (skiing) *teleférico* ⓜ te·le·*fe*·ree·ko
championships *campeonatos* ⓜ pl
  kang·pe·o·*naa*·tos
chance *oportunidade* ①
  o·porr·too·nee·*daa*·de
change *trocar* tro·*kaarr*
change (coins) *troco* ⓜ *tro*·ko
changing room *provador* ⓜ pro·vaa·*dorr*
charming *charmoso/charmosa* ⓜ/①
  shaarr·*mo*·zo/shaarr·*mo*·zaa
chat up *conversar* kong·verr·*saarr*
cheap *barato/barata* ⓜ/①
  baa·*raa*·to/baa·*raa*·taa
cheat *traição* ① tra·ee·*sowng*
check *checar* she·*kaarr*
check-in (desk) *check in* ① she·*keeng*
checkpoint (border) *ponto* ⓜ *de controle*
  pong·to de kong·*tro*·le
cheque (banking) *cheque* ⓜ *she*·ke
cheque (bill) *conta* ① *kong*·taa
cheese *queijo* ⓜ *kay*·zho

cheese shop *queijaria* ① kay·zhaa·*ree*·aa

chef *chefe* ⓜ&① *de cozinha*
she·fe de ko·zee·nyaa

chemist *pharmacista* ⓜ&①
faarr·maa·*sees*·taa

cherry *cereja* ① se·*re*·zhaa

chess *xadrez* ⓜ shaa·*dres*

chess board *tabuleiro* ⓜ *de xadrez*
taa·boo·*lay*·ro de shaa·*dres*

chest (body) *peito* ⓜ *pay*·to

chestnut *castanha* ① *portuguesa*
kaas·*ta*·nyaa porr·too·*ge*·zaa

chewing gum *goma* ① *de mascar*
go·maa de maas·*kaarr*

chicken *galinha* ① gaa·*lee*·nyaa

chicken pox *catapora* ① kaa·taa·*po*·raa

chickpea *grão* ⓜ *de bico*
growng de *bee*·ko

child *criança* ⓜ&① kree·*ang*·saa

child seat *cadeira* ① *de criança*
kaa·*day*·raa de kree·*ang*·saa

childminding *cuidado* ⓜ *da criança*
kooy·*daa*·do da kree·*ang*·saa

children *crianças* ⓜ&① pl kree·*ang*·saas

chilli *pimenta* ① pee·*meng*·taa

chilli sauce *molho* ⓜ *de pimenta* mo·lyo
de pee·*meng*·taa

chiropractor *quiroprático/*
quiroprática ⓜ/① kee·ro·*praa*·tee·ko/
kee·ro·*praa*·tee·kaa

chocolate *chocolate* ⓜ sho·ko·*laa*·te

choose *escolher* es·ko·*lyerr*

Christian *Cristão/Cristã* ⓜ/① krees·*towng*/
krees·*tayng*

Christian name *nome* ⓜ *Cristão • pri-*
meiro nome ⓜ no·me krees·*towng* •
pree·*may*·ro no·me

Christmas Day *Dia* ⓜ *de Natal*
dee·aa de naa·*tow*

Christmas Eve *Noite* ① *de Natal* noy·te
de na·*tow*

church *igreja* ① ee·*gre*·zhaa

cider *cidra* ① *see*·draa

cigar *charuto* ⓜ shaa·*roo*·to

cigarette *cigarro* ⓜ see·*gaa*·ho

cigarette lighter *isqueiro* ⓜ ees·*kay*·ro

cinema *cinema* ⓜ see·ne·maa

circus *circo* ⓜ *seerr*·ko

citizenship *cidadania* ① see·daa·da·*nee*·aa

city *cidade* ① see·*daa*·de

city centre *centro* ⓜ *da cidade*
seng·tro daa see·*daa*·de

civil rights *direitos* ⓜ pl *civis*
dee·*ray*·tos see·*vees*

class (category) *classe* ① *klaa*·se

class system *sistema* ① *de classes*
sees·*te*·maa de *klaa*·ses

classical *clássico/clássica* ⓜ/①
klaa·see·ko/*klaa*·see·kaa

clean *limpo/limpa* ⓜ/①
leeng·po/*leeng*·paa

client *cliente* ⓜ&① klee·*eng*·te

cliff *penhasco* ⓜ pe·*nyaas*·ko

climb *subir* soo·*beerr*

cloakroom *guarda* ⓜ *volumes* gwaarr·daa
vo·*loo*·mes

clock *relógio* ⓜ he·*lo*·zhyo

close *fechar* fe·*shaarr*

closed *fechado/fechada* ⓜ/① fe·*shaa*·do/
fe·*shaa*·daa

clothesline *corda* ① *de roupa*
korr·daa de ho·paa

clothing *roupas* ① pl ho·paas

clothing store *loja* ① *de roupas*
lo·zhaa de ho·paas

cloud *nuvem* ① noo·*veng*

cloudy *nublado/nublada* ⓜ/①
noo·*blaa*·do/noo·*blaa*·daa

clutch (car) *embreagem* ①
eng·bre·*aa*·zheng

coach *técnico/técnica* ⓜ/①
te·kee·nee·ko/*te*·kee·nee·kaa

coast *costa* ① *kos*·taa

coat *casaco* ⓜ kaa·*zaa*·ko

cocaine *cocaína* ① ko·kaa·*ee*·naa

cockroach *barata* ① baa·*raa*·taa

cocoa *cacau* ⓜ ka·*kow*

coconut *côco* ⓜ *ko*·ko

coffee *café* ⓜ kaa·*fe*

coins *moedas* ① pl mo·*e*·daas

cold *frio* ⓜ *free*·o

cold *frio/fria* ⓜ/① *free*·o/*free*·aa

colleague *colega* ⓜ&① ko·*le*·gaa

collect call *ligação* ① *à cobrar*
lee·gaa·*sowng* aa ko·*braarr*

college *academia* ① •
universidade ① aa·kaa·de·*mee*·aa •
oo·nee·verr·see·*daa*·de

colour *cor* ① korr

comb *pente* ⓜ peng·te

come *vir* veerr

comedy *comédia* ① ko·me·dyaa

comfortable *confortável* kong·forr·taa·vel

communications (profession)
comunicação ① ko·moo·nee·kaa·sowng

communion *comunhão* ①
ko·moo·nyowng

communist *comunista* ⓜ&①
ko·moo·nees·taa

companion *companheiro/companheira*
ⓜ/① kong·pa·nyay·ro/kong·pa·nyay·raa

company *companhia* ⓜ&①
kong·paa·nhaa

compass *compasso* ⓜ kong·paa·so

complain *reclamar* he·klaa·marr

computer *computador* ⓜ
kong·poo·taa·dorr

computer game *jogo* ⓜ *de computador*
zho·go de kong·poo·taa·dorr

concert *show* ⓜ show

conditioner *condicionador* ⓜ
kong·dee·syo·naa·dorr

condom *camisinha* ① kaa·mee·zee·nyaa

confession *confissão* ① kong·fee·sowng

conjunctivitis *conjuntivite* ①
kong·zhoong·tee·vee·te

confirm (a booking) *confirmar*
kong·feerr·maarr

connection (phone) *conecção* ①
ko·ne·kee·sowng

conservative *conservador/conservadora*
ⓜ/① kong·serr·vaa·dorr/
kong·serr·vaa·do·raa

constipation *constipação* ①
kongs·tee·paa·sowng

consulate *consulado* ⓜ kong·soo·laa·do

contact lens solution *colírio* ⓜ *para lentes
de contato* ko·lee·ryo paa·raa leng·tes de
kong·taa·to

contact lenses *lentes* ⓜ pl *de contato*
leng·tes de kong·taa·to

contraceptives *anticoncepcional* ⓜ
ang·tee·kong·sep·syo·now

contract *contrato* ⓜ kong·traa·to

convenience store *mercearia* ①
merr·se·aa·ree·aa

convent *convento* ⓜ kong·veng·to

---

cook *cozinheiro/cozinheira* ⓜ/①
ko·zee·nyay·ro/ko·zee·nyay·raa

cook *cozinhar* ko·zee·nyaarr

cookie *biscoito* ⓜ bees·koy·to

corn *milho* ⓜ mee·lyo

cornflakes *cereal* ⓜ se·re·ow

corner *esquina* ① es·kee·naa

corrupt *corrupto/corrupta* ⓜ/①
koo·hoo·pee·to/koo·hoo·pee·taa

cost *custar* koos·taarr

cotton *algodão* ⓜ ow·go·downg

cotton balls *bolas* ① pl *de algodão*
bo·laas de ow·go·downg

cotton buds *cotonete* ⓜ ko·to·ne·te

cough *tossir* to·seerr

cough medicine *xarope* ⓜ shaa·ro·pe

count *contar* kong·taarr

counter (at bar) *balcão* ⓜ bow·kowng

country *país* ⓜ paa·ees

countryside *interior* ⓜ eeng·te·ree·orr

coupon *cupom* ⓜ koo·pong

courgette *abobrinha* ① aa·bo·bree·nyaa

court (legal) *corte* ① korr·te

court (tennis) *quadra* ① kwaa·draa

couscous *cuscuz* ⓜ *marroquino*
koos·koos maa·ho·kee·no

cover charge *couvert* ⓜ *artístico*
koo·verr aarr·tees·tee·ko

cow *vaca* ① vaa·kaa

cracker *biscoito* ⓜ *d'água*
bees·koy·to daa·gwaa

crafts *artesanato* ⓜ aarr·te·zaa·naa·to

crash *batida* ① baa·tee·daa

crazy *louco/louca* ⓜ/① lo·ko/lo·kaa

cream *creme* ⓜ kre·me

creche *creche* ① kre·she

credit card *cartão* ⓜ *de crédito*
kaarr·towng de kre·dee·to

cricket (sport) *cricket* ⓜ kree·ke·tee

crop *tosa* ① to·zaa

cross (religious) *cruz* ① kroos

crowded *lotado/lotada* ⓜ/① lo·taa·do/
lo·taa·daa

cucumber *pepino* ⓜ pe·pee·no

cup *xícara* ① shee·kaa·raa

cupboard *armário* ⓜ aarr·maa·ryo

currency exchange *câmbio* ⓜ *de valores*
kang·byo de vaa·lo·res

current (electricity) *corrente* ① ko·heng·te

current affairs *assuntos* ⓜ pl *atuais*
aa-*soong*-tos aa-*too*-*ais*
curry *caril* ⓜ kaa-*reel*
customs *alfândega* ⓕ aal-*fang*-de-gaa
cut *cortar* korr-*taarr*
cutlery *talheres* ⓜ pl taa-*lye*-res
CV *CV* ⓜ se-*ve*
cycle *andar de bicicleta* ang-*daarr* de
bee-see-*kle*-taa
cycling *ciclismo* ⓜ see-*klees*-mo
cyclist *ciclista* ⓜ&ⓕ see-*klees*-taa
cystitis *cistite* ⓕ sees-*tee*-te

D

dad *pai* ⓜ pai
dance *dançar* dang-*saarr*
dancing *dança* ⓕ *dang*-saa
dangerous *perigoso/perigosa* ⓜ/ⓕ
pe-ree-*go*-zo/pe-ree-*go*-zaa
dark *escuro/escura* ⓜ/ⓕ es-*koo*-ro/
es-*koo*-raa
date (appointment) *hora* ⓕ *marcada*
aw-raa maarr-*kaa*-daa
date (day) *data* ⓕ *daa*-taa
date (fruit) *tâmara* ⓕ *ta*-maa-raa
date (a person) *namorar* naa-mo-*raarr*
date of birth *data* ⓕ *de nascimento*
daa-taa de naa-see-*meng*-to
daughter *filha* ⓕ *fee*-lyaa
dawn *madrugada* ⓕ maa-droo-*gaa*-daa
day *dia* ⓜ *dee*-aa
day after tomorrow *depois* ⓜ *de amanhã*
de-*poys* de aa-maa-*nyang*
day before yesterday *antes* ⓜ *de ontem*
ang-tes de *ong*-teng
dead *morto/morta* ⓜ/ⓕ
morr-to/*morr*-taa
deaf *surdo/surda* ⓜ/ⓕ
soor-do/*soor*-daa
deal (cards) *dar* daarr
December *dezembro* de-*zeng*-bro
decide *decidir* de-see-*deer*
deep *profundo/profunda* ⓜ/ⓕ
pro-*foong*-do/pro-*foong*-daa
deforestation *desflorestamento* ⓜ
des-flo-res-taa-*meng*-to
degrees (temperature) *graus* ⓜ pl grows
delay *atraso* ⓜ aa-*traa*-zo

delicatessen *delicatessen* ⓕ
de-lee-kaa-te-*seng*
deliver *entregar* eng-tre-*gaarr*
democracy *democracia* ⓕ
de-mo-kraa-*see*-aa
demonstration *demonstração* ⓕ
de-mongs-traa-*sowng*
Denmark *Dinamarca* ⓕ
dee-naa-*maarr*-kaa
dental floss *fio* ⓜ *dental*
fee-o deng-*tow*
dentist *dentista* ⓜ&ⓕ deng-*tees*-taa
deodorant *desodorante* ⓜ
de-zo-do-*rang*-te
depart (leave) *partir* paarr-*teerr*
department store *loja* ⓕ *de
departamentos* lo-zhaa de
de-paarr-taa-*meng*-tos
departure *partida* ⓕ paarr-*tee*-daa
departure gate *portão* ⓜ *de partida*
porr-*towng* de paarr-*tee*-daa
deposit *depósito* ⓜ de-po-zee-to
derailleur *câmbio* ⓜ *de marcha* kang-*byo*
de maarr-shaa
descendent *descendente* ⓜ&ⓕ
de-seng-*deng*-te
desert *deserto* de-*zerr*-to
design *design* ⓜ design
dessert *sobremesa* ⓕ so-bre-*me*-zaa
destination *destino* ⓜ des-*tee*-no
details *detalhes* ⓜ pl de-*taa*-lyes
diabetes *diabetes* ⓕ dee-aa-*be*-tes
dial tone *linha* ⓕ *lee*-nyaa
diaper *fralda* ⓕ *frow*-daa
diaphragm *diafragma* ⓜ
dee-aa-*fraa*-gee-maa
diarrhoea *diarréia* ⓕ dee-aa-*hay*-aa
diary *diário* ⓜ dee-*aa*-ryo
dice *dados* ⓜ pl *daa*-dos
dictionary *dicionário* ⓕ dee-syo-*naa*-ryo
die *morrer* mo-*herr*
diet *dieta* ⓕ dee-*e*-taa
different *diferente* dee-fe-*reng*-te
difficult *difícil* dee-*fee*-seel
dining car *vagão* ⓜ *restaurante*
vaa-*gowng* hes-tow-*rang*-te
dinner *jantar* ⓜ zhang-*taarr*
direct *direto/direta* ⓜ/ⓕ
dee-*re*-to/dee-*re*-taa

direct-dial *ligação* ① *direta*
lee-gaa-sowng dee-re-taa

director *diretor/diretora* ⓜ/①
dee-re-torr/dee-re-to-raa

dirty *sujo/suja* ⓜ/① soo-zho/soo-zhaa

disabled *deficiente* de-fee-see-eng-te

disco *disco* ⓜ dees-ko

discount *desconto* ⓜ des-kong-to

discrimination *discriminação* ①
dees-kree-mee-naa-sowng

disease *doença* ① do-eng-saa

disk (computer) *disk* ⓜ deesk

diving *mergulho* ⓜ merr-goo-lyo

diving equipment *equipamento* ⓜ
de mergulho e-kee-paa-meng-to de
merr-goo-lyo

dizzy *tonto/tonta* ⓜ/①
tong-to/tong-taa

do *fazer* faa-zerr

doctor *médico/médica* ⓜ/① me-dee-ko/
me-dee-kaa

documentary *documentário* ⓜ
do-koo-meng-taa-ryo

dog *cachorro* ⓜ/① kaa-sho-ho

dole *seguro social* ⓜ se-goo-ro so-see-ow

doll *boneco/boneca* ⓜ/①
bo-ne-ko/bo-ne-kaa

dollar *dólar* ⓜ do-laarr

door *porta* ① porr-taa

dope (drugs) *bagulho* ⓜ baa-goo-lyo

double *duplo/dupla* ⓜ/①
doo-plo/doo-plaa

double bed *cama* ① *de casal*
ka-maa de kaa-zow

double room *quarto* ⓜ *de casa* kwaarr-to
de kaa-zow

down *baixo* bai-sho

downhill *para baixo* paa-raa bai-sho

dozen *dúzia* ① doo-zyaa

drama *drama* ⓜ dra-maa

dream *sonho* ⓜ so-nyo

dress *vestido* ⓜ ves-tee-do

dried *seco/seca* ⓜ/① se-ko/se-kaa

dried fruit *frutas* ① pl *secas*
froo-taas se-kaas

drink *bebida* ① be-bee-daa

drive *dirigir* dee-ree-zheerr

drivers licence *carteira* ① *de motorista*
kaar-tay-raa de mo-to-rees-taa

drug *droga* ① dro-gaa

drug addiction *vício* ⓜ *de drogas*
vee-syo de dro-gaas

drug dealer *traficante* ⓜ&①
traa-fee-kang-te

drug user *usuário/usuária* ⓜ/① *de
drogas* oo-zoo-aa-ryo/oo-zoo-aa-ryaa
de dro-gaas

drugs *drogas* ① pl dro-gaas

drum *bateria* ① baa-te-ree-aa

drunk *bêbado/bêbada* ⓜ/①
be-baa-do/be-baa-daa

dry *secar* se-kaarr

dry *seco/seca* ⓜ/① se-ko/se-kaa

duck *pato/pata* ⓜ/① paa-to/paa-taa

dummy (for baby) *chupeta* ① shoo-pe-taa

DVD *DVD* ⓜ de-ve-de

E

each *cada* kaa-daa

ear *orelha* ① o-re-lyaa

early *cedo* se-do

earn *ganhar* ga-nyaarr

earplugs *tampões* ⓜ *de ouvido*
tang-powng de o-vee-do

earrings *brincos* ⓜ pl breeng-kos

Earth *Terra* ① te-haa

earthquake *terremoto* ⓜ te-he-mo-to

east *leste* ⓜ les-te

Easter *Páscoa* ① paas-kwaa

easy *fácil* faa-seel

eat *comer* ko-merr

economy class *classe* ① *econômica*
klaa-se e-ko-no-mee-kaa

ecstacy (drug) *êxtase* ⓜ es-taa-ze

eczema *eczema* ⓜ e-kee-ze-maa

editor *editor/editora* ⓜ/①
e-dee-torr/e-dee-to-raa

education *educação* ① e-doo-ka-sowng

egg *ovo* ⓜ o-vo

eggplant *beringela* ⓜ be-reeng-zhe-laa

election *eleição* ① e-lay-sowng

electrical store *loja* ① *de aparelhos
elétricos* lo-zhaa de aa-paa-re-lyos
e-le-tree-kos

electricity *eletricidade* ①
e-le-tree-see-daa-de

elevator *elevador* ⓜ e-le-vaa-dorr

embarrassed *envergonhado/*
envergonhada ⓜ/ⓕ
en-verr-go-*nyaa*-do/en-verr-go-*nyaa*-daa
embassy *embaixada* ⓕ eng-bai-*shaa*-daa
emergency *emergência* ⓕ
e-merr-*zheng*-syaa
emotional *sensível* seng-*see*-vel
employee *empregado/*
empregada ⓜ/ⓕ eng-pre-*gaa*-do/
eng-pre-*gaa*-daa
employer *empregador/*
empregadora ⓜ/ⓕ eng-pre-gaa-dorr/
eng-pre-gaa-do-raa
empty *vazio/vazia* ⓜ/ⓕ
vaa-*zee*-o/vaa-*zee*-aa
end *fim* ⓜ feeng
endangered species *espécies* ⓕ pl
ameaçadas de extinção es-*pe*-syes
aa-me-aa-*saa*-daas de es-*teeng*-sowng
engagement *noivado* ⓜ noy-*vaa*-do
engine *motor* ⓜ mo-torr
engineer *engenheiro/engenheira* ⓜ/ⓕ
eng-zhe-*nyay*-ro/eng-zhe-*nyay*-raa
engineering *engenharia* ⓕ
eng-zhe-nya-*ree*-aa
England *Inglaterra* ⓕ eeng-glaa-*te*-haa
English (language) *Inglês* ⓜ eeng-*gles*
enjoy (oneself) *aproveitar* aa-pro-vay-*taarr*
enough *suficiente* soo-fee-see-*eng*-te
enter *entrar* eng-*traarr*
entertainment guide *guia* ⓜ
de entretenimento gee-aa de
eng-tre-te-nee-*meng*-to
envelope *envelope* ⓜ eng-ve-*lo*-pe
environment *meio* ⓜ *ambiente*
may-o ang-bee-*eng*-te
epilepsy *epilepsia* ⓕ e-pee-le-pee-*see*-aa
equal opportunity
oportunidades ⓕ pl *iguais*
o-porr-too-nee-*daa*-des ee-*gwaa*-ees
equality *igualdade* ⓕ ee-gwow-*daa*-de
equipment *equipamento* ⓜ
e-kee-paa-*meng*-to
escalator *escada rolante* ⓕ
es-*kaa*-daa ho-*lang*-te
euro *euro* ⓜ e-oo-ro
Europe *Europa* ⓕ e-oo-ro-paa
euthanasia *eutanásia* ⓕ e-oo-taa-*naa*-zyaa
evening *noite* ⓕ *noy*-te

everything *tudo* too-do
example *exemplo* ⓜ e-*zeng*-plo
excellent *excelente* e-se-*leng*-te
exchange *troca* ⓕ *tro*-kaa
exchange *trocar* tro-*kaarr*
exchange rate *taxa* ⓕ *de câmbio* taa-shaa
de *kang*-byo
excluded *excluído/excluída* ⓜ/ⓕ
es-kloo-*ee*-do/es-kloo-*ee*-daa
exhaust (car) *exaustor* ⓜ e-zows-*torr*
exhibition *exposição* ⓕ es-po-zee-*sowng*
exit *saída* ⓕ saa-*ee*-daa
expensive *caro/cara* ⓜ/ⓕ
kaa-ro/*kaa*-raa
experience *experiência* ⓕ
es-pe-ree-*eng*-syaa
exploitation *exploração* ⓕ
es-plo-raa-*sowng*
express *expresso/expressa* ⓜ/ⓕ es-*pre*-so/
es-*pre*-saa
express mail *serviço* ⓜ *postal rápido*
serr-*vee*-so pos-*tow* haa-pee-do
extension (visa) *extensão* ⓕ
es-*teng*-sowng
eye *olho* ⓜ o-lyo
eye drops *colírio* ⓜ ko-*lee*-ryo

F

fabric *tecido* ⓜ te-*see*-do
face *rosto* ⓜ *hos*-to
face cloth *toalha* ⓕ *de rosto*
to-*aa*-lyaa de *hos*-to
factory *fábrica* ⓕ *faa*-bree-kaa
factory worker *operário/operária* ⓜ/ⓕ
o-pe-*raa*-ryo/o-pe-*raa*-ryaa
fall (autumn) *outono* ⓜ o-*to*-no
fall (down) *queda* ⓕ *ke*-daa
family *família* ⓕ faa-*mee*-lyaa
family name *sobrenome* ⓜ so-bre-*no*-me
famous *famoso/famosa* ⓜ/ⓕ
faa-*mo*-zo/faa-*mo*-zaa
fan (machine) *ventilador* ⓜ
veng-tee-laa-*dorr*
fan (sport, etc) *fã* ⓜ&ⓕ fang
fanbelt *correia* ⓕ ko-*hay*-aa
far *longe* long-zhe
farm *fazenda* ⓕ faa-*zeng*-daa

farmer *fazendeiro/fazendeira* ⓜ/ⓕ
faa·zeng·*day*·ro/faa·zeng·*day*·raa
fast *rápido/rápida* ⓜ/ⓕ
haa·pee·do/*haa*·pee·daa
fat *gordo/gorda* ⓜ/ⓕ *gorr*·do/*gorr*·daa
father *pai* ⓜ pai
father-in-law *sogro* ⓜ *so*·gro
faucet *torneira* ⓕ torr·*nay*·raa
fault (someone's) *culpa* ⓕ *kool*·paa
faulty *defeituoso/defeituosa* ⓜ/ⓕ
de·fay·too·*o*·zo/de·fay·too·*o*·zaa
February *fevereiro* fe·ve·*ray*·ro
feed *alimentar* aa·lee·meng·*taarr*
feel *sentir* seng·*teerr*
feelings *sentimentos* ⓜ pl
seng·tee·*meng*·tos
fence *cerca* ⓕ *serr*·kaa
fencing (sport) *esgrima* ⓕ es·*gree*·maa
festival *festival* ⓜ fes·tee·*vow*
fever *febre* ⓕ *fe*·bre
few *alguns/algumas* ⓜ/ⓕ
ow·*goons*/ow·goo·maas
fiance *noivo* ⓜ *noy*·vo
fiancee *noiva* ⓕ *noy*·vaa
fiction *ficção* ⓕ feek·*sowng*
fig *figo* ⓜ *fee*·go
fight *luta* ⓕ *loo*·ta
fill *encher* eng·*sherr*
fillet *filé* ⓜ fee·*le*
film (cinema) *filme* ⓜ *feel*·me
film (photography) *filme* ⓜ *fotográfico*
feel·me fo·to·*graa*·fee·ko
film speed *velocidade* ⓕ *do filme*
ve·lo·see·*daa*·de do *feel*·me
filtered *filtrado/filtrada* ⓜ/ⓕ
feel·*traa*·do/feel·*traa*·daa
find *encontrar* eng·kong·*traarr*
fine (payment) *multa* ⓕ *mool*·taa
fine *bom/boa* ⓜ/ⓕ bong/*bo*·aa
finger *dedo* ⓜ *de*·do
finish *término* ⓜ *terr*·mee·no
finish *terminar* terr·mee·*naarr*
fire *fogo* ⓜ *fo*·go
firewood *lenha* ⓕ *le*·nyaa
first *primeiro/primeira* ⓜ/ⓕ
pree·*may*·ro/pree·*may*·raa
first class *primeira classe* ⓕ
pree·*may*·raa *klaa*·se

first-aid kit *kit* ⓜ *de primeiros socorros*
kee·tee de pree·*may*·ros so·*ko*·hos
fish *peixe* ⓜ *pay*·she
fish monger *peixeiro/peixeira* ⓜ/ⓕ
pay·*shay*·ro/pay·*shay*·raa
fish shop *peixaria* ⓕ pay·sha·*ree*·aa
fishing *pesca* ⓕ *pes*·kaa
flag *bandeira* ⓕ bang·*day*·raa
flannel *flanela* ⓕ fla·*ne*·laa
flashlight *flash* ⓜ *luminoso*
flash loo·mee·*no*·zo
flat (apartment) *apartamento* ⓜ
aa·paarr·taa·*meng*·to
flat *plano/plana* ⓜ/ⓕ *pla*·no/*pla*·naa
flea *pulga* ⓕ *pool*·gaa
flight *vôo* ⓜ *vo*·o
flood *enchente* ⓕ eng·*sheng*·te
floor *chão* ⓜ showng
floor (storey) *andar* ⓜ ang·*daarr*
florist (person) *florista* ⓜ&ⓕ flo·*rees*·taa
florist (shop) *floricultura* ⓕ
flo·ree·kool·*too*·raa
flour *farinha* ⓕ faa·*ree*·nyaa
flower *flor* ⓕ florr
fly *voar* vo·*aarr*
foggy *nebuloso/nebulosa* ⓜ/ⓕ
ne·boo·*lo*·zo/ne·boo·*lo*·zaa
follow *seguir* se·*geerr*
food *comida* ⓕ ko·*mee*·daa
foot *pé* ⓜ pe
football (soccer) *futebol* ⓜ foo·te·*bol*
footpath *calçada* ⓕ kow·*saa*·daa
foreign *estrangeiro/estrangeira* ⓜ/ⓕ
es·trang·*zhay*·ro/es·trang·*zhay*·raa
forest *floresta* ⓕ flo·*res*·taa
forever *para sempre* *paa*·raa *seng*·pre
forget *esquecer* es·ke·*serr*
forgive *perdoar* perr·do·*aarr*
fork *garfo* ⓜ *gaarr*·fo
fortnight *quinzena* ⓕ keeng·*ze*·naa
fortune teller *vidente* ⓜ&ⓕ vee·*deng*·te
foul *falta* ⓕ *fow*·taa
foyer *saguão* ⓜ saag·*wowng*
fragile *frágil* *fraa*·zheel
free (gratis) *gratuito/gratuita* ⓜ/ⓕ
graa·*too*·ee·to/graa·*too*·ee·taa
free (not bound) *livre* *lee*·vre
freeze *congelar* kong·zhe·*laarr*
Friday *sexta-feira* ⓕ *ses*·taa·*fay*·raa

fried *frito/frita* ⓜ/ⓕ *free*·to/*free*·taa
friend *amigo/amiga* ⓜ/ⓕ
aa·*mee*·go/aa·*mee*·gaa
frost *geada* ⓕ zhe·*aa*·daa
fruit *fruta* ⓕ *froo*·taa
fruit picking *colheita* ⓕ *de frutas*
ko·*lyay*·taa de *froo*·taas
fry *fritar* free·*taarr*
frying pan *frigideira* ⓕ free·zhee·*day*·raa
full *cheio/cheia* ⓜ/ⓕ *shay*·o/*shay*·aa
full-time *tempo* ⓜ *integral*
teng·po eeng·te·*graal*
fun *divertido/divertida* ⓜ/ⓕ
dee·verr·*tee*·do/dee·verr·*tee*·daa
funeral *enterro* ⓜ eng·*te*·ho
funny *engraçado/engraçada* ⓜ/ⓕ
eng·graa·*saa*·do/eng·graa·*saa*·daa
furniture *móveis* ⓜ pl *mo*·vays
future *futuro* ⓜ foo·*too*·ro

G

game (sport) *jogo* ⓜ *zho*·go
garage *oficina* ⓕ o·fee·*see*·naa
garbage *lixo* ⓜ *lee*·sho
garden *jardim* ⓜ zhaarr·*deeng*
gardener *jardineiro/jardineira* ⓜ/ⓕ
zhaarr·dee·*nay*·ro/zhaarr·dee·*nay*·raa
gardening *jardinagem* ⓕ
zhaarr·dee·*naa*·zheng
garlic *alho* ⓜ *aa*·lyo
gas (for cooking) *gás* ⓜ gas
gas (petrol) *gasolina* ⓕ gaa·zo·*lee*·na
gas cartridge *cartucho* ⓜ *de gás*
kaarr·*too*·sho de gaas
gastroenteritis *gastrenterite* ⓕ
gaas·treng·te·*ree*·te
gate (airport, etc) *portão* ⓜ porr·*towng*
gauze *gaze* ⓕ *gaa*·ze
gay *gay* gay
Germany *Alemanha* ⓕ aa·le·*ma*·nyaa
get *pegar* pe·*gaarr*
gift *presente* ⓜ pre·*zeng*·te
gig *apresentação* ⓕ
aa·pre·seng·*taa*·sowng
gin *gin* ⓜ zheen
girl *menina* ⓕ me·*nee*·naa
girlfriend *namorada* ⓕ naa·mo·*raa*·daa
give *dar* daarr

glandular fever *febre* ⓕ *glandular*
fe·bre glang·doo·*laar*
glass *vidro* ⓜ *vee*·dro
glasses (spectacles) *óculos* ⓜ pl o·koo·los
gloves *luvas* ⓕ pl *loo*·vaas
glue *cola* ⓕ *ko*·laa
go *ir* eerr
go out with *sair* saa·*eerr*
goal *objetivo* ⓜ o·bee·zhe·*tee*·vo
goal (sport) *gol* ⓜ gol
goalkeeper *goleiro/goleira* ⓜ/ⓕ
go·*lay*·ro/go·*lay*·raa
goat *bode* ⓜ *bo*·de
god (general) *deus* ⓜ de·oos
goggles (skiing) *óculos* ⓜ pl *de ski*
o·koo·los de es·*kee*
goggles (swimming) *óculos* ⓜ pl *de*
natação o·koo·los de naa·taa·*sowng*
gold *ouro* ⓜ o·ro
golf ball *bola* ⓕ *de golfe*
bo·laa de *gol*·fee
golf course *campo* ⓕ *de golfe*
kang·po de *gol*·fee
good *bom/boa* ⓜ/ⓕ bong/*bo*·aa
Goodbye. *Tchau/Adeus* ⓜ
tee·*show*/ aa·de·oos
government *governo* ⓜ go·*verr*·no
gram *grama* ⓕ *graa*·maa
grandchild *neto/neta* ⓜ/ⓕ
ne·to/*ne*·taa
grandfather *avô* ⓜ aa·*vo*
grandmother *avó* ⓕ aa·*vaw*
grapefruit *pomelo* ⓜ po·*me*·lo
grapes *uvas* ⓕ pl oo·vaas
grass *grama* ⓕ *gra*·maa
grave *túmulo* ⓜ *too*·moo·lo
gray *cinza* seeng·zaa
great *ótimo/ótima* ⓜ/ⓕ
o·tee·mo/o·tee·maa
green *verde* verr·de
greengrocer *verdureiro/verdureira* ⓜ/ⓕ
verr·doo·ray·ro/verr·doo·ray·raa
grey *cinza* seeng·zaa
grocery *mantimentos* ⓜ pl
mang·tee·meng·tos
groundnut *amendoim* ⓜ
aa·meng·do·*eeng*
grow *crescer* kres·*serr*

g-string *biquíni* ⓜ *fio dental*
bee·*kee*·nee fyo deng·*tow*

guess *adivinhar* aa·dee·vee·*nyaarr*

guide (audio) *guia* ⓜ *auditivo*
gee·aa ow·dee·*tee*·vo

guide (person) *guia* ⓜ&ⓕ *gee*·aa

guide dog *cão-guia* ⓜ kowng·*gee*·aa

guidebook *guia* ⓜ *gee*·aa

guided tour *excursão* ⓕ *guiada*
es·koor·*sowng* gee·*aa*·daa

guilty *culpado/culpada* ⓜ/ⓕ kool·*paa*·do/
kool·*paa*·daa

guitar *violão* ⓜ vee·o·*lowng*

gum *gengiva* ⓕ zheng·*zhee*·vaa

gun *arma* ⓕ *aarr*·maa

gym *ginástica* ⓕ zhee·*naas*·tee·kaa

gymnastics *ginástica* ⓕ *olímpica*
gee·*naas*·tee·kaa o·*leeng*·pee·kaa

gynaecologist *ginecologista* ⓜ&ⓕ
zhee·ne·ko·lo·*zhees*·taa

H

hair *cabelo* ⓜ kaa·*be*·lo

hairbrush *escova* ⓕ es·*ko*·vaa

hairdresser *cabeleireiro/cabeleireira* ⓜ/ⓕ
kaa·be·lay·*ray*·ro/kaa·be·lay·*ray*·raa

halal *halal* aa·*low*

half *metade* ⓕ me·*taa*·de

hallucination *alucinação* ⓕ
aa·loo·see·naa·*sowng*

ham *presunto* ⓜ pre·*zoong*·to

hammer *martelo* ⓜ maarr·*te*·lo

hammock *rede* ⓕ *he*·de

hand *mão* ⓕ mowng

handbag *bolsa* ⓕ *de mão*
bol·saa de mowng

handball *handebol* ⓜ heng·*de*·bol

handicrafts *artesanato* ⓜ
aarr·te·zaa·*naa*·to

handlebars *corrimão* ⓜ ko·hee·*mowng*

handmade *feito à mão*
fay·to aa mowng

handsome *bonito/bonita* ⓜ/ⓕ
bo·*nee*·to/bo·*nee*·taa

happy *feliz* fe·*lees*

harassment *molestamento* ⓜ
mo·les·taa·*meng*·to

harbour *baía* ⓕ baa·*ee*·aa

hard *duro/dura* ⓜ/ⓕ *doo*·ro/*doo*·raa

hard-boiled *cozido/cozida* ⓜ/ⓕ
ko·*zee*·do/ko·*zee*·daa

hardware store *loja* ⓕ *de ferramentas*
lo·zhaa de fe·haa·*meng*·taas

hat *chapéu* ⓜ shaa·*pe*·oo

have *ter* terr

have a cold *estar resfriado* ⓜ/ⓕ
es·*taarr* hes·free·*aa*·do

have fun *divertir-se* dee·verr·*teerr*·se

hay fever *febre* ⓕ *do feno*
fe·bre do *fe*·no

hazelnut *avelã* ⓕ aa·ve·*lang*

he *ele* *e*·le

head *cabeça* ⓕ kaa·*be*·saa

headache *dor* ⓕ *de cabeça*
dorr de kaa·*be*·saa

headlight *faróis* ⓜ pl faa·*roys*

health *saúde* ⓕ sa·oo·de

hear *escutar* es·koo·*taarr*

hearing aid *aparelho* ⓜ *de surdez*
aa·paa·*re*·lyo de soorr·*des*

heart *coração* ⓜ ko·ra·*sowng*

heart attack *ataque* ⓜ *de coração*
aa·*taa*·ke de ko·ra·*sowng*

heart condition *problema* ⓜ *de coração*
pro·*ble*·maa de ko·ra·*sowng*

heating *aquecimento* ⓜ
aa·ke·see·*meng*·to

heater *estufa* ⓕ es·*too*·faa

heavy *pesado/pesada* ⓜ/ⓕ
pe·*zaa*·do/pe·*zaa*·daa

Hello. *Olá.* o·*laa*

Hello. (answering telephone) *Alô.* aa·*lo*

helmet *capacete* ⓜ kaa·paa·*se*·te

help *ajuda* ⓕ aa·*zhoo*·daa

help *ajudar* aa·zhoo·*daarr*

Help! *Socorro!* so·ko·ho

hepatitis *hepatite* ⓕ e·paa·*tee*·te

her *dela* *de*·laa

herbalist *botânico/botânica* ⓜ/ⓕ
bo·*ta*·nee·ko/bo·*ta*·nee·kaa

herb *erva* ⓕ *err*·vaa

here *aqui* aa·*kee*

heroin *heroína* ⓕ e·ro·*ee*·naa

herring *arenque* ⓜ aa·*reng*·ke

high *alto/alta* ⓜ/ⓕ *ow*·to/*ow*·taa

high school *segundo grau* ⓜ
se·*goong*·do grow

highchair *cadeira* ① *para refeição*
kaa-*day*-raa paa-raa he-fay-*sowng*
hike *caminhar* kaa-mee-*nyaarr*
hiking *caminhada* ① kaa-mee-*nyaa*-daa
hiking boots *botas* ① *para caminhadas*
bo-taas paa-raa kaa-mee-*nyaa*-daas
hiking route *rota* ① *de caminhada*
ho-taa de kaa-mee-*nyaa*-daa
hill *morro* ⑩ *mo*-ho
Hindu *Hindu* eeng-*doo*
hire *alugar* aa-loo-*gaarr*
his *dele* de-le
historical *histórico/histórica* ⑩/①
ees-to-ree-ko/ees-to-ree-kaa
history *história* ① ees-to-rya
hitchhike *pegar carona*
pe-*gaarr* kaa-ro-naa
HIV ⑩ *HIV* aa-*gaa* ee ve
hockey *hockey* ⑩ *ho*-kay
holiday *férias* ① pl fe-ryaas
home *casa* ① *kaa*-zaa
homeless *desabrigado/*
desabrigada ⑩/① de-zaa-bree-*gaa*-do/
de-zaa-bree-*gaa*-daa
homemaker *dona* ① *de casa*
do-naa de *kaa*-zaa
homeopathy *homeopatia* ①
o-me-o-paa-*tee*-aa
homosexual *homosexual* o-mo-sek-soo-ow
honey *mel* ⑩ mel
honeymoon *lua* ① *de mel*
loo-aa de mel
horoscope *horóscopo* ⑩ o-ros-ko-po
horse *cavalo* ⑩ kaa-*vaa*-lo
horse riding *cavalgada* ①
kaa-vaal-*gaa*-daa
hospital *hospital* ⑩ os-pee-*tow*
hospitality *hospitalidade* ①
os-pee-taa-lee-*daa*-de
hot *quente* keng-te
hot water *água* ① *quente*
aa-gwaa keng-te
hotel *hotel* ⑩ o-*tel*
house *casa* ① *kaa*-zaa
housework *trabalho* ⑩ *de casa*
traa-*baa*-lyo de *kaa*-zaa
how *como* ko-mo
how much *quanto* kwang-to
hug *abraçar* aa-braa-*saarr*

huge *enorme* e-*norr*-me
human resources *recursos* ⑩ pl *humanos*
he-*koor*-sos oo-ma-nos
human rights *direitos* ⑩ pl *humanos*
dee-*ray*-tos oo-ma-nos
humanities *humanidades* ① pl
oo-ma-nee-*daa*-des
hundred *cem* seng
hungry *faminto/faminta* ⑩/①
faa-meeng-to/faa-*meeng*-taa
hunting *caça* ① *kaa*-saa
hurt *machucar* maa-shoo-*kaarr*
husband *marido* ⑩ maa-*ree*-do

I

I *eu* e-oo
ice *gelo* ⑩ *zhe*-lo
ice axe *quebrador* ⑩ *de gelo*
ke-braa-*dorr* de *zhe*-lo
ice cream *sorvete* ⑩ sorr-*ve*-te
ice-cream parlour *sorveteriu* ①
sorr-ve-le-*ree*-aa
ice hockey *hockey* ⑩ *de gelo*
ho-kay de *zhe*-lo
identification *identificação* ①
ee-deng-tee-fee-kaa-*sowng*
identification card *carteira* ① *de*
identidade kaar-*tay*-raa de
ee-deng-tee-*daa*-de
idiot *idiota* ⑩&① ee-dee-o-taa
if *se* se
ill *mal* mal
immigration *imigração* ①
ee-mee-graa-*sowng*
important *importante* eeng-porr-*tang*-te
in a hurry *com pressa* kong *pre*-saa
in front of *na frente de* naa freng-te de
included *incluso/inclusa* ⑩/①
eeng-*kloo*-zo/eeng-*kloo*-zaa
income tax *imposto* ⑩ *de renda*
eeng-*pos*-to de *heng*-daa
India *Índia* ① *eeng*-dyaa
indicator *indicador* ⑩ eeng-dee-kaa-*dorr*
indigestion *indigestão* ①
eeng-dee-zhes-*towng*
indoors *adentro* aa-*deng*-tro
industry *indústria* ① eeng-*doos*-tryaa
infection *infecção* ① eeng-fek-*sowng*

inflammation *inflamação* ①
eeng·fla·maa·*sowng*

influenza *gripe* ① *gree*·pe

ingredient *ingrediente* ⓜ
eeng·gre·dee·*eng*·te

inject *injetar* eeng·zhe·*taarr*

injection *injeção* ① eeng·zhe·*sowng*

injury *ferimento* ① fe·ree·*meng*·to

inner tube *câmara* ① *de ar*
ka·ma·raa de aarr

innocent *inocente* ee·no·*seng*·te

inside *dentro* deng·tro

instructor *instrutor/instrutora* ⓜ/①
eengs·troo·*torr*/eengs·troo·*to*·raa

insurance *seguro* ⓜ se·*goo*·ro

interesting *interessante* eeng·te·re·*sang*·te

intermission *intervalo* ① eeng·terr·*vaa*·lo

international *internacional*
eeng·terr·naa·syo·*now*

Internet *Internet* ① eeng·terr·*ne*·tee

Internet cafe *Internet café* ⓜ
eeng·terr·*ne*·tee kaa·*fe*

interpreter *intérprete* ⓜ&①
eeng·*terr*·pre·te

interview *entrevista* ① eeng·tre·*vees*·taa

invite *convidar* kong·vee·*daar*

Ireland *Irlanda* ① eerr·*lang*·daa

iron (clothes) *ferro* ⓜ *de passa roupas*
fe·ho de paa·*saarr* ho·paas

island *ilha* ① ee·lyaa

Israel *Israel* ⓜ ees·haa·*el*

it *coisa* ① *koy*·zaa

IT (information technology)
IT ⓜ ai·*tee*

itch *coceira* ① ko·*say*·raa

itemised *listado/listada* ⓜ/①
lees·*taa*·do/lees·*taa*·daa

itinerary *itinerário* ① ee·tee·ne·*raa*·ryo

IUD *DIU* ⓜ *dee*·oo

J

jacket *jaqueta* ① zhaa·*ke*·taa

jail *prisão* ① pree·*zowng*

jam *geléia* ① zhe·*le*·yaa

January *janeiro* ⓜ zhaa·*nay*·ro

Japan *Japão* ⓜ zhaa·*powng*

jar *vidro* ⓜ *vee*·dro

jaw *mandíbula* ① mang·*dee*·boo·laa

jealous *ciumento/ciumenta* ⓜ/①
see·oo·*meng*·to/see·oo·*meng*·taa

jeans *jeans* ⓜ zheens

jeep *jeep* ⓜ *zhee*·pe

jewellery *joalheria* ① zho·a·lye·*ree*·aa

Jewish *Judeu/Judia* ⓜ/①
zhoo·*de*·oo/zhoo·*dee*·aa

job *emprego* ⓜ eng·*pre*·go

jogging *corrida* ① ko·*hee*·daa

joke *piada* ① pee·*aa*·daa

journalist *jornalista* ⓜ&①
zhorr·naa·*lees*·taa

journey *viagem* ① vee·*aa*·zheng

judge *juiz/juiza* ⓜ/①
zhoo·*ees*/zhoo·*ee*·zaa

juice *suco* ⓜ *soo*·ko

July *julho* ⓜ zhoo·lyo

jump *pular* poo·*laarr*

jumper (sweater) *suéter* ① soo·e·terr

jumper leads *recarregador* ⓜ *de bateria*
he·kaa·he·gaa·*dorr* de baa·te·*ree*·aa

June *junho* ⓜ zhoo·nyoo

K

ketchup *ketchup* ⓜ ke·tee·*shoo*·pee

key *chave* ① *shaa*·ve

keyboard *teclado* ① te·*klaa*·do

kick (a ball) *chutar* shoo·*taarr*

kidney *rin* ⓜ pl heeng

kill *matar* maa·*taarr*

kilogram *kilograma* ⓜ kee·lo·*gra*·maa

kilometre *kilômetro* ① kee·*lo*·me·tro

kind *bom/boa* ⓜ/① bong/*bo*·aa

kindergarten *jardim* ⓜ *de infância*
zhaarr·*deeng* de eeng·*fang*·syaa

king *rei* ⓜ hay

kiss *beijo* ⓜ *bay*·zho

kiss *beijar* bay·*zhaarr*

kitchen *cozinha* ① ko·*zee*·nyaa

kiwifruit *kiwi* ⓜ kee·*wee*

knee *joelho* ⓜ zho·e·lyo

knife *faca* ① *faa*·kaa

know *saber* saa·*berr*

kosher *kosher* ko·sherr

L

labourer *trabalhador/trabalhadora* ⓜ/ⓕ *de obra* traa-baa-lyaa-*dorr*/ traa-baa-lyaa-*do*-raa de o-braa
lace *renda* ⓕ *heng*-daa
lake *lago* ⓜ *laa*-go
lamb *ovelha* ⓕ o-*ve*-lyaa
land *terra* ⓕ *te*-haa
landlady *proprietária* ⓕ pro-pree-e-*taa*-ryaa
landlord *proprietário* ⓜ pro-pree-e-*taa*-ryo
language *língua* ⓕ *leeng*-gwaa
laptop *laptop* ⓜ le-pee-to-*pee*
large *grande* grang-de
last *último/última* ⓜ/ⓕ *ool*-tee-mo/*ool*-tee-maa
last (week) *passada (semana)* ⓕ paa-*saa*-daa (se-*ma*-naa)
late *atrasado/atrasada* ⓜ/ⓕ aa-traa-*zaa*-do/aa-traa-*zaa*-daa
laugh *rir* heerr
laundrette *lavanderia* ⓕ laa-vang-de-*ree*-aa
laundry (room) *área* ⓕ *de serviço* *aa*-re-aa de serr-*vee*-so
law *lei* ⓕ lay
lawyer *advogado/advogada* ⓜ/ⓕ aa-dee-vo-*gaa*-do/aa-dee-vo-*gaa*-daa
laxative *laxante* ⓜ la-*shang*-te
lazy *preguiçoso/preguiçosa* ⓜ/ⓕ pre-gee-*so*-zo/pre-gee-*so*-zaa
leader *líder* ⓜ&ⓕ *lee*-derr
leaf *folha* ⓕ fo-lyaa
learn *aprender* aa-preng-*derr*
leather *couro* ⓜ ko-ro
lecturer *professor/professora* ⓜ/ⓕ pro-fe-*sorr*/pro-fe-*so*-raa
ledge *parapeito* ⓜ paa-raa-*pay*-to
leek *alho* ⓜ *porró* aa-lyo po-ho
left (direction) *(à) esquerda* ⓕ (aa) es-*kerr*-daa
left luggage *achados e perdidos* ⓜ pl aa-*shaa*-dos e perr-*dee*-dos
left-wing *esquerdista* es-kerr-*dees*-taa
leg *perna* ⓕ *perr*-naa
legal *legal* le-*gow*
legislation *legislação* ⓕ le-zhees-la-*sowng*
legume *legumes* ⓜ pl le-*goo*-mes

lemon *limão* ⓜ lee-*mowng*
lemonade *limonada* ⓕ lee-mo-*naa*-daa
lens *lentes* ⓕ pl *leng*-tes
lentil *lentilha* ⓕ leng-*tee*-lyaa
lesbian *lésbica* ⓕ *les*-bee-kaa
less *menos* ⓜ *me*-nos
letter (mail) *carta* ⓕ *kaarr*-taa
lettuce *alface* ⓕ ow-*faa*-se
liar *mentiroso/mentirosa* ⓜ/ⓕ meng-tee-*ro*-zo/meng-tee-*ro*-zaa
library *biblioteca* ⓕ bee-blee-o-*te*-kaa
lice *piolho* ⓜ pee-o-lyo
licence *licença* ⓕ lee-*seng*-saa
license plate number *número* ⓜ *da placa* noo-me-ro daa *plaa*-kaa
lie (not stand) *deitar* day-*taarr*
life *vida* ⓕ *vee*-daa
life jacket *colete salva-vidas* ⓜ ko-*le*-te sow-vaa-*vee*-daas
lift (elevator) *elevador* ⓜ e-le-vaa-*dorr*
light *luz* ⓕ looz
light (not heavy) *leve* le-ve
light bulb *lâmpada* ⓕ lang-paa-daa
light meter *fotômetro* ⓜ fo-*to*-me-tro
lighter (cigarette) *isqueiro* ⓜ ees-*kay*-ro
like *gostar* gos-*taarr*
lime *limão* ⓜ lee-*mowng*
lip balm *bálsamo* ⓜ *para lábios* bow-sa-mo paa-raa *laa*-byos
lips *lábios* ⓜ pl *laa*-byos
lipstick *batom* ⓜ ba-*tong*
liquor store *loja* ⓕ *de bebidas* *lo*-zhaa de be-*bee*-daas
listen *escutar* es-koo-*taarr*
little (not much) *pouco/pouca* ⓜ/ⓕ po-ko/*po*-kaa
little (small) *pequeno/pequena* ⓜ/ⓕ pe-*ke*-no/pe-*ke*-naa
live (somewhere) *morar* mo-*raarr*
liver *fígado* ⓜ fee-gaa-do
lizard *lagarto* ⓜ laa-*gaarr*-to
local *local* lo-*kow*
lock *tranca* ⓕ *trang*-kaa
lock *trancar* trang-*kaarr*
locked *trancado/trancada* ⓜ/ⓕ trang-*kaa*-do/trang-*kaa*-daa
lollies *balas* ⓕ pl *baa*-laas
long *longo/longa* ⓜ/ⓕ *long*-go/*long*-gaa

look *ver* verr
look after *cuidar* kooy-*daarr*
look for *procurar* pro-koo-*raarr*
lookout *mirante* ⓜ mee-*rang*-te
loose *solto/solta* ⓜ/ⓕ *sol*-to/*sol*-taa
loose change *trocado* ⓜ tro-*kaa*-do
lose *perder* perr-*derr*
lost *perdido/perdida* ⓜ/ⓕ
  perr-*dee*-do/perr-*dee*-daa
lost property office *escritório* ⓜ *de
  achados e perdidos* es-kree-*to*-ryo de
  aa-*shaa*-dos e perr-*dee*-dos
(a) lot *muito/muita* ⓜ/ⓕ
  mweeng-to/*mweeng*-taa
loud *alto/alta* ⓜ/ⓕ *ow*-to/*ow*-taa
love *amor* ⓜ aa-*morr*
love *amar* aa-*maarr*
lover *amante* ⓜ&ⓕ aa-*mang*-te
low *baixo/baixa* ⓜ/ⓕ *bai*-sho/*bai*-shaa
lubricant *lubrificante* ⓜ
  loo-bree-fee-*kang*-te
luck *sorte* ⓕ *sorr*-te
lucky *sortudo/sortuda* ⓜ/ⓕ
  sorr-*too*-do/sorr-*too*-daa
luggage *bagagem* ⓕ baa-*gaa*-zheng
luggage locker *guarda* ⓜ *volumes*
  gwaar-daa vo-*loo*-mes
luggage tag *etiqueta* ⓕ *de bagagem*
  e-tee-*ke*-taa de baa-*gaa*-zheng
lump *nódulo* ⓜ *no*-doo-lo
lunch *almoço* ⓜ ow-*mo*-so
lung *pulmão* ⓜ pool-*mowng*
luxury *luxo* ⓜ *loo*-sho

M

machine *máquina* ⓕ *maa*-kee-naa
magazine *revista* ⓕ he-*vees*-taa
mail *correspondência* ⓕ
  ko-hes-pong-*deng*-syaa
mailbox *caixa* ⓕ *de correio*
  kai-shaa de ko-*hay*-o
main *principal* preeng-see-*pow*
main road *rua* ⓕ *principal*
  hoo-aa preeng-see-*pow*
make *fazer* faa-*zerr*
make-up *maquiagem* ⓕ
  maa-kee-*aa*-zheng

mammogram *mamograma* ⓜ
  maa-mo-*gra*-maa
man *homem* ⓜ o-meng
manager *gerente* zhe-*reng*-te
mandarin *tangerina* ⓕ tang-zhe-*ree*-naa
mango *manga* ⓕ *mang*-gaa
manual worker *trabalhador/trabalha-
  dora* ⓜ/ⓕ *manual* traa-baa-lyaa-*dorr*/
  traa-baa-lyaa-*do*-raa maa-noo-*ow*
many *vários/várias* ⓜ/ⓕ
  vaa-ryos/*vaa*-ryaas
map *mapa* ⓕ *maa*-paa
March *março* *maar*-so
margarine *margarina* ⓕ
  maarr-gaa-*ree*-naa
marijuana *maconha* ⓕ maa-*ko*-nyaa
marital status *estado* ⓜ *civil*
  es-*taa*-do see-*veel*
market *mercado* ⓜ merr-*kaa*-do
marmalade *marmelada* ⓕ
  maarr-me-*laa*-daa
marriage *casamento* ⓜ kaa-zaa-*meng*-to
marry *casar* kaa-*zaarr*
martial arts *artes* ⓕ pl *marciais*
  aarr-tes maar-see-*ais*
mass (Catholic) *missa* ⓕ *mee*-saa
massage *massagem* ⓕ maa-*saa*-zheng
masseur *massagista* ⓜ&ⓕ
  maa-saa-*zhees*-taa
mat *capacho* ⓜ kaa-*paa*-sho
match (sport) *partida* ⓕ paarr-*tee*-daa
matches *fósforos* ⓜ pl *fos*-fo-ros
mattress *colchão* ⓜ kol-*showng*
May *maio* *maa*-yo
maybe *talvez* tow-*ves*
mayonnaise *maionese* ⓕ maa-yo-*ne*-ze
mayor *prefeito/prefeita* ⓜ/ⓕ
  pre-*fay*-to/pre-*fay*-taa
measles *sarampo* ⓜ saa-*rang*-po
meat *carne* ⓕ *kaar*-ne
mechanic *mecânico/mecânica* ⓜ/ⓕ
  me-*ka*-nee-ko/me-*ka*-nee-kaa
media *mídia* ⓕ *mee*-dyaa
medicine *medicina* ⓕ me-dee-*see*-naa
meditation *meditação* ⓕ
  me-dee-taa-*sowng*
meet *encontrar* eng-kong-*traarr*
melon *melão* ⓜ me-*lowng*
member *membro* ⓜ&ⓕ *meng*-bro

menstruation *menstruação* ①
mengs·troo·aa·sowng

menu *cardápio* ⑩ kaarr·*daa*·pyo

message *mensagem* ① meng·*sa*·zheng

metal *metal* ⑩ me·*tow*

metre *metro* ⑩ me·tro

microwave *microondas* ⑩
mee·kro·ong·daas

midnight *meia-noite* ① *may*·aa·*noy*·te

migraine *enxaqueca* ① en·shaa·*ke*·kaa

military *militar* mee·lee·*taarr*

military service *serviço* ⑩ *militar*
serr·*vee*·so mee·lee·*taarr*

milk *leite* ⑩ *lay*·te

millimetre *milímetro* ⑩ mee·*lee*·me·tro

million *milhão* ⑩ mee·*lowng*

mince *carne* ① *moída*
kaarr·ne mo·*ee*·daa

mineral water *água* ① *mineral*
aa·gwaa mee·ne·*row*

minute *minuto* ⑩ mee·*noo*·to

mirror *espelho* ⑩ es·pe·*lyo*

miscarriage *aborto* ⑩ *espontâneo*
aa·*borr*·to es·pong·*ta*·ne·o

miss (feel absence of) *sentir falta*
seng·*teerr* *fow*·taa

mistake *erro* ⑩ *e*·ho

mix *misturar* mees·too·*raar*

mobile phone *celular* ⑩ se·loo·*laarr*

modem *modem* ⑩ *mo*·deng

moisturiser *hidratante* ⑩ ee·draa·*tang*·te

monastery *monastério* ⑩ mo·naas·*te*·ryo

Monday *segunda-feira* ①
se·*goong*·daa·*fay*·raa

money *dinheiro* ⑩ dee·*nyay*·ro

monk *monge* ⑩ *mong*·zhe

month *mês* ⑩ mes

monument *monumento* ⑩
mo·noo·*meng*·to

moon *lua* ① *loo*·aa

more *mais* mais

morning *manhã* ① ma·*nyang*

morning sickness *enjôo* ⑩ en·*zho*·o

mosque *mosteiro* ⑩ mos·*tay*·ro

mosquito *mosquito* ⑩ mos·*kee*·to

mosquito coil *repelente* ⑩ *em aspiral*
he·pe·*leng*·te eng aas·pee·*row*

mosquito net *mosquiteiro* ⑩
mos·kee·*tay*·ro

mother *mamãe* ① ma·*mayng*

mother-in-law *sogra* ① *so*·graa

motorbike *motocicleta* ①
mo·to·see·*kle*·taa

motorboat *barco* ⑩ *à motor*
baar·ko aa mo·*torr*

motorway (tollway) *auto estrada* ①
ow·to es·*traa*·daa

mountain *montanha* ① mong·*ta*·nyaa

mountain bike *mountain bike* ⑩
maa·oong·tayng *bai*·kee

mountain path *trilha* ① *tree*·lyaa

mountain range *cordilheira* ①
korr·dee·*lyay*·raa

mountaineering *montanhismo* ⑩
mong·ta·*nyees*·mo

mouse *camundongo* ⑩
ka·moong·*dong*·go

mouth *boca* ① bo·*kaa*

movie *cinema* ⑩ see·*ne*·maa

mud *lama* ① *la*·maa

muesli *muesli* ⑩ *moos*·lee

mum *mãe* ① mayng

mumps *caxumba* ① kaa·*shoong*·baa

murder *assassinato* ⑩ aa·saa·see·*naa*·to

murder *assassinar* aa·saa·see·*naarr*

muscle *músculo* ⑩ *moos*·koo·lo

museum *museu* ⑩ mo·*se*·oo

mushroom *cogumelo* ⑩ ko·goo·*me*·lo

music *música* ① *moo*·zee·kaa

music shop *loja* ① *de música*
lo·zhaa de *moo*·zee·kaa

musician *músico/música* ⑩/①
moo·zee·ko/*moo*·zee·kaa

Muslim *Muçulmano/Muçulmana* ⑩/①
moo·sool·*ma*·no/moo·sool·*ma*·naa

mussel *mexilhão* ⑩ me·shee·*lyowng*

mustard *mustarda* ① moos·*taar*·daa

mute *mudo/muda* ⑩/①
moo·do/moo·daa

my *meu/minha* ⑩/① *me*·oo/*mee*·nyaa

N

nail clippers *cortador* ⑩ *de unhas*
korr·taa·*dorr* de oo·*nyaas*

name *nome* ⑩ *no*·me

napkin *guardanapo* ⑩ gwaar·daa·*naa*·po

nappy *fralda* ① *frow*·daa

nappy rash *irritação* ① *à fralda*
ee·hee·ta·*sowng* aa *frow*·daa

national park *parque* ⑩ *nacional*
paar·ke naa·syo·*now*

nationality *nacionalidade* ①
naa·syo·naa·lee·*daa*·de

nature *natureza* ① naa·too·re·*zaa*

naturopathy *naturopatia* ①
naa·too·ro·paa·*tee*·a

nausea *náusea* ① *now*·se·aa

near *perto/perta* ⑩/① *perr*·to/*perr*·taa

nearby *por perto/perta* ⑩/①
porr *perr*·to/*perr*·taa

nearest *mais perto/perta* ⑩/①
mais *perr*·to/*perr*·taa

necessary *necessário/necessária* ⑩/①
ne·se·*sa*·ryo/ne·se·*sa*·ryaa

necklace *colar* ⑩ ko·*laarr*

nectarine *pessego* ⑩ *pe*·se·go

need *precisar* pre·see·*zaarr*

needle (sewing) *agulha* ① aa·*goo*·lyaa

needle (syringe) *agulha* ① aa·*goo*·lyaa

negative *negativo/negativa* ⑩/①
ne·gaa·*tee*·vo/ne·gaa·*tee*·vaa

neither *nenhum deles* ne·*yoom* de·les

net *rede* ① *he*·de

Netherlands *Países* ⑩ pl *Baixos*
paa·*ee*·zes *bai*·shos

never *nunca* *noong*·kaa

new *novo/nova* ⑩/① *no*·vo/*no*·vaa

New Year's Day *Dia* ⑩ *de Ano Novo* dee·aa
de *a*·no *no*·vo

New Year's Eve *Véspera* ① *de Ano Novo*
ves·pe·raa de *a*·no *no*·vo

New Zealand *Nova Zelândia* ①
no·vaa ze·*lang*·dyaa

news *novidades* • *notícias* ① pl
no·vee·*daa*·des • no·*tee*·syaas

news stand *jornaleiro* ⑩ zhorr·na·*lay*·ro

newsagency *jornaleiro* ⑩ zhorr·naa·*lay*·ro

newspaper *jornal* ⑩ zhorr·*now*

next *próximo/próxima* ⑩/①
pro·see·mo/*pro*·see·maa

next to *ao lado de* ow *laa*·do de

nice *bacana* baa·*ka*·naa

nickname *apelido* ⑩ aa·pe·*lee*·do

night *noite* ① *noy*·te

no *não* *nowng*

noisy *barulhento/barulhenta* ⑩/①
baa·roo·*lyeng*·to/baa·roo·*lyeng*·taa

none *nenhum* ne·*yoom*

non-smoking *não-fumante*
nowng·foo·*mang*·te

noodles *macarrão* ⑩ *chinês*
maa·kaa·*howng* shee·*nes*

noon *meio-dia* ⑩ *may*·o dee·aa

Norway *Noruega* ① no·roo·e·gaa

north *norte* ⑩ *norr*·te

nose *nariz* ① naa·*rees*

not *não* nowng

notebook *caderno* ⑩ kaa·*derr*·no

nothing *nada* *naa*·daa

November *novembro* no·*veng*·bro

now *agora* aa·*go*·raa

nuclear energy *energia* ① *nuclear*
e·nerr·*zhee*·aa noo·kle·*aarr*

nuclear testing *teste* ⑩ *nuclear*
tes·te noo·kle·*aarr*

nuclear waste *resíduo* ⑩ *nuclear*
he·*zee*·doo·o noo·kle·*aarr*

number *número* ⑩ *noo*·me·ro

numberplate *número* ⑩ *da placa*
noo·me·ro daa *plaa*·kaa

nun *freira* ① *fray*·raa

nurse *enfermeira* ① eng·ferr·*may*·raa

nut *noz* ① noz

O

oats *aveia* ① aa·*ve*·aa

ocean *oceano* ⑩ o·se·*a*·no

October *outubro* o·*too*·bro

off (food) *estragado/estragada* ⑩/①
es·traa·*gaa*·do/es·traa·*gaa*·daa

office *escritório* ⑩ es·kree·to·ryo

office worker *escriturário/escriturária*
⑩/① es·kree·too·raa·ryo/
es·kree·too·raa·ryaa

often *frequentemente*
fre·kweng·te·*meng*·te

oil *óleo* ⑩ *o*·lyo

old *velho/velha* ⑩/① *ve*·lyo/*ve*·lyaa

olive *azeitona* ① aa·zay·to·naa

olive oil *azeite* ⑩ aa·*zay*·te

Olympic Games *Jogos Olímpidos* ⑩ pl
zho·gos o·*leeng*·pee·kos

on *sobre* *so*·bre

once *uma vez* oo·maa vez
one-way (ticket) *ida* ① ee·daa
onion *cebola* ① se·bo·laa
only *somente* so·meng·te
open *aberto/aberta* ⓜ/① aa·berr·to/aa·berr·taa
open *abrir* aa·breer
opening hours *horário* ⓜ *de funcionamento* o·raa·ryo de foon·syo·naa·meng·to
opera *ópera* ① o·pe·raa
opera house *casa* ① *de ópera* kaa·zaa de o·pe·raa
operation *operação* ① o·pe·raa·sowng
operator *operador/operadora* ⓜ/① o·pe·raa·dorr/o·pe·raa·do·raa
opinion *opinião* ① o·pee·nee·owng
opposite *oposto/oposta* ⓜ/① o·pos·to/o·pos·taa
optometrist *optometrista* ⓜ & ① o·pee·to·me·trees·taa
or *ou* o
orange (fruit) *laranja* ① laa·rang·zhaa
orange (colour) *laranja* laa·rang·zhaa
orange juice *suco* ⓜ *de laranja* soo·ko de laa·rang·zhaa
orchestra *orquestra* ① orr·kes·traa
order (command) *pedido* ⓜ pe·dee·do
order *pedir* pe·deerr
ordinary *ordinário/ordinária* ⓜ/① orr·dee·naa·ryo/orr·dee·naa·ryaa
orgasm *orgasmo* ⓜ orr·gaas·mo
original *original* o·ree·zhee·now
other *outro/outra* ⓜ/① o·tro/o·traa
our *nosso/nossa* ⓜ/① no·so/no·saa
outside *fora* fo·raa
ovarian cyst *cisto* ⓜ *no ovário* sees·to no o·vaa·ryo
ovary *ovário* ⓜ o·vaa·ryo
oven *forno* ⓜ forr·no
overcoat *sobretudo* ⓜ so·bre·too·do
overdose *overdose* ① o·verr·do·ze
owe *dever* de·verr
owner *dono/dona* ⓜ/① do·no/do·naa
oxygen *oxigênio* ⓜ ok·see·zhe·nyo
oyster *ostra* ① os·traa
ozone layer *camada* ① *de ozônio* kaa·maa·daa de o·zo·nyo

P

pacemaker *marca* ⓜ *passo* mar·kaa pa·so
pacifier *chupeta* ① shoo·pe·taa
package *embrulho* ⓜ eng·broo·lyo
packet *pacote* ⓜ pa·ko·te
padlock *cadeado* ⓜ kaa·de·aa·do
page *página* ① paa·zhee·naa
pain *dor* ① dorr
painful *doloroso/dolorosa* ⓜ/① do·lo·ro·zo/do·lo·ro·zaa
painkiller *analgésico* ⓜ aa·now·ge·zee·ko
painter *pintor/pintora* ⓜ/① peeng·torr/peeng·to·raa
painting *pintura* ① peeng·too·raa
pair (couple) *par* ⓜ paarr
Pakistan *Paquistão* ⓜ paa·kees·towng
palace *palácio* ⓜ paa·laa·syo
pan *panela* ① paa·ne·laa
pants (trousers) *calças* ① pl kow·saas
panty liner *absorvente* ⓜ *higiênico* aab·sorr·veng·te ee·zhee·e·nee·ko
pantyhose *meia* ① *calça* may·aa kow·saa
pap smear *exame* ⓜ *papa nicolau* e·za·me paa·paa nee·ko·low
paper *papel* ⓜ paa·pel
paperwork *papelada* ① paa·pe·laa·daa
paraplegic *paraplégico/paraplégica* ⓜ/① paa·raa·ple·zhee·ko/paa·raa·ple·zhee·kaa
parcel *encomenda* ① eng·ko·meng·daa
parents *pais* ⓜ pl paa·ees
park *parque* ⓜ paarr·ke
park (vehicle) *estacionar* es·taa·syo·naarr
parliament *parlamento* ⓜ paarr·laa·meng·to
part (component) *parte* ① paarr·te
part-time *meio expediente* may·o es·pe·dee·eng·te
party (social gathering) *festa* ① fes·taa
party (politics) *partido* ⓜ paarr·tee·do
pass *passar* paa·saarr
passenger *passageiro/passageira* ⓜ/① paa·saa·zhay·ro/paa·saa·zhay·raa
passionfruit *maracujá* ⓜ maa·raa·koo·zhaa
passport *passaporte* ⓜ paa·saa·porr·te

passport number *número* ⓜ *do passaporte* noo·me·ro do paa·saa·*porr*·te

past *passado* ⓜ paa·*saa*·do

pasta *massas* ⓕ pl *maa*·saas

pastry *massa* ⓕ *maa*·saa

path *caminho* ⓜ kaa·*mee*·nyo

pay *pagar* paa·*gaarr*

payment *pagamento* ⓜ paa·gaa·*meng*·to

pea *ervilha* ⓕ err·*vee*·lyaa

peace *paz* ⓕ pas

peach *pêssego* ⓜ *pe*·se·go

peak (mountain) *pico* ⓜ *pee*·ko

peanut *amendoim* ⓜ aa·meng·do·*eeng*

pear *pêra* ⓕ *pe*·raa

pedal *pedal* ⓜ pe·*dow*

pedestrian *pedestre* pe·*des*·tre

pen (ballpoint) *caneta* ⓕ ka·*ne*·taa

pencil *lápis* ⓜ *laa*·pees

penis *pênis* ⓜ *pe*·nees

penknife *canivete* ⓜ kaa·nee·*ve*·te

pensioner *pensionista* ⓜ&ⓕ peng·syo·*nees*·taa

people *pessoas* ⓕ pl pe·*so*·aas

pepper *pimenta* ⓕ pee·*meng*·taa

pepper (bell) *pimentão* ⓜ pee·meng·*towng*

per *por* porr

per cent *porcentagem* ⓕ porr·seng·*taa*·zheng

perfect *perfeito/perfeita* ⓜ/ⓕ perr·*fay*·to/perr·*fay*·taa

performance *performance* ⓕ perr·*forr*·mang·se

perfume *perfume* ⓜ perr·*foo*·me

period pain *cólica* ⓕ *menstrual* ko·lee·kaa mens·troo·*ow*

permission *permissão* ⓕ perr·mee·*sowng*

permit *permissão* ⓕ per·mee·*sowng*

person *pessoa* ⓕ pe·*so*·aa

petition *petição* ⓕ pe·tee·*sowng*

petrol *petróleo* ⓜ pe·*tro*·lyo

pharmacy *farmácia* ⓕ faar·*maa*·syaa

phone book *lista* ⓕ *telefônica* *lees*·taa te·le·fo·nee·kaa

phone box *telefone* ⓜ *público* te·le·*fo*·ne poo·blee·ko

phonecard *cartão* ⓜ *telefônico* kaarr·*towng* te·le·fo·nee·ko

photograph *fotografia* ⓕ fo·to·graa·*fee*·aa

photographer *fotógrafo/fotógrafa* ⓜ/ⓕ fo·*to*·graa·fo/fo·to·gra·faa

photography *fotografia* ⓕ fo·to·graa·*fee*·aa

phrasebook *livro* ⓜ *de frases* *lee*·vro de *fraa*·zes

pickaxe *picareta* ⓕ pee·kaa·*re*·taa

pickles *pikles* ⓜ pl pee·kles

picnic *piquenique* ⓜ pee·ke·*nee*·ke

pie *torta* ⓕ *torr*·taa

piece *pedaço* ⓜ pe·*da*·so

pig *porco/porca* ⓜ/ⓕ *porr*·ko/porr·kaa

pill *pílula* ⓕ *pee*·loo·laa

Pill (the) *pílula* ⓕ *pee*·loo·laa

pillow *travesseiro* ⓜ traa·ve·*say*·ro

pillowcase *fronha* ⓕ *fro*·nyaa

pineapple *abacaxi* ⓜ aa·baa·kaa·*shee*

pink *rosa* ho·za

pistachio *pistáchio* ⓜ pees·*taa*·shyo

place *lugar* ⓜ loo·*gaarr*

place of birth *local* ⓜ *de nascimento* lo·*kow* de naas·see·*meng*·to

planet *planeta* ⓕ pla·*ne*·taa

plant *planta* ⓕ *plang*·taa

plastic *plástico/plástica* ⓜ/ⓕ *plas*·tee·ko/plas·*tee*·kaa

plate *prato* ⓜ *praa*·to

plateau *planalto* ⓜ pla·*now*·to

platform *plataforma* ⓕ plaa·taa·*forr*·maa

play (theatre) *peça* ⓕ pe·saa

play *jogar* zho·*gaarr*

play (guitar) *tocar* to·*kaarr*

plug (bath) *tampa* ⓕ *tang*·paa

plug (electricity) *tomada* ⓕ to·*maa*·daa

plum *ameixa* ⓕ aa·*may*·shaa

poached *poché* po·*she*

pocket *bolso* ⓜ *bol*·so

pocket knife *canivete* ⓜ kaa·nee·*ve*·te

poetry *poesia* ⓕ po·e·*zee*·aa

point *ponto* ⓜ *pong*·to

point *apontar* aa·pong·*taarr*

poisonous *venenoso/venenosa* ⓜ/ⓕ ve·ne·no·zo/ve·ne·no·zaa

police *polícia* ⓕ po·*lee*·syaa

police station *delegacia* ⓕ *de polícia* de·le·gaa·*see*·aa de po·*lee*·sya

policy *regras* ⓕ pl he·*graas*

politician *político/política* ⓜ/ⓕ po·*lee*·tee·ko/po·*lee*·tee·kaa

politics *política* ① po-*lee*-tee-kaa
pollen *pólen* ⓜ po-leng
pollution *poluição* ① po-loo-ee-*sowng*
pool (game) *sinuca* ① see-*noo*-kaa
pool (swimming) *piscina* ① pee-*see*-naa
poor *pobre* po-bre
popular *popular* po-poo-*laarr*
pork *porco/porca* ⓜ/① porr-ko/porr-kaa
pork sausage *linguiça* ① *de porco*
leen-*gwee*-saa de porr-ko
port (sea) *porto* ⓜ porr-to
Portugal *Portugal* ① porr-too-*gow*
positive *positivo/positiva* ⓜ/①
po-zee-*tee*-vo/po-zee-*tee*-vaa
possible *possível* po-*see*-vel
post office *correio* ⓜ ko-*hay*-o
postage *postagem* ① pos-*taa*-zheng
postcard *cartão* ⓜ *postal*
kaarr-*towng* pos-*tow*
postcode *código* ⓜ *postal*
ko-dee-go pos-*tow*
poster *cartaz* ⓜ kaarr-*taz*
pot (ceramics) *louça* ① pl *de barro*
lo-saa de baa-ho
pot (dope) *bagulho* ⓜ baa-*goo*-lyo
potato *batata* ① baa-*taa*-taa
pottery *cerâmica* ① se-*ra*-mee-kaa
pound (money) *libra* ① lee-braa
poverty *pobreza* ① po-*bre*-zaa
powder *pó* ⓜ po
power *poder* ⓜ po-*derr*
prawn *camarão* ⓜ kaa-maa-*rowng*
prayer *reza* ① he-zaa
prefer *preferir* pre-fe-*reerr*
pregnancy test kit *teste* ⓜ *de gravidez*
tes-te de graa-vee-*dez*
pregnant *grávida* ① graa-vee-daa
premenstrual tension *tensão* ①
pré-menstrual teng-*sowng*
pre-mengs-troo-ow
prepare *preparar* pre-paa-*raarr*
present (gift) *presente* ⓜ pre-*zeng*-te
present (time) *presente* ⓜ pre-*zeng*-te
president *presidente* ⓜ&①
pre-zee-*deng*-te
pressure *pressão* ① pre-*sowng*
pretty *bonito/bonita* ⓜ/①
bo-*nee*-to/bo-*nee*-taa
price *preço* ⓜ pre-so

priest *padre* ⓜ paa-dre
prime minister *primeiro ministro* ⓜ •
primeira ministra ① pree-*may*-ro
mee-*nees*-tro • pree-*may*-raa
mee-*nees*-traa
prison *prisão* ① pree-*zowng*
prisoner *prisioneiro/prisioneira* ⓜ/①
pree-zyo-*nay*-ro/pree-zyo-*nay*-raa
private *privado/privada* ⓜ/①
pree-*vaa*-do/pree-*vaa*-daa
produce *produzir* pro-doo-*zeerr*
profit *lucro* ⓜ loo-kro
program *programa* ① pro-*gra*-maa
projector *projetor* ⓜ pro-zhe-*torr*
promise *prometer* pro-me-*terr*
protect *proteger* pro-te-*zherr*
protected *protegido/protegida* ①
pro-te-zhee-do/pro-te-zhee-daa
protest *protesto* ⓜ pro-*tes*-to
protest *protestar* pro-tes-*taarr*
provisions *provisões* ① pl pro-vee-*zoyngs*
prune *ameixa* ① *seca*
aa-*may*-shaa se-kaa
pub *bar* ⓜ baarr
public gardens *jardins* ⓜ pl *públicos*
zhaarr-*deengs* poo-blee-kos
public relations *relações* ① pl *públicas*
he-la-*soyngs* poo-blee-kaas
public telephone *telefone* ⓜ *público*
te-le-*fo*-ne poo-blee-ko
public toilet *banheiro* ⓜ *público*
ba-*nyay*-ro poo-blee-ko
publishing *editoração* ①
e-dee-to-raa-*sowng*
pull *puxar* poo-*shaarr*
pump *bomba* ① bong-baa
pumpkin *abóbora* ① aa-bo-bo-raa
puncture *furo* ⓜ foo-ro
pure *puro/pura* ⓜ/① poo-ro/poo-raa
purple *roxo/roxa* ⓜ/① ho-sho/ho-shaa
push *empurrar* eng-poo-*haarr*
put *colocar* ko-lo-*kaarr*

Q

quadriplegic *quadraplégico/*
quadraplégica ⓜ/①
kwaa-draa-*ple*-zhee-ko/
kwaa-draa-*ple*-zhee-kaa

qualifications *qualificações* ① pl
kwaa·lee·fee·kaa·*soyngs*

quality *qualidade* ① kwaa·lee·*daa*·de

quarantine *quarentena* ①
kwaa·reng·*te*·naa

quarter *quarto* ⑩ *kwaarr*·to

queen *rainha* ① haa·ee·nyaa

question *pergunta* ① • *questão* ①
perr·*goong*·taa • kes·*towng*

queue *fila* ① *fee*·laa

quick *rápido/rápida* ⑩/①
haa·pee·do/*haa*·pee·daa

quiet *quieto/quieta* ⑩/①
kee·*e*·to/kee·*e*·taa

quit *desistir* de·zees·*teerr*

R

rabbit *coelho* ⑩ ko·*e*·lyo

race (sport) *corrida* ① ko·*hee*·daa

racetrack *pista* ① *de corrida*
pees·taa de ko·*hee*·daa

racing bike *bicicleta* ① *de corrida*
bee·see·*kle*·taa de ko·*hee*·daa

racism *racismo* ⑩ haa·*sees*·mo

racquet *raquete* ① haa·*ke*·te

radiator *radiador* ⑩ haa·dee·aa·*dorr*

radish *rabanete* ⑩ haa·baa·*ne*·te

railway station *estação* ① *de trem*
es·taa·*sowng* de treng

rain *chuva* ① *shoo*·vaa

raincoat *casaco* ⑩ *de chuva*
kaa·*zaa*·ko de *shoo*·vaa

raisin *passas* ① pl *paa*·saas

rally *comício* ⑩ ko·*mee*·syo

rape *estrupo* ⑩ es·*troo*·po

rape *estrupar* es·troo·*paarr*

rare (food) *mal passado/passada* ⑩/①
mow paa·*saa*·do/paa·*saa*·daa

rare (uncommon) *raro/rara* ⑩/①
haa·ro/*haa*·raa

rash *irritação* ① *na pele*
ee·hee·taa·*sowng* naa *pe*·le

raspberry *framboesa* ① fraang·bo·e·zaa

rat *rato/ratazana* ⑩/①
haa·to/haa·taa·*za*·naa

raw *cru/crua* ⑩/① kroo/*kroo*·aa

razor *raspador* ⑩ haas·paa·*dorr*

razor blade *gilete* ① zhee·*le*·te

read *ler* lerr

ready *pronto/pronta* ⑩/①
prong·to/*prong*·taa

real estate agent *agente* ⑩&①
imobiliário aa·*zheng*·te
ee·mo·bee·lee·*aa*·ryo

realistic *realista* he·aa·*lees*·taa

reason *razão* ① haa·*zowng*

receipt *recibo* ⑩ he·*see*·bo

recently *recentemente* he·seng·te·*meng*·te

recommend *recomendar*
he·ko·meng·*daarr*

record *gravar* graa·*vaarr*

recording *gravação* ① graa·vaa·*sowng*

recyclable *reciclável* he·see·*klaa*·vel

recycle *reciclar* he·see·*klaar*

red *vermelho/vermelha* ⑩/①
verr·*me*·lyo/verr·*me*·lyaa

referee *juiz/juíza* ⑩/①
zhoo·ees/zhoo·ee·zaa

reference *referência* ① he·fe·*reng*·syaa

reflexology *reflexologia* ①
he·flek·so·lo·*zhee*·aa

refrigerator *geladeira* ① zhe·laa·*day*·raa

refugee *refugiado/refugiada* ⑩/①
he·foo·zhee·aa·do/he·foo·zhee·*aa*·daa

refund *reembolso* ⑩ he·eng·*bol*·so

refuse *recusar* he·koo·*zaarr*

regional *regional* he·zhyo·*now*

registered mail *correio* ⑩ *registrado*
ko·*hay*·o he·zhees·*traa*·do

rehydration salts *sais* ⑩ pl *de hidratação*
sais de ee·draa·taa·*sowng*

reiki *reiki* ① *hay*·kee

relationship *relacionamento* ⑩
he·laa·syo·na·*meng*·to

relax *relaxar* he·la·*shaarr*

relic *rélica* ① he·*lee*·kaa

religion *religião* ① he·lee·zhee·*owng*

religious *religioso/religiosa* ⑩/①
he·lee·zhee·o·zo/he·lee·zhee·o·zaa

remote *remoto/remota* ⑩/①
he·*mo*·to/he·*mo*·taa

remote control *controle* ⑩ *remoto*
kong·*tro*·le he·*mo*·to

rent *alugar* aa·loo·*gaarr*

repair *consertar* kong·serr·*taarr*

republic *república* ① he·*poo*·blee·kaa

reservation (booking) *reserva* ①
he·*zerr*·vaa

rest *descansar* des·kang·*saarr*

restaurant *restaurante* ⓜ hes·tow·*rang*·te

resume (CV) *currículum* ⓜ
koo·*hee*·koo·loom

retired *aposentado/aposentada* ⓜ/①
aa·po·seng·*taa*·do/aa·po·seng·*taa*·daa

return *retornar* he·torr·*naarr*

return (ticket) *ida e volta*
ee·daa e *vol*·taa

review *revisão* ① he·vee·*zowng*

rhythm *ritmo* ⓜ *hee*·tee·mo

rib *costela* ① kos·*te*·laa

rice *arroz* ⓜ aa·hos

rich (wealthy) *rico/rica* ⓜ/①
hee·ko/*hee*·kaa

ride (car) *volta* ① *vol*·taa

ride (horse) *andar à cavalo*
ang·*daarr* aa kaa·*vaa*·lo

right (direction) (à) *direita* ①
(aa) dee·*ray*·taa

right (correct) *correto/correta* ⓜ/①
ko·*he*·to/ko·*he*·taa

right-wing *direitista* dee·ray·*tees*·taa

ring (on finger) *anel* ⓜ aa·*nel*

ring (phone) *tocar* to·*kaarr*

rip-off *roubo* ⓜ *ho*·bo

risk *risco* ⓜ *hees*·ko

river *rio* ⓜ *hee*·o

road *estrada* ① es·*traa*·daa

road map *mapa* ① *da estrada*
maa·paa daa es·*traa*·daa

rob *roubar* ho·*baarr*

rock *pedra* ① *pe*·draa

rock (music) *rock* ⓜ *ho*·kee

rock climbing *alpinismo* ⓜ
ow·pee·*nees*·mo

rock group *banda* ① *de rock*
bang·daa de *ho*·kee

rockmelon *melão* ⓜ me·*lowng*

roll (bread) *pão* ⓜ *powng*

rollerblading *patinaçao*
paa·tee·naa·*sowng*

romantic *romântico/romântica* ⓜ/①
ho·*mang*·tee·ko/ho·*mang*·tee·kaa

room *quarto* ⓜ *kwaarr*·to

room number *número* ⓜ *do quarto*
noo·me·ro do *kwaarr*·to

rope *corda* ① *korr*·daa

round *redondo/redonda* ⓜ/①
he·*dong*·do/he·*dong*·daa

route *rota* ① *ho*·taa

rowing *remo* ⓜ *he*·mo

rubbish *lixo* ⓜ *lee*·sho

rubella *rubéola* ① hoo·*be*·o·laa

rug *tapete* ⓜ taa·*pe*·te

rugby *rugby* ⓜ *hoo*·gee·bee

ruins *ruínas* ① pl hoo·*ee*·naas

rule *regra* ① *he*·graa

rum *rum* ⓜ hoom

run *correr* ko·*herr*

running *corrida* ① ko·*hee*·daa

runny nose *coriza* ① ko·*ree*·zaa

S

sad *triste* *trees*·te

saddle *sela* ① *se*·laa

safe *seguro/segura* ⓜ/①
se·*goo*·ro/se·*goo*·raa

safe *cofre* ⓜ *ko*·fre

safe sex *sexo* ⓜ *com proteção*
sek·so kong pro·te·*sowng*

saint *santo/santa* ⓜ/①
sang·to/*sang*·taa

salad *salada* ① sa·*laa*·daa

salami *salaminho* ⓜ saa·laa·*mee*·nyo

salary *salário* ⓜ saa·*laa*·ryo

sale *liquidação* ① lee·kee·daa·*sowng*

sales tax *imposto* ⓜ *sobre venda*
eeng·*pos*·to *so*·bre *veng*·daa

salmon *salmão* ⓜ sow·*mowng*

salt *sal* ⓜ sow

same *mesmo/mesma* ⓜ/①
mes·mo/*mes*·maa

sand *areia* ① aa·*re*·yaa

sandal *sandália* ① sang·*daa*·lyaa

sanitary napkin *toalha* ⓜ *higiênica*
to·*aa*·lyaa ee·zhee·*e*·nee·kaa

sardine *sardinha* ① saarr·*dee*·nyaa

Saturday *sábado* ⓜ *saa*·baa·do

sauce *molho* ⓜ *mo*·lyo

sauna *sauna* ① *sow*·naa

sausage *salsicha* ① sow·*see*·shaa

say *dizer* dee·*zerr*

scalp *couro* ⓜ *cabeludo*
ko·ro kaa·be·*loo*·do

scarf *lenço* ⓜ leng·so
school *escola* ⓕ es·ko·laa
science *ciências* ⓕ pl see·eng·syaas
scientist *cientista* ⓜ&ⓕ see·eng·tees·taa
scissors *tesoura* ⓕ te·zo·raa
score *contar os pontos* kong·taarr os pong·tos
scoreboard *painel* ⓜ *de marcação* pai·nel de maarr·kaa·sowng
Scotland *Escócia* ⓕ es·ko·syaa
scrambled *mexido/mexida* ⓜ/ⓕ me·shee·do/me·shee·daa
sculptor *escultor/escultora* ⓜ/ⓕ es·kool·toorr/es·kool·too·ra
sculpture *escultura* ⓕ es·kool·too·raa
sea *mar* ⓜ maarr
seasick *enjoado/enjoada* ⓜ/ⓕ en·zho·aa·do/en·zho·aa·daa
seaside *beira mar* ⓕ bay·raa maarr
season *estação* ⓕ es·taa·sowng
seat *assento* ⓜ aa·seng·to
seatbelt *cinto* ⓜ *de segurança* seeng·to de se·goo·rang·saa
second (time) *segundo* ⓜ se·goong·do
second *segundo/segunda* ⓜ/ⓕ se·goong·do/se·goong·daa
second-hand *de segunda mão* de se·goong·daa mowng
second-hand shop *loja* ⓕ *de segunda mão* lo·zhaa de se·goon·daa mowng
secretary *secretário/secretária* ⓜ/ⓕ se·kre·taa·ryo/se·kre·taa·ryaa
see *ver* verr
self-employed *autônomo/autônoma* ⓜ/ⓕ ow·to·no·mo/ow·to·no·maa
selfish *egoísta* e·go·ees·taa
self-service *auto-serviço* ⓜ ow·to·serr·vee·so
sell *vender* veng·derr
send *enviar* eng·vee·aarr
sensible *sensível* seng·see·vel
sensual *sensual* seng·soo·ow
separate *separado/separada* ⓜ/ⓕ se·paa·raa·do/se·paa·raa·daa
September *setembro* se·teng·bro
serious *sério/séria* ⓜ/ⓕ se·ryo/se·ryaa
service charge *taxa* ⓕ *de serviço* taa·shaa de serr·veee·so

service station *posto* ⓜ *de gasolina* pos·to de gaa·zo·lee·naa
serviette *guardanapo* ⓜ gwaarr·daa·naa·po
several *diversos/diversas* ⓜ/ⓕ pl dee·verr·sos/dee·verr·saas
sew *costurar* kos·too·raarr
sex *sexo* ⓜ sek·so
sexism *machismo* ⓜ maa·shees·mo
sexy *sexy* sek·see
shadow *sombra* ⓕ song·braa
shampoo *xampú* ⓜ shang·poo
shape *forma* ⓕ forr·maa
share (with) *dividir* dee·vee·deerr
shave *fazer a barba* faa·zerr aa baarr·baa
shaving cream *creme* ⓜ *de barbear* kre·me de baarr·be·aarr
she *ela* e·laa
sheep *ovelha* ⓕ o·ve·lyaa
sheet (bed) *lençol* ⓜ leng·sow
shelf *prateleira* ⓕ praa·te·lay·raa
shiatsu *shiatsu* ⓕ shee·aa·tee·zoo
shingles (illness) *cobreiro* ⓜ ko·bray·ro
ship *navio* ⓜ naa·vee·o
shirt *camisa* ⓕ kaa·mee·zaa
shoe *sapato* ⓜ saa·paa·to
shoe shop *sapataria* ⓕ saa·paa·taa·ree·aa
shoot *atirar* aa·tee·raarr
shop *loja* ⓕ lo·zhaa
shopping centre *shopping centre* ⓜ sho·peeng seng·terr
short *curto/curta* ⓜ/ⓕ koor·to/koor·taa
shortage *escassez* ⓕ es·kaa·ses
shorts *bermuda* ⓕ berr·moo·daa
shoulder *ombro* ⓜ pl ong·bro
shout *gritar* gree·taarr
show *mostrar* mos·traarr
shower *chuveiro* ⓜ shoo·vay·ro
shrine *relicário* ⓜ he·lee·kaa·ryo
shut *fechado/fechada* ⓜ/ⓕ fe·shaa·do/fe·shaa·daa
shy *tímido/tímida* ⓜ/ⓕ tee·mee·do/tee·mee·daa
sick *doente* do·eng·te
side *lado* ⓜ laa·do
sign *aviso* ⓜ aa·vee·zo
signature *assinatura* ⓕ aa·see·naa·too·raa
silk *seda* ⓕ se·daa
silver *prata* ⓕ praa·taa

similar *parecido/parecida* ⓜ/ⓕ
paa·re·see·do/paa·re·see·daa

simple *simples* seeng·ples

since *desde* des·de

sing *cantar* kang·taarr

Singapore *Cingapura* seen·gaa·poo·raa

singer *cantor/cantora* ⓜ/ⓕ
kang·torr/kang·to·raa

single *solteiro/solteira* ⓜ/ⓕ
sol·tay·ro/sol·tay·raa

singlet *camiseta* ⓕ kaa·mee·ze·taa

sister *irmã* ⓕ eer·ma

sit *sentar* seng·taarr

size *tamanho* ⓜ ta·ma·nyo

skate *andar de skate*
ang·daarr de ees·kay·te

skateboarding *skate* ⓜ ees·kay·te

ski *esquiar* es·kee·aarr

skiing *esqui* ⓜ es·kee

skim milk *leite* ⓜ *desnatado*
lay·te des·naa·taa·do

skin *pele* ⓕ pe·le

skirt *saia* ⓕ saa·yaa

skull *crânio* ⓜ kra·nyo

sky *céu* ⓜ se·oo

sleep *dormir* dorr·meerr

sleeping bag *saco* ⓜ *de dormir*
saa·ko de dorr·meerr

sleeping berth *leito* ⓜ lay·to

sleeping car *vagão* ⓜ *de dormir*
va·gowng de dorr·meerr

sleeping pills *pílula* ⓕ *para dormir*
pee·loo·laa paa·raa dorr·meerr

sleepy *sonolento/sonolenta* ⓜ/ⓕ
so·no·leng·to/so·no·leng·taa

slide (film) *slide* ⓜ ees·lai·de

slow *devagar* de·vaa·gaarr

slowly *vagarosamente*
vaa·gaa·ro·zaa·meng·te

small *pequeno/pequena* ⓜ/ⓕ
pe·ke·no/pe·ke·na

smell *cheiro* ⓜ shay·ro

smile *sorrir* so·heerr

smoke *fumar* foo·maarr

snack *lanche* ⓜ lang·she

snail *lesma* ⓕ les·maa

snake *cobra* ⓕ ko·braa

snorkelling *snorkel* ⓜ ees·norr·kel

snow *neve* ⓕ ne·ve

snow pea *vagem* ⓕ *chinesa* vaa·zheng
shee·ne·zaa

snowboarding *snowboarding* ⓜ
snow·borr·deeng

soap *sabonete* ⓜ saa·bo·ne·te

soap opera *novela* ⓕ no·ve·laa

soccer *futebol* ⓜ foo·te·bol

social welfare *seguro* ⓜ *social*
se·goo·ro so·see·ow

socialist *socialista* so·see·aa·lees·taa

sock *meia* ⓕ may·aa

soft drink *refrigerante* ⓜ
he·free·zhe·rang·te

soft-boiled *mole* mo·le

soldier *soldado* ⓜ&ⓕ sol·daa·do

some *alguns/algumas* ⓜ/ⓕ
ow·goons/ow·goo·maas

someone *alguém* ow·geng

something *alguma coisa*
ow·goo·maa koy·zaa

sometimes *às vezes* aas ve·zes

son *filho* ⓜ fee·lyo

song *canção* ⓕ kang·sowng

soon *em breve* eng bre·ve

sore *dolorido/dolorida* ⓜ/ⓕ
do·lo·ree·do/do·lo·ree·daa

soup *sopa* ⓕ so·paa

sour cream *creme* ⓜ *azedo*
kre·me aa·ze·do

south *sul* ⓜ sool

souvenir *souvenir* ⓜ soo·ve·neerr

souvenir shop *loja* ⓕ *de souvenir*
lo·zhaa de soo·ve·neerr

soy milk *leite* ⓜ *de soja* lay·te de so·zhaa

soy sauce *molho* ⓜ *de soja*
mo·lyo de so·zhaa

space *espaço* ⓜ es·pa·so

Spain *Espanha* ⓕ es·pa·nyaa

sparkling wine *vinho* ⓜ *espumante*
vee·nyo es·poo·mang·te

speak *falar* faa·laarr

special *especial* es·pe·see·ow

specialist *especialista* ⓜ&ⓕ
es·pe·see·aa·lees·taa

speed *velocidade* ⓕ ve·lo·see·daa·de

speed limit *limite* ⓜ *de velocidade*
lee·mee·te de ve·lo·see·daa·de

speedometer *mostrador* ⓜ *de velocidade*
mos·traa·dorr de ve·lo·see·daa·de

spider *aranha* ⓕ aa·*ra*·nyaa

spinach *espinafre* ⓜ es·pee·*naa*·fre

spoiled *mimado/mimada* ⓜ/ⓕ
  mee·*maa*·do/mee·*maa*·daa

spoke (wheel) *trave* ⓕ *de roda*
  traa·ve de *ho*·daa

spoon *colher* ⓕ ko·*lyerr*

sport *esporte* ⓜ es·*porr*·te

sports store *loja* ⓕ *de esportes*
  lo·zhaa de es·*porr*·tes

sportsperson *esportista* ⓜ&ⓕ
  es·porr·*tees*·taa

sprain *torcimento* ⓜ · *deslocamento* ⓜ
  torr·see·*meng*·to · des·lo·kaa·*meng*·to

spring (coil) *molas* ⓕ pl *mo*·laas

spring (season) *primavera* ⓕ
  pree·maa·*ve*·raa

square (town) *praça* ⓕ *praa*·saa

stadium *estádio* ⓜ es·*taa*·dyo

stairway *escadaria* ⓕ es·kaa·daa·*ree*·aa

stale *velho/velha* ⓜ/ⓕ *ve*·lyo/*ve*·lyaa

stamp *selo* ⓜ *se*·lo

standby ticket *bilhete* ⓜ *de stand by*
  bee·*lye*·te de ees·*tang*·dee bai

(four-)star *(quatro) estrelas* ⓕ pl *(kwaa*·tro)
  es·*tre*·laas

star *estrela* ⓕ es·*tre*·laa

start *começo* ⓜ ko·*me*·so

start *começar* ko·me·*saarr*

station *estação* ⓕ es·taa·*sowng*

stationery shop *papelaria* ⓕ
  paa·pe·laa·*ree*·aa

statue *estátua* ⓕ es·*taa*·twaa

stay (at a hotel) *ficar* fee·*kaarr*

stay (in one place) *ficar* fee·*kaarr*

steak (beef) *bife* ⓜ *bee*·fe

steal *roubar* ho·*baarr*

steep *íngreme* *eeng*·gre·me

step *passo* ⓜ *paa*·so

stereo *estéreo* ⓜ es·*te*·ryo

still water *água* ⓕ *sem gás*
  aa·gwaa seng gaas

stock (food) *caldo* ⓜ *kow*·do

stockings *meias* ⓕ pl *finas*
  may·aas *fee*·naas

stomach *estômago* ⓜ es·*to*·maa·go

stomachache *dor* ⓕ *de estômago*
  dorr de es·*to*·maa·go

stone *pedra* ⓕ *pe*·draa

stoned (drugged) *fumado/fumada* ⓜ/ⓕ
  foo·*maa*·do/foo·*maa*·daa

stop (bus) *ponto* ⓜ *de ônibus*
  pong·to de *o*·nee·boos

stop (cease) *parar* paa·*raarr*

stop (prevent) *evitar* e·vee·*taarr*

Stop! *Pare!* *paa*·re

storm *tempestade* ⓕ teng·pes·*taa*·de

story *estória* ⓕ es·*to*·ryaa

stove *fogão* ⓜ fo·*gowng*

straight *direto/direta* ⓜ/ⓕ
  dee·*re*·to/dee·*re*·taa

strange *estranho/estranha* ⓜ/ⓕ
  es·*tra*·nyo/es·*tra*·nyaa

stranger *estranho/estranha* ⓜ/ⓕ
  es·*tra*·nyo/es·*tra*·nyaa

strawberry *morango* ⓜ mo·*rang*·go

stream *vapor* ⓜ vaa·*porr*

street *rua* ⓕ *hoo*·aa

strike *ataque* ⓜ aa·*taa*·ke

string *barbante* ⓜ baarr·*bang*·te

stroke (health) *derrame* ⓜ de·*ha*·me

strong *forte* *forr*·te

stubborn *teimoso/teimosa* ⓜ/ⓕ
  tay·mo·zo/tay·*mo*·zaa

student *estudante* ⓜ&ⓕ es·too·*dang*·te

studio *estúdio* ⓜ es·*too*·dyo

stupid *burro/burra* ⓜ/ⓕ
  boo·ho/*boo*·haa

style *estilo* ⓜ es·*tee*·lo

subtitles *sub-títulos* ⓜ pl
  soo·bee·*tee*·too·los

suburb *bairro* ⓜ *bai*·ho

sugar *açúcar* ⓜ aa·*soo*·kaarr

suitcase *mala* ⓕ *maa*·laa

sultana *passas* ⓕ pl *pa*·saas

summer *verão* ⓜ ve·*rowng*

sun *sol* ⓜ sol

Sunday *domingo* ⓜ do·*meeng*·go

sunblock *proteção* ⓕ *contra sol*
  pro·te·*sowng* kong·traa sol

sunburnt *queimado/queimada* ⓜ/ⓕ
  de sol kay·*maa*·do/kay·*maa*·daa de sol

sunglasses *óculos* ⓜ pl *de sol*
  o·koo·los de sol

sunny *ensolarado/ensolarada* ⓜ/ⓕ
  eng·so·laa·*raa*·do/eng·so·laa·*raa*·daa

sunrise *nascer* ⓜ *do sol* naa·serr do sol

sunset *pôr* ⓜ *do sol* porr do sol

sunstroke *insolação* ⓕ eeng·so·laa·sowng
supermarket *supermercado* ⓜ soo·perr·merr·kaa·do
superstition *superstição* ⓕ soo·pers·tee·sowng
supporter (sport) *torcedor/ torcedora* ⓜ/ⓕ torr·se·dorr/ torr·se·do·raa
supporter (politics) *apoio* ⓜ *ao partido* aa·po·yo ow paarr·tee·do
surf *surfar* soorr·faarr
surface mail *correspondência* ⓕ *via terrestre* ko·hes·pong·deng·syaa vee·aa te·hes·tre
surfboard *prancha* ⓕ *de surfe* prang·shaa de soorr·fee
surfing *surfe* ⓜ soorr·fee
surname *sobrenome* ⓜ so·bre·no·me
surprise *surpresa* ⓕ soor·pre·zaa
sweater *suéter* ⓜ soo·e·terr
Sweden *Suécia* ⓕ soo·e·syaa
sweet *doce* do·se
sweets *doces* ⓜ pl do·ses
swelling *inchaço* ⓜ eeng·shaa·so
swim *nadar* naa·daarr
swimming pool *piscina* ⓕ pee·see·naa
swimsuit *roupa* ⓕ *de banho* ho·paa de ba·nyo
Switzerland *Suíça* ⓕ soo·ee·saa
synagogue *sinagoga* ⓕ see·naa·go·gaa
synthetic *sintético/sintética* ⓜ/ⓕ seeng·te·tee·ko/seeng·te·tee·kaa
syringe *seringa* ⓕ se·reeng·gaa

T

table *mesa* ⓕ me·zaa
table tennis *tênis* ⓜ *de mesa* te·nees de me·zaa
tablecloth *toalha* ⓕ *de mesa* to·aa·lyaa de me·zaa
tail *rabo* ⓜ haa·bo
tailor *alfaiate* ⓜ ow·faa·yaa·te
take *levar* le·vaarr
take (photo) *tirar* tee·raarr
talk *falar* faa·laarr
tall *alto/alta* ⓜ/ⓕ ow·to/ow·taa
tampon *tampão* ⓜ tang·powng

tanning lotion *loção* ⓕ *de bronzear* lo·sowng de brong·ze·aarr
tap *torneira* ⓕ torr·nay·raa
tap water *água* ⓕ *da torneira* aa·gwaa daa torr·nay·raa
tasty *gostoso/gostosa* ⓜ/ⓕ gos·to·zo/gos·to·zaa
tax *imposto* ⓜ eeng·pos·to
taxi *táxi* ⓜ taak·see
taxi stand *fila* ⓕ *de táxi* fee·laa de taak·see
tea *chá* ⓜ shaa
teacher *professor/professora* ⓜ/ⓕ pro·fe·sorr/pro·fe·so·raa
team *time* ⓜ tee·me
teaspoon *colher* ⓕ *de chá* ko·lyerr de shaa
technique *técnica* ⓕ te·kee·nee·kaa
teeth *dentes* ⓜ pl deng·tes
telegram *telegrama* ⓜ te·le·gra·maa
telephone *telefone* ⓜ te·le·fo·ne
telephone *telefonar* te·le·fo·naarr
telephone centre *central* ⓕ *telefônica* seng·trow te·le·fo·nee·kaa
telescope *telescópio* ⓜ te·les·ko·pyo
television *televisão* ⓕ te·le·vee·sowng
tell *dizer* dee·zerr
temperature *temperatura* ⓕ teng·pe·raa·too·raa
temple *têmpora* ⓕ teng·po·raa
tennis *tênis* ⓜ te·nees
tennis court *quadra* ⓕ *de tênis* kwaa·draa de te·nees
tent *barraca* ⓕ baa·haa·kaa
tent peg *estaca* ⓕ es·taa·kaa
terrible *terrível* te·hee·vel
test *teste* ⓜ tes·te
thank *agradecer* aa·graa·de·serr
theatre *teatro* ⓜ te·aa·tro
their *deles* de·les
they *eles* e·les
thick *grosso/grossa* ⓜ/ⓕ gro·so/gro·saa
thief *ladrão/ladra* ⓜ/ⓕ laa·drowng/laa·dra
thin *fino/fina* ⓜ/ⓕ fee·no/fee·naa
think *pensar* peng·saarr
third *terceiro/terceira* ⓜ/ⓕ terr·say·ro/terr·say·raa

thirsty *sedento/sedenta* Ⓜ/Ⓕ
se·*deng*·to/se·*deng*·taa

this *este/esta* Ⓜ/Ⓕ *es*·te/es·taa

throat *garganta* Ⓕ gaarr·*gang*·taa

thrush (health) *cândida* Ⓕ • *corrimento* Ⓜ
kang·dee·daa • ko·hee·*meng*·to

Thursday *quinta-feira* Ⓕ *kween*·ta·*fay*·raa

ticket *bilhete* Ⓜ bee·*lye*·te

ticket machine *máquina* Ⓕ *de vender
passagem* *maa*·kee·naa de *veng*·derr
paa·*saa*·zheng

ticket office *bilheteria* Ⓕ bee·lye·te·*ree*·aa

tide *maré* Ⓕ maa·*re*

tight *apertado/apertada* Ⓜ/Ⓕ
aa·perr·*taa*·do/aa·perr·*taa*·daa

time *tempo* Ⓜ *teng*·po

time difference *diferença* Ⓕ *de horário*
dee·fe·*reng*·saa de o·*raa*·ryo

timetable *horário* Ⓜ o·*raa*·rio

tin (can) *lata* Ⓕ *laa*·taa

tin opener *abridor* Ⓜ *de lata*
aa·bree·dorr de *laa*·taa

tiny *mínimo/mínima* Ⓜ/Ⓕ
mee·nee·mo/*mee*·nee·maa

tip (gratuity) *gorgeta* Ⓕ gorr·*zhe*·taa

tired *cansado/cansada* Ⓜ/Ⓕ
kang·*saa*·do/kang·*saa*·daa

tissue *lencinho* Ⓜ *de papel*
leng·*see*·nyo de paa·*pel*

toast *torrada* Ⓕ to·*haa*·daa

toaster *torradeira* Ⓕ to·haa·*day*·raa

tobacco *tabaco* Ⓜ taa·*baa*·ko

tobacconist *tabaconista* Ⓜ
taa·baa·ko·*nees*·taa

tobogganing *tobogã* Ⓜ to·bo·*gang*

today *hoje* o·*zhee*

toe *dedos* Ⓜ pl *do pé* *de*·dos do pe

tofu *tofu* Ⓜ to·*foo*

together *junto/junta* Ⓜ/Ⓕ
zhoong·to/*zhoong*·taa

toilet *banheiro* Ⓜ ba·*nyay*·ro

toilet paper *papel* Ⓜ *higiênico*
paa·*pel* ee·gee·*e*·nee·ko

tomato *tomate* Ⓜ to·*maa*·te

tomato sauce *molho* Ⓜ *de tomate*
mo·lyo de to·*maa*·te

tomorrow *amanhã* aa·ma·*nyang*

tomorrow afternoon *amanhã à tarde*
aa·ma·*nyang* aa *taarr*·de

tomorrow evening *amanhã à noite*
aa·ma·*nyang* aa *noy*·te

tomorrow morning *amanhã de manhã*
aa·ma·*nyang* de ma·*nyang*

tonight *hoje à noite* o·zhee aa *noy*·te

too (also) *também* tang·*beng*

too (much) *demais* de·*mais*

tooth *dente* Ⓜ *deng*·te

toothache *dor* Ⓕ *de dente*
dorr de *deng*·te

toothbrush *escova* Ⓕ *de dentes*
es·*ko*·vaa de *deng*·tes

toothpaste *pasta* Ⓕ *de dentes*
pas·taa de *deng*·tes

toothpick *palito* Ⓜ *de dentes*
paa·*lee*·to de *deng*·tes

torch (flashlight) *lanterna* Ⓕ lang·*terr*·naa

touch *tocar* to·*kaarr*

tour *excursão* Ⓕ es·koorr·*sowng*

tourist *turista* Ⓜ&Ⓕ too·*rees*·taa

tourist office *escritório* Ⓜ *de turismo*
es·kree·*to*·ryo de too·*rees*·mo

towards *em direção à*
eng dee·re·*sowng* aa

towel *toalha* Ⓕ to·*aa*·lyaa

tower *torre* Ⓕ *to*·he

toxic waste *resíduo* Ⓜ *tóxico*
he·*zee*·dwo tok·*see*·ko

toy shop *loja* Ⓕ *de brinquedos*
lo·zhaa de breeng·*ke*·dos

track (path) *caminho* Ⓜ kaa·*mee*·nyo

track (sport) *pista* Ⓕ *pees*·taa

trade *comércio* Ⓜ ko·*merr*·syo

traffic *tráfico* Ⓜ *traa*·fee·ko

traffic light *sinal* Ⓜ *de trânsito*
see·*now* de *trang*·zee·to

trail *vestígio* Ⓜ ves·*tee*·zhyo

train *trem* Ⓜ treng

train station *estação* Ⓕ *de trem*
es·taa·*sowng* de treng

tram *bonde* Ⓜ *bong*·de

transit lounge *sala* Ⓕ *de trânsito*
saa·laa de *trang*·zee·to

translate *traduzir* traa·doo·*zeerr*

transport *transporte* Ⓜ trans·*porr*·te

travel *viajar* vee·aa·*zhaarr*

travel agency *agência* Ⓕ *de viagens*
aa·*zheng*·syaa de vee·*aa*·zhengs

travel sickness *enjôo* Ⓜ *de viagem*
eng·*jo*·o de vee·*aa*·zheng
travellers cheques *travellers*
cheques Ⓜ pl traa·ve·*ler she*·kes
tree *árvore* Ⓕ *aarr*·vo·re
trip (journey) *viagem* Ⓕ vee·*aa*·zheng
trousers *calças* Ⓕ pl *kow*·saas
truck *caminhão* Ⓜ kaa·mee·*nyowng*
trust *crer* krerr
try (attempt) *tentar* teng·*taarr*
T-shirt *camiseta* Ⓕ kaa·mee·ze·taa
tube (tyre) *câmara* Ⓕ *ka*·maa·raa
Tuesday *terça-feira* Ⓕ *terr*·saa·*fay*·raa
tumour *tumor* Ⓜ too·*morr*
tuna *atum* Ⓜ aa·*toong*
tune *tom* Ⓜ tong
turkey *perú* Ⓜ pe·*roo*
turn *virar* vee·*raarr*
TV *tevê* Ⓜ te·*ve*
tweezers *pinça* Ⓕ *peeng*·saa
twice *duas vezes* *doo*·aas *ve*·zes
twin beds *camas* Ⓕ pl *gêmeas*
ka·maas *zhe*·me·aas
twins *gêmeos/gêmeas* Ⓜ/Ⓕ
zhe·me·os/*zhe*·me·aas
type *tipo* Ⓜ *tee*·po
typical *típico/típica* Ⓜ/Ⓕ
tee·pee·ko/*tee*·pee·kaa
tyre *pneu* Ⓜ pee·*ne*·oo

U

ultrasound *ultrasom* Ⓜ ool·traa·*song*
umbrella *guarda-chuva* Ⓜ
gwaarr·daa·*shoo*·vaa
uncomfortable *desconfortável*
des·kong·forr·*taa*·vel
understand *compreender*
kong·pre·eng·*derr*
underwear *roupa* Ⓕ *de baixo*
ho·paa de *bai*·sho
unemployed *desempregado/*
desempregada Ⓜ/Ⓕ
de·zeng·pre·*gaa*·do/
de·zeng·pre·*gaa*·daa
unfair *injusto/injusta* Ⓜ/Ⓕ
eeng·*zhoos*·to/eeng·*zhoos*·taa
uniform *uniforme* Ⓜ oo·nee·*forr*·me
universe *universo* Ⓜ oo·nee·*verr*·so

university *universidade* Ⓕ
oo·nee·verr·see·*daa*·de
unleaded *sem chumbo* seng *shoong*·bo
unsafe *inseguro/insegura* Ⓜ/Ⓕ
eeng·se·*goo*·ro/eeng·se·*goo*·raa
until *até* aa·*te*
unusual *atípico/atípica* Ⓜ/Ⓕ
aa·*tee*·pee·ko/aa·*tee*·pee·kaa
up *em cima* eng *see*·maa
uphill *para cima* paa·raa *see*·maa
urgent *urgente* oorr·zheng·te
urinary infection *infecção* Ⓕ *urinária*
een·fek·*sowng* oo·ree·*naa*·ryaa
the USA *os EUA* Ⓜ pl os *e*·waa
useful *útil* oo·til

V

vacant *vago/vaga* Ⓜ/Ⓕ
vaa·go/*vaa*·gaa
vacation *férias* Ⓕ pl *fe*·ryaas
vaccination *vacina* Ⓕ vaa·*see*·naa
vagina *vagina* Ⓕ vaa·*zhee*·naa
validate *validar* vaa·lee·*daarr*
valley *vale* Ⓜ *vaa*·le
valuable *valioso/valiosa* Ⓜ/Ⓕ
vaa·lee·o·zo/vaa·lee·o·zaa
value (price) *valor* vaa·*lorr*
van *van* Ⓕ van
veal *bezerro/bezerra* Ⓜ/Ⓕ
be·ze·ho/be·ze·haa
vegetable *legumes* Ⓜ pl le·*goo*·mes
vegetarian *vegetariano/*
vegetariana Ⓜ/Ⓕ ve·zhe·taa·ree·*a*·no/
ve·zhe·taa·ree·*a*·naa
vein *veia* Ⓕ *ve*·aa
venereal disease *doença* Ⓕ *venérea*
do·*eng*·saa ve·ne·ryaa
venue *local* Ⓜ lo·kow
very *muito/muita* Ⓜ/Ⓕ
mweeng·to/*mweeng*·taa
video tape *fita* Ⓕ *de vídeo*
fee·taa de *vee*·de·o
view *vista* Ⓕ *vees*·taa
village *vilarejo* Ⓜ vee·laa·*re*·zho
vine *vinho* Ⓜ *vee*·nyo
vinegar *vinagre* Ⓜ ve·*naa*·gre
vineyard *vinha* Ⓕ *vee*·nyaa
virus *vírus* Ⓜ *vee*·roos

visa *visto* ⓜ vees·to
visit *visitar* vee·zee·*taarr*
vitamin *vitamina* ⓕ vee·taa·*mee*·naa
vodka *vodka* ⓕ vo·dee·kaa
voice *voz* ⓕ voz
volleyball (sport) *vôlei* ⓜ *vo*·lay
volume *volume* ⓜ vo·*loo*·me
vote *votar* vo·*taarr*

W

wage *salário* ⓜ saa·*laa*·ryo
wait *esperar* es·pe·*raarr*
waiter *garçon/garçonete* ⓜ/ⓕ gaarr·*song*/ gaarr·so·*ne*·te
waiting room *sala* ⓕ *de espera* *saa*·laa de es·*pe*·raa
walk *andar* ang·*daarr*
wall (outer) *parede* ⓕ paa·*re*·de
want *querer* ke·*rerr*
war *guerra* ⓕ *ge*·haa
wardrobe *armário* ⓜ aarr·*maa*·ryo
warm *morno/morna* ⓜ/ⓕ *morr*·no/*morr*·naa
warn *avisar* aa·vee·*zaarr*
wash *lavar* laa·*vaarr*
wash cloth (flannel) *pano* ⓜ *de limpeza* *pa*·no de leeng·*pe*·zaa
washing machine *máquina* ⓕ *de lavar roupa* *maa*·kee·naa de laa·*vaarr* ho·paa
watch *relógio* ⓜ he·*lo*·zhyo
watch *cuidar • vigiar* kooy·*daarr* • vee·zhee·*aarr*
water *água* ⓕ *aa*·gwaa
water bottle *garrafa* ⓕ *d'água* gaa·*haa*·faa *daa*·gwaa
waterfall *cachoeira* ⓕ kaa·sho·ay·raa
watermelon *melancia* ⓕ me·lang·*see*·aa
waterproof *à prova d'água* aa *pro*·vaa *daa*·gwaa
waterskiing *eski* ⓜ *aquático* es·*kee* aa·*kwaa*·tee·ko
wave *onda* ⓕ *ong*·daa
way *caminho* ⓜ kaa·*mee*·nyo
we *nós* nos
weak *fraco/fraca* ⓜ/ⓕ *fraa*·ko/*fraa*·kaa
wealthy *rico/rica* ⓜ/ⓕ *hee*·ko/*hee*·kaa
wear *vestir* ves·*teerr*
weather *tempo* ⓜ *teng*·po

wedding *casamento* ⓜ kaa·zaa·*meng*·to
wedding cake *bolo* ⓜ *de casamento* *bo*·lo de kaa·zaa·*meng*·to
wedding present *presente* ⓜ *de casamento* pre·*zeng*·te de kaa·zaa·*meng*·to
Wednesday *quarta-feira* ⓕ *kwaarr*·taa·*fay*·raa
week *semana* ⓕ se·*ma*·naa
weekend *final* ⓜ *de semana* fee·*now* de se·*ma*·naa
weigh *pesar* pe·*zaarr*
weight *peso* ⓜ *pe*·zo
weights *pesos* ⓜ pl *pe*·zos
welcome *receber* he·se·*berr*
welfare *bem* ⓜ *social* beng so·see·*ow*
well *bem* ⓜ beng
west *oeste* ⓜ o·*es*·te
wet *molhado/molhada* ⓜ/ⓕ mo·*lyaa*·do/mo·*lyaa*·daa
what *que* ke
wheel *roda* ⓕ *ho*·daa
wheelchair *cadeira* ⓕ *de rodas* kaa·*day*·raa de *ho*·daas
when *quando* *kwang*·do
where *onde* *ong*·de
whisky *whisky* ⓜ oo·*ees*·kee
white *branco/branca* ⓜ/ⓕ *brang*·ko/*brang*·kaa
who *quem* keng
wholemeal bread *pão* ⓜ *integral* powng eeng·te·*grow*
why *por que* porr ke
wide *largo/larga* ⓜ/ⓕ *laarr*·go/*laarr*·gaa
wife *esposa* ⓕ es·*po*·zaa
win *ganhar* ga·*nyaarr*
wind *vento* ⓜ *veng*·to
window *janela* ⓕ zhaa·*ne*·laa
windscreen *parabrisa* ⓜ paa·raa·*bree*·zaa
windsurfing *windsurfe* ⓜ wind·*soorr*·fee
wine *vinho* ⓜ *vee*·nyo
wings *asas* ⓕ pl *aa*·zaas
winner *ganhador/ganhadora* ⓜ/ⓕ ga·nyaa·*dorr*/ga·nyaa·*do*·raa
winter *inverno* ⓜ eeng·*verr*·no
wire *arame* ⓜ aa·*ra*·me
wish *desejar* de·ze·*zhaarr*
with *com* kong

within (an hour) *dentro de (uma hora)*
deng·tro de (oo·maa *aw*·raa)
without *sem* seng
woman *mulher* ① moo·*lyerr*
wonderful *maravilhoso/maravilhosa* ⓜ/①
maa·raa·vee·*lyo*·zo/maa·raa·vee·*lyo*·zaa
wood *madeira* ① maa·*day*·raa
wool *lã* ① lang
word *palavra* ① paa·*laa*·vraa
work *trabalho* ⓜ traa·*baa*·lyo
work *trabalhar* traa·baa·*lyaarr*
work experience *experiência* ① de
trabalho es·pe·ree·*eng*·syaa de
traa·*baa*·lyo
work permit *permissão* ① *para trabalhar*
perr·mee·*sowng* paa·raa traa·baa·*lyaarr*
workout *resolução* ① he·zo·loo·*sowng*
workshop *oficina* ① o·fee·*see*·naa
world *mundo* ⓜ *moong*·do
World Cup *Copa do Mundo* ①
ko·paa do *moong*·do
worms *minhocas* ① pl mee·*nyo*·kaas
worried *preocupado/preocupada* ⓜ/①
pre·o·koo·*paa*·do/pre·o·koo·*paa*·daa
worship *reverenciar* he·ve·reng·see·*aarr*
wrist *punho* ⓜ *poo*·nyo
write *escrever* es·kre·*verr*

writer *escritor/escritora* ⓜ/①
es·kree·*torr*/es·kree·*to*·raa
wrong *errado/errada* ⓜ/①
e·*haa*·do/e·*haa*·daa

Y

year *ano* ⓜ *a*·no
yellow *amarelo/amarela* ⓜ/①
aa·maa·*re*·lo/aa·maa·*re*·laa
yes *sim* seeng
yesterday *ontem* ong·teng
(not) yet *ainda (não)*
aa·*eeng*·daa (nowng)
yoga *ioga* ① ee·o·gaa
yogurt *iogurte* ⓜ ee·o·*goorr*·te
you *você/vocês* sg/pl vo·*se*/vo·*ses*
young *jovem* zho·veng
your *seu/sua* ⓜ/① *se*·oo/*soo*·aa
youth hostel *albergue* ⓜ *da juventude*
ow·*berr*·ge daa zhoo·veng·*too*·de

Z

zodiac *zodíaco* ⓜ zo·*dee*·aa·ko
zoo *zoológico* ⓜ zo·o·*lo*·zhee·ko
zucchini *abobrinha* ① aa·bo·*bree*·nyaa

Nouns in the dictionary have their gender indicated by ⓜ or ⓕ. If it's a plural noun, you'll also see pl. Where a word that could be either a noun or a verb has no gender indicated, it's the verb. For all words relating to local food, see the **menu decoder**, page 159.

A

a bordo aa *borr*-do *aboard*

à direita ⓕ aa dee-*ray*-taa *right (direction)*

à esquerda ⓕ aa es-*kerr*-daa *left (direction)*

a prova d'água aa *pro*-vaa *daa*-gwaa *waterproof*

abacate ⓜ aa-baa-*kaa*-te *avocado*

abacaxi ⓜ aa-baa-kaa-*shee* *pineapple*

abaixo aa-*bai*-sho *below*

abelha ⓕ aa-*be*-lyaa *bee*

aberto/aberta ⓜ/ⓕ aa-*berr*-to/aa-*berr*-taa *open*

abóbora ⓕ aa-*bo*-bo-raa *pumpkin*

abobrinha ⓕ aa-bo-*bree*-nyaa *courgette • zucchini*

aborto ⓜ aa-*borr*-to *abortion*
  — espontâneo es-pong-*ta*-ne-o *miscarriage*

abraçar aa-braa-*saarr* *hug*

abridor ⓜ **de garrafas** aa-bree-*dorr* de gaa-*haa*-faas *bottle opener*

abridor ⓜ **de lata** aa-bree-*dorr* de *laa*-taa *can opener • tin opener*

abril aa-*breel* *April*

abrir aa-*breerr* *open*

absorvente ⓜ **higiênico** aab-sorr-*veng*-te ee-zhee-e-nee-ko *panty liner*

academia ⓕ aa-kaa-de-*mee*-aa *college*

acampamento ⓜ aa-kang-paa-*meng*-to *camping ground*

acampar aa-kang-*paarr* *camp*

achados e perdidos ⓜ pl aa-*shaa*-dos e perr-*dee*-dos *left luggage*

acidente ⓜ aa-see-*deng*-te *accident*

açougue ⓜ aa-*so*-ge *butcher's shop*

açougueiro/açougueira ⓜ/ⓕ aa-so-*gay*-ro/aa-so-*gay*-raa *butcher*

açúcar ⓜ aa-*soo*-kaarr *sugar*

acupuntura ⓕ aa-koo-poom-*too*-raa *acupuncture*

adaptador ⓜ aa-daa-pee-taa-*dorr* *adaptor*

adentro aa-*deng*-tro *indoors*

adivinhar aa-dee-vee-*nyaarr* *guess*

administração ⓕ aa-dee-mee-nees-traa-*sowng* *administration*

admitir aa-dee-mee-*teerr* *admit (acknowledge)*

adulto/adulta ⓜ/ⓕ aa-*dool*-to/aa-*dool*-taa *adult*

advogado/advogada ⓜ/ⓕ aa-dee-vo-*gaa*-do/aa-dee-vo-*gaa*-daa *lawyer*

aeróbica ⓕ aa-e-ro-bee-kaa *aerobics*

aeroplano ⓜ aa-e-ro-*pla*-no *aeroplane*

aeroporto ⓜ aa-e-ro-*porr*-to *airport*

África ⓕ *aa*-free-kaa *Africa*

agência ⓕ **de viagens** aa-*zheng*-syaa de vee-*aa*-zhengs *travel agency*

agente ⓜ&ⓕ **imobiliário** aa-*zheng*-te ee-mo-bee-lee-*aa*-ryo *real estate agent*

agora aa-*go*-raa *now*

agosto aa-*gos*-to *August*

agradecer aa-graa-de-*serr* *thank*

agricultura ⓕ aa-gree-kool-*too*-raa *agriculture*

água ⓕ *aa*-gwaa *water*
  — da torneira daa torr-*nay*-raa *tap water*
  — mineral mee-ne-*row* *mineral water*
  — quente *keng*-te *hot water*
  — sem gás seng gaas *still water*

agulha ⓕ aa-*goo*-lyaa *needle (sewing/syringe)*

Aids ⓕ *ai*-dees *AIDS*

ainda (não) aa-*eeng*-daa (nowng) *(not) yet*

ajuda ① aa-*zhoo*-daa *help*

ajudar aa-zhoo-*daarr help*

albergue ⑩ **da juventude** ow-*berr*-ge daa zhoo-veng-*too*-de *youth hostel*

álcool ⑩ *ow*-kol *alcohol*

Alemanha ① aa-le-*le*-ma-nyaa *Germany*

alergia ① aa-lerr-*zhee*-aa *allergy*

alface ⑩ ow-*faa*-se *lettuce*

alfaiate ⑩ ow-faa-*yaa*-te *tailor*

alfândega ① aal-*fang*-de-gaa *customs*

algodão ⑩ ow-go-*downg* cotton

alguém ow-*geng someone*

alguma coisa ow-*goo*-maa *koy*-zaa *something*

alguns/algumas ⑩/①
ow-*goons*/ow-goo-maas *few* • *some*

alho ⑩ *aa*-lyo *garlic*

alimentar aa-lee-meng-*taarr feed*

almoço ⑩ ow-*mo*-so *lunch*

alpinismo ⑩ ow-pee-*nees*-mo *rock climbing*

altar ⑩ ow-*taarr altar*

altitude ① ow-tee-*too*-de *altitude*

alto/alta ⑩/① *ow*-to/*ow*-taa *high* • *loud* • *tall*

alucinação ① aa-loo-see-naa-*sowng hallucination*

alugar aa-loo-*gaarr hire* • *rent*

aluguel ⑩ **de carro** aa-loo-*gel* de *kaa*-ho *car hire*

amanhã aa-ma-*nyang tomorrow*
— **à noite** aa *noy*-te *tomorrow evening*
— **à tarde** aa *taarr*-de *tomorrow afternoon*
— **de manhã** de ma-*nyang tomorrow morning*

amante ⑩&① aa-*mang*-te *lover*

amar aa-*maarr love*

amarelo/amarela ⑩/①
aa-maa-*re*-lo/aa-maa-*re*-laa *yellow*

ambos/ambas ⑩/① *ang*-bos/*ang*-baas *both*

ameixa ① aa-*may*-shaa *plum*
— **seca** *se*-kaa *prune*

amêndoa ① aa-*meng*-dwaa *almond*

amendoim ⑩ aa-meng-do-*eeng groundnut* • *peanut*

amigo/amiga ⑩/①
aa-*mee*-go/aa-*mee*-gaa *friend*

amor ⑩ aa-*morr love*

analgésico ⑩ aa-now-*ge*-zee-ko *painkiller*

anarquista ⑩&① aa-naarr-*kees*-taa *anarchist*

ancião/anciã ⑩/① ang-see-*owng*/ ang-see-*ang ancient*

andar ⑩ ang-*daarr floor (storey)*

andar ang-*daarr walk*
— **à cavalo** aa kaa-*vaa*-lo *ride (horse)*
— **de bicicleta** de bee-see-*kle*-taa *cycle*
— **de skate** de ees-*kay*-te *skate*

anel ⑩ aa-*nel ring (on finger)*

anemia ① aa-ne-*mee*-aa *anaemia*

animal ⑩&① aa-nee-*mow animal*

aniversário ⑩ aa-nee-verr-*saa*-ryo *birthday*

ano ⑩ *a*-no *year*

antes *ang*-tes *before*

antes ⑩ **de ontem** *ung*-tes de *ong*-teng *day before yesterday*

antibióticos ⑩ pl ang-tee-bee-o-tee-kos *antibiotics*

anticoncepcional ⑩
ang-tee-kong-sep-syo-*now contraceptives*

antigo/antiga ⑩/①
ang-*tee*-go/ang-*tee*-gaa *antique*

antinuclear ang-tee-noo-kle-*aarr antinuclear*

anti-séptico ⑩ ang-tee-*sep*-tee-ko *antiseptic*

anúncio ⑩ aa-*noom*-see-o *advertisement*

ao lado de ow *laa*-do de *next to*

aparelho ⑩ **de surdez** aa-paa-*re*-lyo de soorr-*des hearing aid*

apartamento ⑩ aa-paarr-taa-*meng*-to *apartment* • *flat*

apelido ⑩ aa-pe-*lee*-do *nickname*

apêndice ⑩ aa-*peng*-dee-se *appendix (body)*

apertado/apertada ⑩/① aa-perr-*taa*-do/ aa-perr-*taa*-daa *tight*

apoio ⑩ **ao partido** aa-*po*-yo ow paarr-*tee*-do *supporter (politics)*

pontar aa·pong·taarr *point*
posentado/aposentada ⓜ/ⓕ
  aa·po·seng·*taa*·do/aa·po·seng·*taa*·daa
  retired
posta ⓕ aa·*pos*·taa *bet*
prender aa·preng·*derr* *learn*
presentação ⓕ aa·pre·seng·taa·*sowng*
  gig
proveitar aa·pro·vay·*taarr* *enjoy (oneself)*
quecimento ⓜ aa·ke·see·*meng*·to
  heating
qui aa·*kee* *here*
r ⓜ aarr *air*
r condicionado ⓜ aarr
  kong·dee·syo·*naa*·do *air-conditioning*
rame ⓜ aa·*ra*·me *wire*
ranha ⓕ aa·*ra*·nyaa *spider*
rea ⓕ **de serviço** *aa*·re·aa de serr·*vee*·so
  laundry (room)
reia ⓕ aa·*re*·yaa *sand*
renque ⓜ aa·*reng*·ke *herring*
rma ⓕ aarr·maa *gun*
rmário ⓜ aarr·*maa*·ryo
  cupboard • wardrobe
romaterapia ⓕ
  aa·ro·maa·te·raa·*pee*·aa *aromatherapy*
queológico/arqueológica ⓜ/ⓕ
  aarr·ke·o·*lo*·zhee·ko/
  aarr·ke·o·*lo*·zhee·kaa *archaeological*
quiteto/arquiteta ⓜ/ⓕ
  aarr·kee·*te*·to/aarr·kee·*te*·taa *architect*
quitetura ⓕ aar·kee·te·*too*·raa
  architecture
roz ⓜ aa·*hos* *rice*
te ⓕ *aarr*·te *art*
tes ⓜ pl **marciais** *aarr*·tes maar·see·*ais*
  martial arts
tesanato ⓜ aarr·te·zaa·*naa*·to *crafts •*
  handicrafts
tista ⓜ&ⓕ aar·*tees*·taa *artist*
  — de rua de hoo·aa *busker*
vore ⓕ *aarr*·vo·re *tree*
vezes aas *ve·zes sometimes*
as ⓕ pl *aa·zaas wings*
ia ⓕ *aa*·zyaa *Asia*
ma ⓕ *aas*·maa *asthma*
pargo ⓜ aas·*paarr*·go *asparagus*
pirina ⓕ aas·pee·ree·*naa* *aspirin*

assassinar aa·saa·see·*naarr* *murder*
assassinato ⓜ aa·saa·see·*naa*·to *murder*
assento ⓜ aa·*seng*·to *seat*
assinatura ⓕ aa·see·naa·*too*·raa *signature*
assuntos ⓜ pl **atuais** aa·*soong*·tos
  aa·too·*ais current affairs*
ataque ⓜ aa·*taa*·ke *strike*
  — de coração de ko·ra·*sowng*
  heart attack
até aa·*te until*
atípico/atípica ⓜ/ⓕ
  aa·*tee*·pee·ko/aa·*tee*·pee·kaa *unusual*
atirar aa·tee·*raarr shoot*
ativista ⓜ&ⓕ aa·tee·*vees*·taa *activist*
atletismo ⓜ aat·le·*tees*·mo *athletics*
atmosfera ⓕ aa·tee·mos·*fe*·raa
  atmosphere
atrás aa·*traas behind*
atrasado/atrasada ⓜ/ⓕ
  aa·traa·*zaa*·do/aa·traa·*zaa*·daa *late*
atraso ⓜ aa·*traa*·zo *delay*
através aa·traa·*ves across*
atum ⓜ aa·*toong tuna*
austrália ⓕ ows·*traa*·lya *Australia*
auto estrada ⓕ ow·to es·*traa*·daa
  motorway (tollway)
autônomo/autônoma ⓜ/ⓕ
  ow·to·no·mo/ow·to·no·maa
  self-employed
auto-serviço ⓜ ow·to·serr·*vee*·so
  self-service
aveia ⓕ aa·*ve*·aa *oats*
avelã ⓕ aa·ve·*lang hazelnut*
avenida ⓕ aa·ve·*nee*·daa *avenue*
avião ⓜ aa·vee·*owng airplane*
avisar aa·vee·*zaarr warn*
aviso ⓜ aa·*vee*·zo *sign*
avó ⓕ aa·*vaw grandmother*
avô ⓜ aa·*vo grandfather*
azeite ⓜ aa·*zay*·te *olive oil*
azeitona ⓕ aa·zay·to·*naa olive*
azul aa·*zool blue*

B

babá ⓕ baa·*baa babysitter*
bacana baa·*ka*·naa *nice*
bacon ⓜ *bay*·kong *bacon*

bagagem ① baa-*gaa*-zheng
  baggage • luggage
bagulho ⑩ baa-*goo*-lyo dope (drugs)
baía ① baa-*ee*-aa harbour
bairro ⑩ *bai*-ho suburb
baixo *bai*-sho down
baixo/baixa ⑩/① *bai*-sho/*bai*-shaa low
bala ① *baa*-laa candy
balanço ⑩ baa-*lang*-so balance (account)
balas ① pl *baa*-laas lollies
balcão ⑩ bow-*kowng* balcony •
  counter (at bar)
balde ⑩ *bow*-de bucket
balé ⑩ ba-*le* ballet
bálsamo ⑩ **para lábios** *bow*-sa-mo
  paa-raa *laa*-byos lip balm
banana ① baa-*na*-naa banana
banco ⑩ *bang*-ko bank
banda ① **(de música)** *bang*-daa (de
  moo-zee-kaa) band (music)
band-aid ⑩ *bang*-*day*-dee Band-Aid
bandeira ① bang-*day*-raa flag
banheira ① ba-*nyay*-raa bath
banheiro ⑩ ba-*nyay*-ro bathroom • toilet
  — público ba-*nyay*-ro poo-blee-ko
  public toilet
bar ⑩ baarr bar • pub
barata ① baa-*raa*-taa cockroach
barato/barata ⑩/①
  baa-*raa*-to/baa-*raa*-taa cheap
barbante ⑩ baarr-*bang*-te string
barbeiro ⑩ baarr-*bay*-ro barber
barco ⑩ *baar*-ko boat
barco ⑩ **à motor** *baar*-ko aa mo-*torr*
  motorboat
barraca ① baa-*haa*-kaa tent
barulhento/barulhenta ⑩/①
  baa-roo-*lyeng*-to/baa-roo-*lyeng*-taa noisy
baseball ⑩ *bay*-ze-bol baseball
basquete ⑩ baas-*ke*-te basketball
batata ① baa-*taa*-taa potato
bateria ① baa-te-*ree*-aa drum
batida ① baa-*tee*-daa crash
batismo ⑩ baa-*tees*-mo baptism
batom ⑩ ba-*tong* lipstick
bêbado/bêbada ⑩/①
  be-baa-do/be-baa-daa drunk
bebê ⑩&① be-*be* baby

bebida ① be-*bee*-daa drink
beijar bay-*zhaarr* kiss
beijo ⑩ *bay*-zho kiss
beira mar ① bay-raa maarr seaside
bem beng well
bem ⑩ **social** beng so-see-*ow* welfare
beringela ① be-reeng-*zhe*-la
  aubergine • eggplant
bermuda ① berr-*moo*-daa shorts
beterraba ① be-te-*haa*-baa beetroot
bexiga ① be-*shee*-gaa bladder
bezerro/bezerra ⑩/①
  be-ze-ho/be-ze-haa veal
bíblia ① *bee*-blyaa bible
biblioteca ① bee-blee-o-*te*-kaa library
bicho ⑩ *bee*-sho bug
bicicleta ① bee-see-*kle*-taa bicycle • bike
  — de corrida de ko-*hee*-daa racing bike
bife ⑩ *bee*-fe beef • steak
bilhete ⑩ bee-*lye*-te ticket
  — de stand by de ees-*tang*-dee bai
  standby ticket
bilheteria ① bee-lye-te-*ree*-aa ticket office
binóculos ⑩ pl bee-no-koo-los binocular
biquíni ⑩ **fio dental** bee-*kee*-nee fyo
  deng-*tow* g-string
biscoito ⑩ bees-*koy*-to biscuit • cookie
  — d'água *daa*-gwaa cracker
bloqueado/bloqueada ⑩/①
  blo-ke-*aa*-do/blo-ke-*aa*-daa blocked
boarding pass ⑩ borr-deeng paas
  boarding pass
boca ① *bo*-kaa mouth
bode ⑩ *bo*-de goat
bola ① *bo*-laa ball
  — de golfe de *gol*-fee golf ball
bolas ① pl **de algodão**
  bo-laas de ow-go-*downg* cotton balls
bolha ① *bo*-lyaa blister
bolo ⑩ *bo*-lo cake
  — de casamento de kaa-zaa-*meng*-to
  wedding cake
bolsa ① **de mão** *bol*-saa de mowng
  handbag
bolso ⑩ *bol*-so pocket
bom/boa ⑩/① bong/*bo*-aa
  fine • good • kind
bomba ① *bong*-baa pump

bonde m *bong-de cable car • tram*
boneco/boneca m/f
  bo-ne-ko/bo-ne-kaa doll
bonito/bonita m/f *bo-nee-to/bo-nee-taa handsome • beautiful*
borboleta f *borr-bo-le-taa butterfly*
borda f *borr-daa border*
borracha f *bo-haa-shaa gum*
bota f *bo-taa boot (footwear)*
botânico/botânica m/f
  bo-ta-nee-ko/bo-ta-nee-kaa herbalist
botas f pl *bo-taas boots (footwear)*
botões m pl *bo-toyngs buttons*
boxe m *bo-kee-see boxing*
braço m *braa-so arm*
branco/branca m/f
  brang-ko/brang-kaa white
brandy m *brang-dee brandy*
brilhante *bree-lyang-te brilliant*
brincos m pl *breeng-kos earrings*
brochura f *bro-shoo-raa brochure*
brócolis m pl *bro-ko-lees broccoli*
bronquite f *brong-kee-te bronchitis*
broto m **de feijão** *bro-to de fay-zhowng beansprout*
Budista *boo-dees-taa Buddhist*
buffet m *boo-fe buffet*
burro/burra m/f *boo-ho/boo-haa stupid*
business class f *bee-zee-nes klaas business class*

C

cabeça f *kaa-be-saa head*
cabeleireiro/cabeleireira m/f
  kaa-be-lay-ray-ro/kaa-be-lay-ray-raa hairdresser
cabelo m *kaa-be-lo hair*
caça f *kaa-saa hunting*
cacau m *ka-kow cocoa*
cachoeira f *kaa-sho-ay-raa waterfall*
cachorro m *kaa-sho-ho dog*
cada *kaa-daa each*
cadeado m *kaa-de-aa-do padlock*

cadeira f *kaa-day-raa chair*
  — de criança *de kree-ang-saa child seat*
  — de rodas *de ho-daas wheelchair*
  — para refeição *paa-raa he-fay-sowng highchair*
caderno m *kaa-derr-no notebook*
café m *kaa-fe cafe • coffee*
  — da manhã *da ma-nyang breakfast*
caixa f *kai-shaa box • cashier*
  — automático *ow-to-maa-tee-ko automatic teller machine (ATM)*
  — registradora *he-gees-traa-do-raa cash register*
  — de correio *de ko-hay-o mailbox*
  — de papelão *de paa-pe-lowng carton*
calçada f *kow-saa-daa footpath*
calças f pl *kow-saas pants • trousers*
calculadora f *kow-koo-laa-do-raa calculator*
caldo m *kow-do stock (food)*
calendário m *kaa-leng-daa-ryo calendar*
cama f *ka-maa bed*
  — de casal *de kaa-zow double bed*
camada f **de ozônio** *kaa-maa-daa de o-zo-nyo ozone layer*
câmara f *ka-maa-raa tube (tyre)*
  — de ar *de aarr inner tube*
camarão m *kaa-maa-rowng prawn*
camas f pl **gêmeas** *ka-maas zhe-me-aas twin beds*
câmbio m **de marcha** *kang-byo de maarr-shaa derailleur*
câmbio m **de valores** *kang-byo de vaa-lo-res currency exchange*
câmera f *ka-me-raa camera*
caminhada f *kaa-mee-nyaa-daa hiking*
caminhão m *kaa-mee-nyowng truck*
caminhar *kaa-mee-nyaarr hike*
caminho m *kaa-mee-nyo path • track • way*
camisa f *kaa-mee-zaa shirt*
camiseta f *kaa-mee-ze-taa singlet • T-shirt*
camisinha f *kaa-mee-zee-nyaa condom*
campeonatos m pl *kang-pe-o-naa-tos championships*
campo m **de golfe** *kang-po de gol-fee golf course*

camundongo ⓜ ka·moong·*dong*·go mouse

Canadá ⓜ kaa·naa·*daa* Canada

canção ⓕ kang·*sowng* song

cancelar kang·se·*laarr* cancel

câncer ⓜ *kang*·serr cancer

cândida ⓕ *kang*·dee·daa thrush (health)

caneta ⓕ ka·*ne*·taa pen (ballpoint)

canivete ⓜ kaa·nee·*ve*·te penknife • pocket knife

cansado/cansada ⓜ/ⓕ kang·*saa*·do/kang·*saa*·daa tired

cantar kang·*taarr* sing

cantor/cantora ⓜ/ⓕ kang·*torr*/kang·to·raa singer

cão-guia ⓜ kowng·*gee*·aa guide dog

capacete ⓜ kaa·paa·*se*·te helmet

capacho ⓜ kaa·*paa*·sho mat

caravan ⓕ kaa·raa·*vang* caravan

cardápio ⓜ kaarr·*daa*·pyo menu

caril ⓜ kaa·*reel* curry

carne ⓕ *kaar*·ne meat

— **moída** mo·ee·daa mince

caro/cara ⓜ/ⓕ *kaa*·ro/*kaa*·raa expensive

carpinteiro ⓜ karr·peeng·*tay*·ro carpenter

carregar kaa·he·*gaarr* carry

carro ⓜ *kaa*·ho car

carta ⓕ *kaarr*·taa letter (mail)

cartão ⓜ kaarr·*towng* credit card

— **de crédito** de *kre*·de·to credit card

— **postal** kaarr·*towng* pos·*tow* postcard

— **telefônico** kaarr·*towng* te·le·fo·nee·ko phonecard

cartas ⓕ pl *kaarr*·tas cards (playing)

cartaz ⓜ kaarr·*taz* poster

carteira ⓕ **de identidade** kaar·*tay*·raa de ee·deng·tee·*daa*·de identification card

carteira ⓕ **de motorista** kaar·*tay*·raa de mo·to·*rees*·taa drivers licence

cartucho ⓜ **de gás** kaarr·*too*·sho de gaas gas cartridge

casa ⓕ *kaa*·zaa home • house

— **de cômodos** de *ko*·mo·dos boarding house

— **de ópera** de o·pe·raa opera house

casaco ⓜ kaa·*zaa*·ko coat

— **de chuva** de *shoo*·vaa raincoat

casamento ⓜ kaa·zaa·*meng*·to marriage • wedding

casar kaa·*zaarr* marry

casino ⓜ kaa·*see*·no casino

castanha ⓕ **de cajú** kas·*ta*·nyaa de kaa·*zhoo* cashew

castanha ⓕ **portuguesa** kaas·*ta*·nyaa porr·too·ge·zaa chestnut

castelo ⓜ kaas·*te*·lo castle

catapora ⓕ kaa·taa·po·raa chicken pox

catedral ⓕ kaa·te·*drow* cathedral

Católico/Católica ⓜ/ⓕ kaa·to·lee·ko/kaa·to·lee·kaa Catholic

cavalgada ⓕ kaa·vaal·*gaa*·daa horse riding

cavalo ⓜ kaa·*vaa*·lo horse

caverna ⓕ kaa·*verr*·naa cave

caxumba ⓕ kaa·*shoong*·baa mumps

CD ⓜ se·*de* CD

cebola ⓕ se·*bo*·laa onion

cedo *se*·do early

cego/cega ⓜ/ⓕ se·*gò*/se·gaa blind

celular ⓜ se·loo·*laarr* mobile phone

cem seng hundred

cenoura ⓕ se·*no*·raa carrot

centavos ⓜ pl seng·*taa*·vos cent

centímetro ⓜ seng·*tee*·me·tro centimetre

central ⓕ **telefônica** seng·*trow* te·le·fo·nee·kaa telephone centre

centro ⓜ *seng*·tro centre

— **da cidade** daa see·*daa*·de city centre

cerâmica ⓕ se·*ra*·mee·kaa ceramics • pottery

cerca ⓕ *serr*·kaa fence

cereal ⓜ se·re·*ow* cereal

cereja ⓕ se·*re*·zhaa cherry

certidão ⓕ **de nascimento** serr·tee·*downg* de naa·see·*meng*·to birth certificate

certificado ⓜ serr·tee·fee·*kaa*·do certificate

cerveja ⓕ serr·*ve*·zhaa beer

cesta ⓕ *ses*·taa basket

céu ⓜ se·oo sky

chá ⓜ shaa tea

chão ⓜ showng floor

chapéu ⓜ shaa·*pe*·oo hat

charmoso/charmosa ⓜ/ⓕ shaarr·mo·zo/shaarr·mo·zaa *charming*

charuto ⓜ shaa·roo·to *cigar*

chave ⓕ shaa·ve *key*

checar she·kaarr *check*

check in ⓜ she·keeng *check-in (desk)*

chefe ⓜ&ⓕ de cozinha she·fe de ko·zee·nyaa *chef*

chegada(s) ⓕ sg/pl she·gaa·daa(s) *arrival*

chegar she·gaarr *arrive*

cheio/cheia ⓜ/ⓕ shay·o/shay·aa *full*

cheiro ⓜ shay·ro *smell*

cheque ⓜ she·ke *cheque (banking)*

chocolate ⓜ sho·ko·laa·te *chocolate*

chupeta ⓕ shoo·pe·taa *dummy • pacifier*

chutar shoo·taarr *kick (a ball)*

chuva ⓕ shoo·vaa *rain*

chuveiro ⓜ shoo·vay·ro *shower*

ciclismo ⓜ see·klees·mo *cycling*

ciclista ⓜ&ⓕ see·klees·taa *cyclist*

cidadania ⓕ see·daa·da·nee·aa *citizenship*

cidade ⓕ see·daa·de *city*

cidra ⓕ see·draa *cider*

ciências ⓕ pl see·eng·syaas *science*

cientista ⓜ&ⓕ see·eng·tees·taa *scientist*

cigarro ⓜ see·gaa·ho *cigarette*

cinema ⓜ see·ne·maa *cinema • movie*

Cingapura seen·gaa·poo·raa *Singapore*

cinto ⓜ de segurança seeng·to de se·goo·rang·saa *seatbelt*

cinza ⓕ seeng·zaa *gray*

cinzeiro ⓜ seen·zay·ro *ashtray*

circo ⓜ seerr·ko *circus*

ciroula ⓕ se·ro·laa *boxer shorts*

cistite ⓕ sees·tee·te *cystitis*

cisto ⓜ no ovário sees·to no o·vaa·ryo *ovarian cyst*

ciumento/ciumenta ⓜ/ⓕ see·oo·meng·to/see·oo·meng·taa *jealous*

classe ⓕ klaa·se *class (category)*

— econômica e·ko·no·mee·kaa *economy class*

clássico/clássica ⓜ/ⓕ klaa·see·ko/klaa·see·kaa *classical*

cliente ⓜ&ⓕ klee·eng·te *client*

cobertor ⓜ ko·berr·torr *blanket*

cobra ⓕ ko·braa *snake*

cobreiro ⓜ ko·bray·ro *shingles (illness)*

cocaína ⓕ ko·kaa·ee·naa *cocaine*

coceira ⓕ ko·say·raa *itch*

côco ⓜ ko·ko *coconut*

código postal ko·dee·go pos·tow *postcode*

coelho ⓜ ko·e·lyo *rabbit*

cofre ⓜ ko·fre *safe*

cogumelo ⓜ ko·goo·me·lo *mushroom*

coisa ⓕ koy·zaa *it*

cola ⓕ ko·laa *glue*

colar ⓜ ko·laarr *necklace*

colchão ⓜ kol·showng *mattress*

colega ⓜ&ⓕ ko·le·gaa *colleague*

colete salva-vidas ⓜ ko·le·te sow·vaa·vee·daas *life jacket*

colheita ⓕ de frutas ko·lyay·taa de froo·taas *fruit picking*

colher ⓕ ko·lyerr *spoon*

— de chá de shaa *teaspoon*

cólica ⓕ menstrual ko·lee·kaa mengs·troo·ow *period pain*

colírio ⓜ ko·lee·ryo *eye drops*

colocar ko·lo·kaarr *put*

com kong *with*

com pressa kong pre·saa *in a hurry*

começar ko·me·saarr *start*

começo ⓜ ko·me·so *start*

comédia ⓕ ko·me·dyaa *comedy*

comemoração ⓕ ko·me·mo·raa·sowng *celebration*

comer ko·merr *eat*

comércio ⓜ ko·merr·syo *trade*

comício ⓜ ko·mee·syo *rally*

comida ⓕ ko·mee·daa *food*

— de bebê de be·be *baby food*

como ko·mo *how*

companheiro/companheira ⓜ/ⓕ kong·pa·nyay·ro/kong·pa·nyay·raa *companion*

companhia ⓕ kong·paa·nhaa *company*

compasso ⓜ kong·paa·so *compass*

comprar kong·praarr *buy*

compreender kong·pre·eng·derr *understand*

computador ⓜ kong·poo·taa·dorr *computer*

comunhão ⓕ ko·moo·nyowng *communion*

comunicação ① ko·moo·nee·kaa·*sowng* communication • communications (profession)

comunista ⓜ&① ko·moo·nees·taa communist

concordar kong·korr·*daarr* agree

condicionador ⓜ kong·dee·syo·naa·*dorr* conditioner

conecção ① ko·ne·kee·*sowng* connection (phone)

confeitaria ① kong·fay·taa·*ree*·aa cake shop

confirmar kong·feerr·*maarr* confirm (a booking)

confissão ① kong·fee·*sowng* confession

confortável kong·forr·*taa*·vel comfortable

congelar kong·zhe·*laarr* freeze

conjuntivite ① kong·zhoong·tee·*vee*·te conjunctivitis

conselho ⓜ kong·se·lyo advice

consertar kong·serr·*taarr* repair

conservador/conservadora ⓜ/① kong·serr·vaa·*dorr*/kong·serr·vaa·do raa conservative

constipação ① kongs·tee·paa·*sowng* constipation

construir kongs·troo·*eerr* build

construtor ⓜ kongs·troo·*tor* builder

consulado ⓜ kong·soo·*laa*·do consulate

consulta ① kong·*sool*·taa appointment

conta ① kong·taa bill • cheque
— **bancária** bang·*kaa*·rya bank account

contar kong·*taarr* count

contar os pontos kong·*taarr* os *pong*·tos score

contrato ⓜ kong·*traa*·to contract

controle ⓜ **remoto** kong·*tro*·le he·*mo*·to remote control

convento ⓜ kong·*veng*·to convent

conversar kong·verr·*saarr* chat

convidar kong·vee·*daar* invite

Copa do Mundo ① ko·paa do *moong*·do World Cup

cor ① korr colour

coração ⓜ ko·ra·*sowng* heart

corajoso/corajosa ⓜ/① ko·raa·*zho*·zo/ko·raa·*zho*·zaa brave

corda ① korr·*daa* rope
— **de roupa** de *ho*·paa clothesline

cordilheira ① korr·dee·*lyay*·raa mountain range

coriza ① ko·ree·zaa runny nose

corpo ⓜ korr·po body

corredor ⓜ ko·he·dorr aisle

correia ① ko·hay·aa fanbelt

correio ⓜ ko·hay·o post office
— **registrado** he·zhees·*traa*·do registered mail

corrente ① ko·heng·te chain • current (electricity)
— **de bicicleta** de bee·see·*kle*·taa bike chain

correr ko·*herr* run

correspondência ① ko·hes·pong·*deng*·syaa mail
— **via aéreo/aérea** ⓜ/① vee·aa aa·e·re·o/aa·e·re·aa airmail
— **via terrestre** vee·aa te·*hes*·tre surface mail

correto/correta ⓜ/① ko he·to/ko·he·taa right (correct)

corrida ① ko·hee·daa jogging • race • running

corrimão ⓜ ko·hee·*mowng* handlebars

corrimento ⓜ ko·hee·*meng*·to thrush (health)

corrupto/corrupta ⓜ/① koo·hoo·pee·to/koo·hoo·pee·taa corrupt

cortador ⓜ **de unhas** korr·taa·*dorr* de oo·nyaas nail clippers

cortar korr·*taarr* cut

corte ① korr·te court (legal)

costa ① kos·taa coast

costas ① kos·taas back (body)

costela ① kos·*te*·laa rib

costurar kos·too·*raarr* sew

cotonete ⓜ ko·to·*ne*·te cotton buds

couro ⓜ ko·ro leather
— **cabeludo** kaa·be·*loo*·do scalp

couve ① **flor** ko·ve florr cauliflower

couvert ⓜ **artístico** koo·*verr* aarr·*tees*·tee·ko cover charge

cozido/cozida ⓜ/① ko·zee·do/ko·zee·daa hard-boiled

cozinha ① ko-*zee*-nyaa *kitchen*

cozinhar ko-zee-*nyaar* *cook*

cozinheiro/cozinheira ⓜ/①
ko-zee-*nyay*-ro/ko-zee-*nyay*-raa *cook*

crânio ⓜ *kra*-nyo *skull*

creche ① *kre*-she *creche*

creme ⓜ *kre*-me *cream*

— **azedo** aa-*ze*-do *sour cream*

— **de barbear** de baarr-be-*aarr*
shaving cream

crer krerr *trust*

crescer kres-*serr* *grow*

criança kree-*ang*-saa *child*

crianças pl kree-*ang*-saas *children*

cricket ⓜ *kree*-ke-tee *cricket (sport)*

Cristão/Cristã ⓜ/①
krees-*towng*/krees-*tayng* *Christian*

cru/crua ⓜ/① kroo/*kroo*-aa *raw*

cruz ① kroos *cross (religious)*

cuidado ⓜ **da criança** kooy-*daa*-do de
kree-*ang*-saa *childminding*

cuidar kooy-*daarr* *look after* • *watch*

culpa ① *kool*-paa *(someone's) fault*

culpado/culpada ⓜ/① kool-*paa*-do/
kool-*paa*-daa *guilty*

cupom ⓜ koo-*pong coupon*

curativo ⓜ koo-raa-*tee*-vo *bandage*

currículum ⓜ koo-*hee*-koo-loom
resume (CV)

curto/curta ⓜ/① *koor*-to/*koor*-taa *short*

cuscuz ⓜ **marroquino** koos-*koos*
maa-ho-*kee*-no *couscous*

custar koos-*taarr cost*

CV ⓜ se-*ve CV*

D

dados ⓜ pl *daa*-dos *dice*

damasco ⓜ daa-*maas*-ko *apricot*

dança ① *dang*-saa *dancing*

dançar dang-*saarr dance*

dar daarr *give • deal (cards)*

data ① *daa*-taa *date (day)*

— **de nascimento** de naa-see-*meng*-to
date of birth

de costas de kos-*taas back (position)*

de segunda mão de se-*goong*-daa
mowng *second-hand*

decidir de-see-*deer* decide

dedo ⓜ *de*-do *finger*

— **do pé** do pe *toe*

defeituoso/defeituosa ⓜ/①
de-fay-too-*o*-zo/de-fay-too-*o*-zaa *faulty*

deficiente de-fee-see-*eng*-te *disabled*

deitar day-*taarr lie (not stand)*

dela *de*-laa *her*

dele *de*-le *his*

delegacia ① **de polícia** de-le-gaa-*see*-aa
de po-*lee*-sya *police station*

deles *de*-les *their*

delicatessen ① de-lee-kaa-*te*-seng
delicatessen

demais de-*mais too (much)*

democracia ① de-mo-kraa-*see*-aa
democracy

demonstração ① de-mongs-traa-*sowng*
demonstration

dente(s) ⓜ *deng*-te(s) *tooth (teeth)*

dentista ⓜ&① deng-*tees*-taa *dentist*

dentro *deng*-tro *inside*

— **de (uma hora)** de (*oo*-maa *aw*-raa)
within (an hour)

depois de-*poys after*

— **de amanhã** de aa-maa-*nyang*
day after tomorrow

depósito ⓜ de-po-*zee*-to *deposit*

derrame ⓜ de-*ha*-me *stroke (health)*

desabrigado/desabrigada ⓜ/①
de-zaa-bree-*gaa*-do/de-zaa-bree-*gaa*-daa
homeless

descansar des-kang-*saarr rest*

descendente ⓜ&① de-seng-*deng*-te
descendent

desconfortável des-kong-forr-*taa*-vel
uncomfortable

descontar des-kong-*taarr*
(um cheque) (oom *she*-ke) *cash (a cheque)*

desconto ⓜ des-*kong*-to *discount*

desde *des*-de *since*

desejar de-ze-*zhaarr wish*

deserto ⓜ de-*zerr*-to *desert*

desflorestamento ⓜ
des-flo-res-taa-*meng*-to *deforestation*

design ⓜ design *design*

desistir de-zees-*teerr quit*

deslocamento ⓜ des·lo·kaa·*meng*·to
   sprain
desodorante ⓜ de·zo·do·*rang*·te
   deodorant
despertador ⓜ des·perr·taa·*dorr*
   alarm clock
destino ⓜ des·*tee*·no *destination*
detalhes ⓜ pl de·*taa*·lyes *details*
deus ⓜ *de*·oos *god*
devagar de·vaa·*gaarr* *slow*
dever de·*verr* *owe*
dezembro de·*zeng*·bro *December*
dia ① *dee*·aa *day*
Dia ① **de Ano Novo** *dee*·aa de a·no no·vo
   New Year's Day
Dia ⓜ **de Natal** *dee*·aa de naa·*tow*
   Christmas Day
diabetes ① dee·aa·*be*·tes *diabetes*
diafragma ⓜ dee·aa·*fraa*·gee·maa
   diaphragm
diário ⓜ dee·*aa*·ryo *diary*
diarréia ① dee·aa·*hay*·aa *diarrhoea*
dicionário ⓜ dee·syo·*naa*·ryo *dictionary*
dieta ① dee·*e*·taa *diet*
diferença ① **de horário** dee·fe·*reng*·saa
   de o·*raa*·ryo *time difference*
diferente dee·fe·*reng*·te *different*
difícil dee·*fee*·seel *difficult*
Dinamarca ① dee·naa·*maarr*·kaa
   Denmark
dinheiro ⓜ dee·*nyay*·ro *money*
(à) direita ① (aa) dee·*ray*·taa *right*
   (direction)
direitista dee·ray·*tees*·taa *right-wing*
direto/direta ⓜ/① dee·*re*·to/dee·*re*·taa
   direct • straight
diretor/diretora ⓜ/① dee·re·*torr*/
   dee·re·to·raa *director*
direitos ⓜ pl **civis** dee·*ray*·tos see·*vees*
   civil rights
direitos ⓜ pl **humanos** dee·*ray*·tos
   oo·*ma*·nos *human rights*
dirigir dee·ree·*zheerr* *drive*
disco ⓜ *dees*·ko *disco*
discriminação ①
   dees·kree·mee·naa·*sowng*
   discrimination
discutir dees·koo·*teerr* *argue*

disk ⓜ deesk *disk (computer)*
DIU ⓜ *dee*·oo *IUD*
diversos/diversas ⓜ/① pl
   dee·*verr*·sos/dee·*verr*·saas *several*
divertido/divertida ⓜ/①
   dee·verr·*tee*·do/dee·verr·*tee*·daa *fun*
divertir-se dee·verr·*teerr*·se *have fun*
dividir dee·vee·*deerr* *share (with)*
dizer dee·*zerr* *say • tell*
doce ① *do*·se *sweet*
documentário ⓜ do·koo·meng·*taa*·ryo
   documentary
doença ① do·*eng*·saa *disease*
   — venérea ve·ne·ryaa *venereal disease*
doente do·*eng*·te *sick*
dólar ⓜ *do*·laarr *dollar*
dolorido/dolorida ⓜ/①
   do·lo·*ree*·do/do·lo·*ree*·daa *sore*
doloroso/dolorosa ⓜ/①
   do·lo·ro·zo/do·lo·ro·zaa *painful*
domingo ⓜ do·*meeng*·go *Sunday*
dona ① **de casa** *do*·naa de *kaa*·zaa
   homemaker
dono/dona ⓜ/① *do*·no/*do*·naa *owner*
dor ① dorr *pain*
   — de cabeça de kaa·*be*·saa *headache*
   — de dente de *deng*·te *toothache*
   — de estômago de es·*to*·maa·go
   stomachache
dormir dorr·*meerr* *sleep*
drama ⓜ *dra*·maa *drama*
droga ① *dro*·gaa *drug*
duas vezes *doo*·aas *ve*·zes *twice*
duplo/dupla ⓜ/① *doo*·plo/*doo*·plaa
   double
duro/dura ⓜ/① *doo*·ro/*doo*·raa *hard*
dúzia ① *doo*·zyaa *dozen*
DVD ⓜ de·ve·*de* *DVD*

E

e e *and*
eczema ⓜ e·*kee*·ze·maa *eczema*
editor/editora ⓜ/①
   e·dee·*torr*/e·dee·to·raa *editor*
editoração ① e·dee·to·raa·*sowng*
   publishing
educação ① e·doo·ka·*sowng* *education*

egoísta e-go-ees-taa *selfish*

ela e-laa *she*

ele e-le *he*

eleição ⓕ e-lay-sowng *election*

eles e-les *they*

eletricidade ⓕ e-le-tree-see-daa-de *electricity*

elevador ⓜ e-le-vaa-dorr *elevator • lift (elevator)*

em eng *in*
— **em breve** bre-ve *soon*
— **cima** see-maa *up*
— **direção à** dee-re-sowng aa *towards*
— **espécie** es-pe-sye *cash*
— **frente** freng-te *ahead*

embaixada ⓕ eng-bai-shaa-daa *embassy*

embaixador/embaixadora ⓜ/ⓕ eng-bai-shaa-dorr/eng-bai-shaa-do-raa *ambassador*

embreagem ⓕ eng-bre-aa-zheng *clutch (car)*

embrulho ⓜ eng-broo-lyo *package*

emergência ⓕ e-merr-zheng-syaa *emergency*

empregado/empregada ⓜ/ⓕ eng-pre-gaa-do/eng-pre-gaa-daa *employee*

empregador/empregadora ⓜ/ⓕ eng-pre-gaa-dorr/eng-pre-gaa-do-raa *employer*

emprego ⓜ eng-pre-go *job*

emprestar eng-pres-taarr *borrow*

empurrar eng-poo-haarr *push*

enchente ⓕ eng-sheng-te *flood*

encher eng-sherr *fill*

encomenda ⓕ eng-ko-meng-daa *parcel*

encontrar eng-kong-traarr *find • meet*

endereço ⓜ eng-de-re-so *address*

energia ⓕ **nuclear** e-nerr-zhee-aa noo-kle-aarr *nuclear energy*

enfermeira ⓕ eng-ferr-may-raa *nurse*

engenharia ⓕ eng-zhe-nya-ree-aa *engineering*

engenheiro/engenheira ⓜ/ⓕ eng-zhe-nyay-ro/eng-zhe-nyay-raa *engineer*

engraçado/engraçada ⓜ/ⓕ eng-graa-saa-do/eng-graa-saa-daa *funny*

enguiçar eng-gee-saarr *break down*

enjoado/enjoada ⓜ/ⓕ en-zho-aa-do/en-zho-aa-daa *seasick*

enjôo ⓜ en-zho-o *morning sickness*
— **de viagem** de vee-aa-zheng *travel sickness*

enorme e-norr-me *huge*

ensolarado/ensolarada ⓜ/ⓕ eng-so-laa-raa-do/eng-so-laa-raa-daa *sunny*

entediado/entediada ⓜ/ⓕ eng-te-dee-aa-do/eng-te-dee-aa-daa *bored*

entediante eng-te-dee-ang-te *boring*

enterro ⓜ eng-te-ho *funeral*

entrar eng-traarr *enter*

entre eng-tre *between*

entregar eng-tre-gaarr *deliver*

entrevista ⓕ eeng-tre-vees-taa *interview*

envelope eng-ve-lo-pe *envelope*

envergonhado/envergonhada ⓜ/ⓕ en-verr-go-nyaa-do/en-verr-go-nyaa-daa *embarrassed*

enviar eng-vee-aarr *send*

enxaqueca ⓕ en-shaa-ke-kaa *migraine*

epilepsia ⓕ e-pe-le-pee-see-aa *epilepsy*

equipamento ⓜ e-kee-paa-meng-to *equipment*
— **de mergulho** de merr-goo-lyo *diving equipment*

errado/errada ⓜ/ⓕ e-haa-do/e-haa-daa *wrong*

erro ⓜ e-ho *mistake*

ervilha ⓕ err-vee-lyaa *pea*

escada ⓕ **rolante** es-kaa-daa ho-lang-te *escalator*

escadaria ⓕ es-kaa-daa-ree-aa *stairway*

escassez ⓕ es-kaa-ses *shortage*

Escócia ⓕ es-ko-syaa *Scotland*

escola ⓕ es-ko-laa *school*

escolher es-ko-lyerr *choose*

escova ⓕ es-ko-vaa *brush (hair)*
— **de dentes** de deng-tes *toothbrush*

escrever es-kre-verr *write*

E

brazilian portuguese–english

235

escritor/escritora ⓜ/ⓕ
es·kree·*torr*/es·kree·to·raa *writer*

escritório ⓜ es·kree·to·ryo *office*
— **de achados e perdidos** de
aa·*shaa*·dos e perr·*dee*·dos
lost-property office
— **de turismo** de too·*rees*·mo
tourist office

escriturário/escriturária ⓜ/ⓕ
es·kree·too·*raa*·ryo/es·kree·too·*raa*·ryaa
office worker

escultor/escultor ⓜ/ⓕ
es·kool·*toorr*/es·kool·*too*·ra *sculptor*

escultura ⓕ es·kool·*too*·raa *sculpture*

escuro/escura ⓜ/ⓕ es·koo·ro/es·*koo*·raa
dark

escutar es·koo·*taarr* *hear • listen*

esempregado/desempregada ⓜ/ⓕ
de·zeng·pre·*gaa*·do/
de·zeng·pre·*gaa*·daa *unemployed*

esgotado/esgotada ⓜ/ⓕ es·go·*taa*·do/
es·go·*taa*·daa *booked out*

esgrima ⓕ es·*gree*·maa *fencing (sport)*

eski ⓝ **aquático** es·kee aa·*kwaa*·tee·ku
waterskiing

espaço ⓜ es·*pa*·so *space*

Espanha ⓕ es·*pa*·nyaa *Spain*

especial es·pe·see·*ow* *special*

especialista ⓜ&ⓕ es·pe·see·aa·*lees*·taa
specialist

espécies ⓕ pl **ameaçadas de extinção**
es·*pe*·syes aa·me·aa·*saa*·daas de
es·teeng·*sowng endangered species*

espelho ⓜ es·*pe*·lyo *mirror*

esperar es·pe·*raarr hope • wait*

espinafre ⓜ es·pee·*naa*·fre *spinach*

esporte ⓜ es·*porr*·te *sport*

esportista ⓜ&ⓕ es·porr·*tees*·taa
sportsperson

esposa ⓕ es·*po*·zaa *wife*

esquecer es·ke·*serr forget*

(à) esquerda ⓕ (aa) es·*kerr*·daa *left
(direction)*

esquerdista es·kerr·*dees*·taa *left-wing*

esqui ⓜ es·*kee skiing*

esquiar es·kee·*aarr ski*

esquina ⓕ es·*kee*·naa *corner*

esta ⓕ es·*taa this*

estaca ⓕ es·*taa*·kaa *tent peg*

estação ⓕ es·*taa*·sowng *season • station*
— **de trem** de treng *railway station*

estacionamento ⓜ
es·*taa*·syo·naa·*meng*·to *car park*

estacionar es·*taa*·syo·*naarr park (vehicle)*

estádio ⓜ es·*taa*·dyo *stadium*

estado ⓜ **civil** es·*taa*·do see·*veel
marital status*

estar es·*taarr be (temporary)*
— **resfriado** hes·free·*aa*·do *have a cold*

estátua ⓕ es·*taa*·twaa *statue*

este ⓜ es·te *this*

estéreo ⓜ es·*te*·ryo *stereo*

estilo ⓜ es·*tee*·lo *style*

estômago ⓜ es·*to*·maa·go *stomach*

estória ⓕ es·*to*·ryaa *story*

estrada ⓕ es·*traa*·daa *road*

estragado/estragada ⓜ/ⓕ
es·traa·*gaa*·do/es·traa·*gaa*·daa *off (food)*

estrangeiro/estrangeira ⓜ/ⓕ
es·trang·*zhay*·ro/es·trang·*zhay*·raa
foreign

estranho/estranha ⓜ/ⓕ es·*tra*·nyo/
es·*tra*·nyaa *strange • stranger*

estrela ⓕ es·*tre*·laa *star*

estrupar es·troo·*paarr rape*

estrupo ⓜ es·*troo*·po *rape*

estudante es·too·*dang*·te *student*

estúdio ⓜ es·*too*·dyo *studio*

estufa ⓕ es·*too*·faa *heater*

etiqueta ⓕ **de bagagem** e·tee·*ke*·taa de
baa·gaa·*zheng luggage tag*

eu e·oo *I*

EUA ⓜ pl e·waa *USA*

euro ⓜ *e·oo*·ro *euro*

Europa ⓕ e·oo·ro·paa *Europe*

eutanásia ⓕ e·oo·taa·*naa*·zyaa
euthanasia

evitar e·vee·*taarr stop (prevent)*

exame ⓜ **de sangue** e·za·me de *sang*·ge
blood test

exame ⓜ **papa nicolau** e·za·me paa·paa
nee·ko·*low pap smear*

exaustor ⓜ e·zows·*torr exhaust (car)*

excelente e·se·*leng*·te *excellent*

excluído/excluída ⓜ/ⓕ es·kloo·*ee*·do/
es·kloo·*ee*·daa *excluded*

excursão ① es·koorr·*sowng tour*
— **guiada** ① gee·*aa*·daa *guided tour*
exemplo ⑩ e·*zeng*·plo *example*
experiência ① es·pe·ree·*eng*·syaa
experience
exploração ① es·plo·raa·*sowng*
exploitation
exposição ① es·po·zee·*sowng exhibition*
expresso/expressa ⑩/①
es·*pre*·so/es·*pre*·saa *express*
êxtase ⑩ es·*taa*·ze *ecstasy (drug)*
extensão ① es·teng·*sowng*
extension
exterior es·te·ree·*orr abroad*

F

fã ⑩&① fang *fan (sport, etc)*
fábrica ① faa·*bree*·kaa *factory*
faca ① faa·kaa *knife*
fácil faa·*seel easy*
falar faa·*laarr speak • talk*
falta ① fow·taa *foul*
família ① faa·*mee*·lyaa *family*
faminto/faminta ⑩/① faa·meeng·to/
faa·*meeng*·taa *hungry*
famoso/famosa ⑩/① faa·*mo*·zo/
faa·*mo*·zaa *famous*
farinha ① faa·*ree*·nyaa *flour*
farmácia ① faar·*maa*·syaa *pharmacy*
faróis ⑩ pl faa·*roys headlight*
fazenda ① faa·*zeng*·daa *farm*
fazendeiro/fazendeira ⑩/①
faa·zeng·*day*·ro/faa·zeng·*day*·raa *farmer*
fazer faa·*zerr do • make*
febre ① fe·bre *fever*
— **do feno** do fe·no *hay fever*
— **glandular** glang·doo·*laar*
glandular fever
fechado/fechada ⑩/① fe·*shaa*·do/
fe·*shaa*·daa *closed • shut*
fechar fe·*shaarr close*
feijão ⑩ fay·*zhowng bean*
feito/feita ⑩/① à mão fay·to/fay·taa aa
mowng *handmade*
feliz fe·*lees happy*
férias ① pl fe·*ryaas holiday • vacation*
ferimento ⑩ fe·ree·*meng*·to *injury*

ferro ⑩ **de passa roupas** fe·ho de
paa·*saarr* ho·paas *iron (clothes)*
festa ① fes·taa *party (social gathering)*
festival ⑩ fes·tee·*vow festival*
fevereiro fe·ve·*ray*·ro *February*
ficar fee·*kaarr stay*
ficção ① feek·*sowng fiction*
fígado ⑩ fee·gaa·do *liver*
figo ⑩ fee·go *fig*
fila ① fee·laa *queue*
— **de táxi** de taak·*see taxi stand*
filé ⑩ fee·*le fillet*
filha ① fee·lyaa *daughter*
filho ① fee·lyo *son*
filme ⑩ feel·me *film (cinema)*
— **fotográfico** fo·to·*graa*·fee·ko
film (photography)
filtrado/filtrada ⑩/① feel·*traa*·do/
feel·*traa*·daa *filtered*
fim ⑩ feeng *end*
final ⑩ **de semana** fee·*now* de se·*ma*·naa
weekend
fino/fina ⑩/① fee·no/fee·naa *thin*
fio ⑩ **dental** fee·o deng·tow *dental floss*
fita ① **cassete** fee·taa kaa·se·te *cassette*
fita ① **de vídeo** fee·taa de *vee*·de·o
video tape
flanela ① fla·*ne*·laa *flannel*
flash luminoso flash loo·mee·*no*·zo
flashlight
flor ① florr *flower*
floresta ① flo·*res*·taa *forest*
floricultura ① flo·ree·kool·*too*·raa
florist (shop)
florista ⑩&① flo·*rees*·taa *florist (person)*
fogão ⑩ fo·*gowng stove*
fogo ⑩ fo·go *fire*
folha ① fo·lyaa *leaf*
fora fo·raa *outside*
forma ① forr·maa *shape*
formiga ① forr·*mee*·gaa *ant*
forno ⑩ forr·no *oven*
forte forr·te *strong*
fósforos ⑩ pl fos·fo·ros *matches*
fotografia ① fo·to·graa·*fee*·aa *photograph •*
photography
fotógrafo/fotógrafa ⑩/① fo·to·graa·fo/
fo·to·gra·faa *photographer*

fotômetro ⓜ fo·to·me·tro *light meter*

fraco/fraca ⓜ/ⓕ fraa·ko/fraa·kaa *weak*

frágil fraa·zheel *fragile*

fralda ⓕ frow·daa *diaper • nappy*

framboesa ⓕ frang·bo·e·zaa *raspberry*

freio ⓜ fray·o *brake*

freira ⓕ fray·raa *nun*

frequentemente fre·kweng·te·meng·te *often*

frigideira ⓕ free·zhee·day·raa *frying pan*

frio ⓜ free·o *cold*

frio/fria ⓜ/ⓕ free·o/free·aa *cold*

fritar free·taarr *fry*

frito/frita ⓜ/ⓕ free·to/free·taa *fried*

fronha ⓕ fro·nyaa *pillowcase*

fruta ⓕ froo·taa *fruit*

frutas ⓕ pl **secas** froo·taas se·kaas *dried fruit*

fumado/fumada ⓜ/ⓕ foo·maa·do/foo·maa·daa *stoned (drugged)*

fumar foo·maarr *smoke*

furo ⓜ foo·ro *puncture*

futebol americano foo·te·bol aa·me·ree·ka·no *American football*

futebol ⓜ foo·te·bol *football • soccer*

futuro ⓜ foo·too·ro *future*

G

galeria ⓕ **de arte** gaa·le·ree·aa de aarr·te *art gallery*

galinha ⓕ gaa·lee·nyaa *chicken*

ganhador/ganhadora ⓜ/ⓕ ga·nyaa·dorr/ga·nyaa·do·raa *winner*

ganhar ga·nyaarr *earn • win*

garçon/garçonete ⓜ/ⓕ gaarr·song/gaarr·so·ne·te *waiter*

garfo ⓜ gaarr·fo *fork*

garganta ⓕ gaarr·gang·taa *throat*

garrafa ⓕ gaa·haa·faa *bottle*

— d'água daa·gwaa *water bottle*

gás ⓜ gas *gas (for cooking)*

gasolina ⓕ gaa·zo·lee·naa *gas (petrol)*

gastrenterite ⓕ gaas·treng·te·ree·te *gastroenteritis*

gato/gata ⓜ/ⓕ gaa·to/gaa·taa *cat*

gay gay *gay*

gaze ⓕ gaa·ze *gauze*

geada ⓕ zhe·aa·daa *frost*

geladeira ⓕ zhe·laa·day·raa *refrigerator*

geléia ⓕ zhe·le·yaa *jam*

gelo ⓜ zhe·lo *ice*

gêmeos/gêmeas ⓜ/ⓕ zhe·me·os/zhe·me·aas *twins*

gengiva ⓕ zheng·zhee·vaa *gum (part of mouth)*

gerente ⓜ&ⓕ zhe·reng·te *manager*

gilete ⓕ zhee·le·te *razor blade*

gin ⓜ zheen *gin*

ginástica ⓕ zhee·naas·tee·kaa *gym*

— olímpica o·leeng·pee·kaa *gymnastics*

ginecologista ⓜ&ⓕ zhee·ne·ko·lo·zhees·taa *gynaecologist*

gol ⓜ gol *goal (sport)*

goleiro/goleira ⓜ/ⓕ go·lay·ro/go·lay·raa *goalkeeper*

goma ⓕ **de mascar** go·maa de maas·kaarr *chewing gum*

gordo/gorda ⓜ/ⓕ gorr·do/gorr·daa *fat*

gorgeta ⓕ gorr·zhe·taa *tip (gratuity)*

gostar gos·taarr *like*

gostar (de alguém) gos·taarr (de ow·geng) *care (for someone)*

gostoso/gostosa ⓜ/ⓕ gos·to·zo/gos·to·zaa *tasty*

governo ⓜ go·verr·no *government*

grama ⓕ graa·maa *gram • grass*

grande grang·de *large • big*

grão ⓜ **de bico** growng de bee·ko *chickpea*

gratuito/gratuita graa·too·ee·to/graa·too·ee·taa *free (gratis)*

graus ⓜ pl grows *degrees (temperature)*

gravação ⓕ graa·vaa·sowng *recording*

gravar graa·vaarr *record*

grávida ⓕ graa·vee·daa *pregnant*

gripe ⓕ gree·pe *influenza*

gritar gree·taarr *shout*

grosso/grossa ⓜ/ⓕ gro·so/gro·saa *thick*

grupo ⓜ **sanguíneo** groo·po sang·gwee·ne·o *blood group*

guarda ⓜ **volumes** gwaarr·daa vo·loo·mes *cloakroom • luggage locker*

guarda-chuva ⓜ gwaarr·daa·shoo·vaa *umbrella*

guardanapo ⓜ gwaar-daa-*naa*-po
  napkin • serviette
guerra ⓕ ge-haa war
guia ⓜ/ⓕ gee-aa guide (person)
guia ⓜ/ⓕ gee-aa guidebook
  — **auditivo** ⓜ ow-dee-*tee*-vo
  guide (audio)
  — **de entretenimento** de
  eng-tre-te-nee-*meng*-to
  entertainment guide
guitarra ⓕ gee-*taa*-haa guitar

H

há (três dias) aa (tres *dee*-aas)
  (three days) ago
halal aa-*low* halal
handebol ⓜ *heng*-de-bol handball
hematoma ⓜ e-maa-*to*-maa bruise
hepatite ⓕ e-paa-*tee*-te hepatitis
heroína ⓕ e-ro-ee-naa heroin
hidratante ⓜ ee-draa-*tang*-te moisturiser
Hindu eeng-*doo* Hindu
história ⓕ ees-*to*-rya history
histórico/histórica ⓜ/ⓕ ees-*to*-ree-ko/
  ees-*to*-ree-kaa historical
HIV ⓜ aa-*gaa* ee ve HIV
hockey ⓜ ho-*kay* hockey
hoje o-zhee today
hoje à noite o-zhee aa *noy*-te tonight
homem ⓜ o-meng man
  — **de negócios** de ne-*go*-syos
  businessman
homeopatia ⓕ o-me-o-paa-*tee*-aa
  homeopathy
homosexual o-mo-sek-soo-*ow*
  homosexual
hora ⓕ **marcada** aw-raa maarr-*kaa*-daa
  date (appointment)
horário ⓜ o-*raa*-rio timetable
horário ⓜ **de funcionamento** o-*raa*-ryo
  de foon-syo-naa-*meng*-to opening hours
horóscopo ⓜ o-*ros*-ko-po horoscope
horrível o-*hee*-vel awful
hospedagem ⓕ os-pe-*daa*-zheng
  accommodation
hospital ⓜ os-pee-*tow* hospital

hospitalidade ⓕ os-pee-taa-lee-*daa*-de
  hospitality
hotel ⓜ o-*tel* hotel
humanidades ⓕ pl oo-ma-nee-*daa*-des
  humanities

I

ida ⓕ ee-daa one-way (ticket)
ida e volta ⓕ ee-daa e *vol*-taa return (ticket)
idade ⓕ ee-*daa*-de age
identificação ⓕ ee-deng-tee-fee-kaa-*sowng*
  identification
idiota ⓜ&ⓕ ee-dee-o-taa idiot
igreja ⓕ ee-*gre*-zhaa church
igualdade ⓕ ee-gwow-*daa*-de equality
ilha ⓕ ee-*lyaa* island
imigração ⓕ ee-mee-graa-*sowng*
  immigration
importante eeng-porr-*tang*-te important
imposto ⓜ eeng-*pos*-to tax
  — **de renda** de *heng*-daa income tax
  — **sobre venda** so-bre *veng*-daa
  sales tax
inchaço ⓜ eeng-*shaa*-so swelling
incluso/inclusa ⓜ/ⓕ eeng-*kloo*-zo/
  eeng-*kloo*-zaa included
Índia ⓕ *eeng*-dyaa India
indicador ⓜ eeng-dee-kaa-*dorr* indicator
indigestão ⓕ eeng-dee-zhes-*towng*
  indigestion
indústria ⓕ eeng-*doos*-tryaa industry
infecção ⓕ eeng-fek-*sowng* infection
  — **urinária** oo-ree-*naa*-ryaa
  urinary infection
inflamação ⓕ eeng-fla-maa-*sowng*
  inflammation
Inglaterra ⓕ eeng-glaa-*te*-haa England
Inglês ⓜ eeng-*gles* English (language)
ingrediente ⓜ eeng-gre-dee-*eng*-te
  ingredient
íngreme eeng-*gre*-me steep
injeção ⓕ eeng-zhe-*sowng* injection
injetar eeng-zhe-*taarr* inject
injusto/injusta ⓜ/ⓕ eeng-*zhoos*-to/
  eeng-*zhoos*-taa unfair
inocente ee-no-*seng*-te innocent

inseguro/insegura ⓜ/ⓕ eeng·se·goo·ro/
eeng·se·goo·raa *unsafe*
insolação ⓕ eeng·so·laa·sowng *sunstroke*
instrutor/instrutora ⓜ/ⓕ
eengs·troo·torr/eengs·troo·to·raa
instructor
interessante eeng·te·re·sang·te *interesting*
interior ⓜ eeng·te·ree·orr *countryside*
internacional eeng·terr·naa·syo·now
international
Internet ⓕ eeng·terr·ne·te *Internet*
intérprete ⓜ&ⓕ eeng·terr·pre·te
interpreter
intervalo ⓜ eeng·terr·vaa·lo *intermission*
inverno ⓜ eeng·verr·no *winter*
ioga ⓕ ee·o·gaa *yoga*
iogurte ⓜ ee·o·goorr·te *yogurt*
ir eerr *go*
Irlanda ⓕ eerr·lang·daa *Ireland*
irmã ⓕ eer·ma *sister*
irmão ⓜ eerr·mowng *brother*
irritação ⓕ ee·hee·ta·sowng *irritation*
— **à fralda** aa *frow*·daa *nappy rash*
— **na pele** naa *pe*·le *rash*
isqueiro ⓜ ees·kay·ro *cigarette lighter*
Israel ⓜ ees·haa·el *Israel*
IT ⓜ ai·tee *IT (information technology)*
itinerário ⓜ ee·tee·ne·raa·ryo *itinerary*

J

já zhaa *already*
janeiro ⓜ zhaa·nay·ro *January*
janela ⓕ zhaa·ne·laa *window*
jantar ⓜ zhang·taarr *dinner*
Japão ⓜ zhaa·powng *Japan*
jaqueta ⓕ zhaa·ke·taa *jacket*
jardim ⓜ zhaarr·deeng *garden*
— **botânico** bo·ta·nee·ko
botanic garden
— **de infância** de eeng·fang·syaa
kindergarten
jardineiro/jardineira ⓜ/ⓕ
zhaarr·dee·nay·ro/zhaarr·dee·nay·raa
gardener
jardins ⓜ pl **públicos** zhaarr·deengs
poo·blee·kos *public gardens*
jeans ⓜ zheens *jeans*

jeep ⓜ zhee·pe *jeep*
joalheria ⓕ zho·a·lye·ree·aa *jewellery*
joelho ⓜ zho·e·lyo *knee*
jogar zho·gaarr *play*
jogo ⓜ zho·go *game (sport)*
— **de computador** de
kong·poo·taa·dorr *computer game*
Jogos Olímpicos ⓜ pl zho·gos
o·leeng·pee·kos *Olympic Games*
jornal ⓜ zhorr·now *newspaper*
jornaleiro ⓜ zhorr·na·lay·ro
news stand • newsagency
jornalista ⓜ&ⓕ zhorr·naa·lees·taa
journalist
jovem zho·veng *young*
Judeu/Judia ⓜ/ⓕ zhoo·de·oo/
zhoo·dee·aa *Jewish*
juiz/juíza ⓜ/ⓕ zhoo·ees/zhoo·ee·zaa
judge • referee
julho ⓜ zhoo·lyo *July*
junho ⓜ zhoo·nyoo *June*
junto/junta ⓜ/ⓕ zhoong·to/zhoong·taa
together

K

ketchup ⓜ ke·tee·shoo·pee *ketchup*
kilograma ⓜ kee·lo·gra·maa *kilogram*
kilômetro ⓜ kee·lo·me·tro *kilometre*
kit ⓜ **de primeiros socorros** kee·tee de
pree·may·ros so·ko·hos *first-aid kit*
kiwi ⓜ kee·wee *kiwifruit*
kosher ko·sherr *kosher*

L

lã ⓕ lang *wool*
lábios ⓜ pl laa·byos *lips*
lado ⓜ laa·do *side*
ladrão/ladra ⓜ/ⓕ laa·drowng/laa·dra
thief
lagarto ⓜ laa·gaarr·to *lizard*
lago ⓜ laa·go *lake*
lama ⓕ la·maa *mud*
lâmpada ⓕ lang·paa·daa *light bulb*
lanche ⓜ lang·she *snack*
lanterna ⓕ lang·terr·naa *torch (flashlight)*
lápis ⓜ laa·pees *pencil*

laptop ⓜ le-pee-to-*pee laptop*
laranja ① laa-*rang*-zhaa *orange*
laranja laa-*rang*-zhaa *orange*
largo/larga ⓜ/① laarr-go/laarr-gaa *wide*
lata ① *laa*-taa *can · tin*
lavanderia ① laa-vang-de-*ree*-aa *laundrette*
lavar laa-*vaarr wash*
laxante ⓜ laa-*shang*-te *laxative*
legal le-*gow legal*
legislação ① le-zhees-la-*sowng legislation*
legumes ⓜ pl le-*goo*-mes *legumes · vegetables*
lei ① lay *law*
leite ⓜ *lay*-te *milk*
   — de soja de *so*-zhaa *soy milk*
   — desnatado des-naa-*taa*-do *skim milk*
leito ⓜ *lay*-to *sleeping berth*
lencinho ⓜ **de papel** leng-*see*-nyo de paa-*pel tissue*
lenço ⓜ *leng*-so *scarf*
lençol ⓜ leng-*sow sheet (bed)*
lenha ① *le*-nyaa *firewood*
lentes ① pl *leng*-tes *lenses*
   — de contato de kong-*taa*-to *contact lenses*
lentilha ① leng-*tee*-lyaa *lentil*
ler lerr *read*
lésbica ① *les*-bee-kaa *lesbian*
lesma ① *les*-maa *snail*
leste ⓜ *les*-te *east*
levar le-*vaarr take*
leve *le*-ve *light (not heavy)*
libra ① *lee*-braa *pound (money)*
licença ① lee-*seng*-saa *licence*
líder ⓜ&① *lee*-derr *leader*
ligação ① **à cobrar** lee-gaa-*sowng* aa ko-*braarr collect call*
ligação ① **direta** lee-gaa-*sowng* dee-*re*-taa *direct-dial call*
limão ⓜ lee-*mowng lemon · lime*
limité ⓜ **de peso** lee-*mee*-te de *pe*-zo *baggage allowance*
limite ⓜ **de velocidade** lee-*mee*-te de ve-lo-see-*daa*-de *speed limit*
limonada ① lee-mo-*naa*-daa *lemonade*
limpo/limpa ⓜ/① *leeng*-po/*leeng*-paa *clean*

língua ① *leeng*-gwaa *language · tongue*
linguiça ① **de porco** leen-*gwee*-saa de *porr*-ko *pork sausage*
linha ① *lee*-nyaa *dial tone*
linha aérea ① pl *lee*-nyaa aa-*e*-re-aa *airline*
liquidação ① lee-kee-daa-*sowng sale*
lista ① **telefônica** *lees*-taa te-le-*fo*-nee-kaa *phone book*
listado/listada ⓜ/① lees-*taa*-do/ lees-*taa*-daa *itemised*
livraria ① lee-vraa-*ree*-aa *book shop*
livre *lee*-vre *free (not bound)*
livro ⓜ *lee*-vro *book*
   — de frases de *fraa*-zes *phrasebook*
lixo ⓜ *lee*-sho *garbage · rubbish*
local lo-*kow local*
local ⓜ lo-*kow venue*
   — de nascimento de naas-see-*meng*-to *place of birth*
   — para acampar *paa*-raa aa-kang-*paarr camp site*
loção ① **de bronzear** lo-*sowng* de brong-ze-*aarr tanning lotion*
loja ① *lo*-zhaa *shop*
   — de aparelhos elétricos de aa-paa-*re*-lyos e-*le*-tree-kos *electrical store*
   — de bebidas de be-*bee*-daas *bottle shop · liquor store*
   — de bicicleta de bee-see-*kle*-taa *bike shop*
   — de brinquedos de breeng-*ke*-dos *toy shop*
   — de departamentos de de-paarr-taa-*meng*-tos *department store*
   — de equipamentos fotográficos de e-kee-pa-*meng*-tos fo-to-*graa*-fee-kos *camera shop*
   — de esportes de es-*porr*-tes *sports store*
   — de ferramentas de fe-haa-*meng*-taas *hardware store*
   — de música de *moo*-zee-kaa *music shop*

— **de roupas** de ho-paas *clothing store*

— **de segunda mão** de se-goon-daa mowng *second-hand shop*

— **de souvenir** de soo-ve-neerr *souvenir shop*

— **de acampamento** de aa-kam-paa-meng-to *camping store*

longe long-zhe *far*

longo/longa ⓜ/ⓕ long-go/long-gaa *long*

lotado/lotada ⓜ/ⓕ lo-taa-do/lo-taa-daa *crowded*

louça ⓕ **de barro** lo-saa de baa-ho *pot (ceramics)*

louco/louca ⓜ/ⓕ lo-ko/lo-kaa *crazy*

lua ⓕ loo-aa *moon*

— **de mel** de mel *honeymoon*

lubrificante loo-bree-fee-kang-te *lubricant*

lucro ⓜ loo-kro *profit*

lugar ⓜ loo-gaarr *place*

luta ⓕ loo-ta *fight*

luvas ⓕ pl loo-vaas *gloves*

luxo ⓜ loo-sho *luxury*

luz ⓕ looz *light*

M

maçã ⓕ maa-sang *apple*

macarrão ⓜ **chinês** maa-kaa-howng shee-nes *noodles*

machismo ⓜ maa-shees-mo *sexism*

machucar maa-shoo-kaarr *hurt*

maconha ⓕ maa-ko-nyaa *marijuana*

madeira ⓕ maa-day-raa *wood*

madrugada ⓕ maa-droo-gaa-daa *dawn*

mãe ⓕ mayng *mum*

maio maa-yo *May*

maionese ⓕ maa-yo-ne-ze *mayonnaise*

mais mais *more*

— **perto/perta** ⓜ/ⓕ perr-to/perr-ta *nearest*

mal maa-l *ill*

mal passado/passada ⓜ/ⓕ mow paa-saa-do/paa-saa-daa *rare (food)*

mala ⓕ maa-laa *suitcase*

mamãe ⓕ ma-mayng *mother*

mamograma ⓜ maa-mo-gra-maa *mammogram*

mandíbula ⓕ mang-dee-boo-laa *jaw*

manga ⓕ mang-gaa *mango*

manhã ⓕ ma-nyang *morning*

manteiga ⓕ man-tay-gaa *butter*

mantimentos ⓜ pl mang-tee-meng-tos *groceries*

mão ⓕ mowng *hand*

mapa ⓕ maa-paa *map*

— **da estrada** daa es-traa-daa *road map*

maquiagem ⓕ maa-kee-aa-zheng *make-up*

máquina ⓕ maa-kee-naa *machine*

— **de lavar roupa** de laa-vaarr ho-paa *washing machine*

— **de vender passagem** de veng-derr paa-saa-zheng *ticket machine*

mar ⓜ maarr *sea*

maracujá ⓜ maa-raa-koo-zhaa *passionfruit*

maravilhoso/maravilhosa ⓜ/ⓕ maa-raa-vee-lyo-zo/maa-raa-vee-lyo-zaa *wonderful*

marca ⓜ **passo** mar-kaa pa-so *pacemaker*

março maar-so *March*

maré ⓕ maa-re *tide*

margarina ⓕ maarr-gaa-ree-naa *margarine*

marido ⓜ maa-ree-do *husband*

marmelada ⓕ maarr-me-laa-daa *marmalade*

marron maa-hong *brown*

martelo ⓜ maarr-te-lo *hammer*

mas maas *but*

massa ⓕ maa-saa *pastry*

massagem ⓕ maa-saa-zheng *massage*

massagista ⓜ&ⓕ maa-saa-zhees-taa *masseur*

massas ⓕ pl maa-saas *pasta*

matar maa-taarr *kill*

mecânico/mecânica ⓜ/ⓕ me-ka-nee-ko/ me-ka-nee-kaa *mechanic*

medicina ⓕ me-dee-see-naa *medicine*

médico/médica ⓜ/ⓕ me-dee-ko/ me-dee-kaa *doctor*

meditação ⓕ me-dee-taa-sowng *meditation*

meia ⓕ may-aa *sock*

— **calça** kow-saa *pantyhose*

meia-noite ① *may-aa-noy-*te *midnight*

meio ambiente *may-*o ang*-bee-eng-*te *environment*

meio expediente *may-*o es-pe-dee-*eng-*te *part-time*

meio-dia ⓜ *may-*o dee-*aa noon*

mel ⓜ mel *honey*

melancia ① me-lang-*see-*aa *watermelon*

melão ⓜ me-*lowng cantaloupe • melon • rockmelon*

melhor me-*lyorr best • better*

membro ⓜ&① *meng-*bro *member*

menina ① me-*nee-*naa *girl*

menino ⓜ me-*nee-*no *boy*

menos me-nos *less*

mensagem ① meng-*sa-*zheng *message*

menstruação ① mengs-troo-aa-*sowng menstruation*

mentiroso/mentirosa ⓜ/① meng-tee-ro-zo/meng-tee-ro-zaa *liar*

mercado ⓜ merr-*kaa-*do *market*

mercearia ① merr-se-aa-*ree-*aa *convenience store*

mergulho ⓜ merr-*goo-*lyo *diving*

mês ⓜ mes *month*

mesa ① me-zaa *table*

mesmo/mesma ⓜ/① mes-mo/mes-maa *same*

metade ① me-*taa-*de *half*

metal ⓜ me-tow *metal*

metro ⓜ me-tro *metre*

meu/minha ⓜ/① me-oo/mee-nyaa *my*

mexido/mexida ⓜ/① me-shee-do/me-shee-daa *scrambled*

mexilhão ⓜ me-shee-*lyowng mussel*

microondas ⓜ mee-kro-ong-daas *microwave*

mídia ① mee-dyaa *media*

milhão ⓜ mee-*lowng million*

milho ⓜ mee-lyo *corn*

milímetro ⓜ mee-lee-me-tro *millimetre*

militar mee-lee-*taarr military*

mimado/mimada ⓜ/① mee-*maa-*do/mee-*maa-*daa *spoiled*

minhocas ① pl mee-*nyo-*kaas *worms*

mínimo/mínima ⓜ/① mee-*nee-*mo/mee-*nee-*maa *tiny*

minuto ⓜ mee-*noo-*to *minute*

mirante ⓜ mee-*rang-*te *lookout*

missa ① mee-saa *mass (Catholic)*

misturar mees-*too-*raar *mix*

mochila ① mo-*shee-*la *backpack*

modem ⓜ mo-deng *modem*

moedas ① pl mo-e-daas *coins*

molas ① pl mo-laas *spring (coil)*

mole mo-le *soft-boiled*

molestamento ⓜ mo-les-taa-*meng-*to *harassment*

molhado/molhada ⓜ/① mo-*lyaa-*do/mo-*lyaa-*daa *wet*

molho ⓜ mo-lyo *sauce*

— **de pimenta** de pee-*meng-*taa *chilli sauce*

— **de soja** de so-zhaa *soy sauce*

— **de tomate** de to-*maa-*te *tomato sauce*

monastério ⓜ mo-naas-*te-*ryo *monastery*

monge ⓜ mong-zhe *monk*

montanha ① mong-*ta-*nyaa *mountain*

montanhismo ⓜ mong-ta-*nyees-*mo *mountaineering*

monumento ⓜ mo-noo-*meng-*to *monument*

morango ⓜ mo-*rang-*go *strawberry*

morar mo-*raarr live (somewhere)*

mordida ① morr-*dee-*daa *bite (dog/insect)*

morno/morna ⓜ/① morr-no/morr-naa *warm*

morrer mo-*herr die*

morro ⓜ mo-ho *hill*

morto/morta ⓜ/① morr-to/morr-taa *dead*

mosquiteiro ⓜ mos-kee-*tay-*ro *mosquito net*

mosquito ⓜ mos-*kee-*to *mosquito*

mosteiro ⓜ mos-*tay-*ro *mosque*

mostrador de velocidade · mos-traa-*dorr* de ve-lo-see-*daa-*de *speedometer*

mostrar mos-*traarr show*

motocicleta ① mo-to-see-*kle-*taa *motorbike*

motor ⓜ mo-torr *engine*

mountain bike ⓜ maa-oong-tayng bai-kee *mountain bike*

móveis ⓜ pl mo-vays *furniture*

Muçulmano/Muçulmana ⓜ/ⓕ moo-sool-*ma*-no/moo-sool-*ma*-naa *Muslim*

mudo/muda ⓜ/ⓕ *moo*-do/*moo*-daa *mute*

muesli ⓜ *moos*-lee *muesli*

muito/muita ⓜ/ⓕ *mweeng*-to/*mweeng*-taa (a) *lot • very*

mulher ⓕ moo-*lyerr woman*
— **de negócios** de ne-*go*-syos *business person*

multa ⓕ *mool*-taa *fine (payment)*

mundo ⓜ *moong*-do *world*

músculo ⓜ *moos*-koo-lo *muscle*

museu ⓜ mo-*se*-oo *museum*

música ⓕ *moo*-zee-kaa *music*

músico/música ⓜ/ⓕ *moo*-zee-ko/*moo*-zee-kaa *musician*

mustarda ⓕ moos-*taar*-daa *mustard*

N

na frente de naa *freng*-te de *in front of*

nacionalidade ⓕ naa-syo-naa-lee-*daa*-de *nationality*

nada *naa*-daa *nothing*

nadar naa-*daarr swim*

namorada ⓕ naa-mo-*raa*-daa *girlfriend*

namorado ⓜ na-mo-*raa*-do *boyfriend*

namorar naa-mo-*raarr date (a person)*

não nowng *no • not*

não-fumante nowng-foo-*mang*-te *non-smoking*

nariz ⓜ naa-*rees nose*

nascer ⓜ **do sol** naa-serr do sol *sunrise*

natureza ⓕ naa-too-*re*-zaa *nature*

naturopatia ⓕ naa-too-ro-paa-*tee*-a *naturopathy*

náusea ⓕ *now*-se-aa *nausea*

navio ⓜ naa-*vee*-o *ship*

nebuloso/nebulosa ⓜ/ⓕ ne-boo-*lo*-zo/ne-boo-*lo*-zaa *foggy*

necessário/necessária ⓜ/ⓕ ne-se-*sa*-ryo/ne-se-*sa*-ryaa *necessary*

negativo/negativa ⓜ/ⓕ ne-gaa-*tee*-vo/ne-gaa-*tee*-vaa *negative*

negócios ⓜ pl ne-*go*-syos *business*

nenhum ne-*yoom none*

nenhum deles ne-*yoom de*-les *neither*

neto/neta ⓜ/ⓕ *ne*-to/*ne*-taa *grandchild*

neve ⓕ *ne*-ve *snow*

nódulo ⓜ *no*-doo-lo *lump*

noite ⓕ *noy*-te *evening • night*

Noite ⓕ **de Natal** *noy*-te de na-*tow Christmas Eve*

noiva ⓕ *noy*-vaa *fiancee*

noivado ⓜ noy-*vaa*-do *engagement*

noivo ⓜ *noy*-vo *fiance*

nome ⓜ *no*-me *name*
— **Cristão** ⓜ krees-*towng Christian name*

norte ⓜ *norr*-te *north*

Noruega ⓕ no-roo-e-gaa *Norway*

nós nos *we*

nosso/nossa ⓜ/ⓕ *no*-so/*no*-saa *our*

nota ⓕ *no*-taa *banknote*

notícias ⓕ pl no-*tee*-syaas *news*

Nova Zelândia ⓕ no-vaa ze-*lang*-dyaa *New Zealand*

novamente no-vaa-*meng*-te *again*

novela ⓕ no-ve-laa *soap opera*

novembro no-*veng*-bro *November*

novidades ⓕ pl no-vee-*daa*-des *news*

novo/nova ⓜ/ⓕ *no*-vo/*no*-vaa *new*

noz ⓕ noz *nut*

nublado/nublada ⓜ/ⓕ noo-*blaa*-do/noo-*blaa*-daa *cloudy*

número ⓜ *noo*-me-ro *number*
— **da placa** daa *plaa*-kaa *license plate number • numberplate*
— **do passaporte** do paa-saa-*porr*-te *passport number*
— **do quarto** do *kwaarr*-to *room number*

nunca *noong*-kaa *never*

nuvem ⓕ noo-*veng cloud*

O

objetivo ⓜ o-bee-zhe-*tee*-vo *goal*

oceano ⓜ o-se-a-no *ocean*

óculos ⓜ pl o-koo-los *glasses (spectacles)*
— **de natação** de naa-taa-*sowng goggles (swimming)*
— **de ski** de es-*kee goggles (skiing)*
— **de sol** de sol *sunglasses*

ocupado/ocupada ⓜ/ⓕ oo-koo-*paa*-do/
o-koo-*paa*-daa *busy*

oeste ⓜ o-*es*-te *west*

oficina ⓕ o-fee-*see*-naa *garage • workshop*

óleo ⓜ o-lyo *oil*

olho ⓜ o-lyo *eye*

ombro ⓜ it ong-bro *shoulder*

onda ⓕ ong-daa *wave*

onde ong-de *where*

ônibus ⓜ o-nee-boos *bus*

ontem ong-teng *yesterday*

ópera ⓕ o-pe-raa *opera*

operação ⓕ o-pe-raa-*sowng* *operation*

operador/operadora ⓜ/ⓕ o-pe-raa-*dorr*/
o-pe-raa-*do*-raa *operator*

operário/operária ⓜ/ⓕ o-pe-*raa*-ryo/
o-pe-*raa*-ryaa *factory worker*

opinião ⓕ o-pee-nee-*owng* *opinion*

oportunidade ⓕ o-porr-too-nee-*daa*-de
chance

oportunidades ⓕ pl **iguais**
o-porr-too-nee-*daa*-des ee-*gwaa*-ees
equal opportunity

oposto/oposta ⓜ/ⓕ o-*pos*-to/o-*pos*-taa
opposite

optometrista ⓜ&ⓕ o-pee-to-me-*trees*-taa
optometrist

ordinário/ordinária ⓜ/ⓕ
orr-dee-*naa*-ryo/orr-dee-*naa*-ryaa
ordinary

orelha ⓕ o-*re*-lyaa *ear*

orgasmo ⓜ orr-*gaas*-mo *orgasm*

original o-ree-zhee-*now* *original*

orquestra ⓕ orr-*kes*-traa *orchestra*

os EUA ⓜ pl os e-waa *the USA*

osso ⓜ o-so *bone*

ostra ⓕ os-traa *oyster*

ótimo/ótima ⓜ/ⓕ o-tee-mo/o-tee-maa
great

ou o o *or*

ouro ⓜ o-ro *gold*

outono ⓜ o-*to*-no *autumn • fall*

outro/outra ⓜ/ⓕ o-tro/o-traa *other*

outubro o-*too*-bro *October*

ovário ⓜ o-*vaa*-ryo *ovary*

ovelha ⓕ o-*ve*-lyaa *lamb • sheep*

ovo ⓜ o-vo *egg*

oxigênio ⓜ ok-see-*zhe*-nyo *oxygen*

P

pacote ⓜ pa-*ko*-te *packet*

padaria ⓕ paa-daa-*ree*-aa *bakery*

padre ⓜ *paa*-dre *priest*

pães ⓜ pl payngs *bread rolls*

pagamento ⓜ paa-gaa-*meng*-to *payment*

pagar paa-*gaarr* *pay*

página ⓕ *paa*-zhee-naa *page*

pai ⓜ pai *father*

painel de marcação pai-*nel* de
maarr-kaa-*sowng* *scoreboard*

país ⓜ paa-*ees* *country*

pais ⓜ pl paa-*ees* *parents*

Países Baixos paa-*ee*-zes bai-shos
Netherlands

palácio ⓜ paa-*laa*-syo *palace*

palavra ⓕ paa-*laa*-vraa *word*

palito de dentes paa-*lee*-to de *deng*-tes
toothpick

panela ⓕ paa-*ne*-laa *pan*

pano de limpeza *pa*-no de
leeng-pe-zaa *wash cloth (flannel)*

pão ⓜ powng *bread*

— **integral** eeng-te-*grow*
wholemeal bread

papel ⓜ paa-*pel* *paper*

— **higiênico** ee-zhee-e-nee-ko
toilet paper

papelada ⓕ paa-pe-*laa*-daa *paperwork*

papelaria ⓕ paa-pe-laa-*ree*-aa *stationery
shop*

Paquistão ⓜ paa-kees-*towng* *Pakistan*

par ⓜ paarr *pair (couple)*

para *paa*-raa *for*

— **baixo** *bai*-sho *downhill*

— **cima** *see*-maa *uphill*

— **sempre** *seng*-pre *forever*

parabrisa ⓕ paa-raa-*bree*-zaa *windscreen*

parada cardíaca paa-*raa*-daa
kaarr-*dee*-aa-kaa *cardiac arrest*

parapeito ⓜ paa-raa-*pay*-to *ledge*

paraplégico/paraplégica ⓜ/ⓕ
paa-raa-*ple*-zhee-ko/paa-raa-*ple*-zhee-kaa
paraplegic

parar paa-*raarr* *stop (cease)*

parecido/parecida ⓜ/ⓕ
paa·re·*see*·do/paa·re·*see*·daa *similar*

parede ⓕ paa·*re*·de *wall (outer)*

parlamento ⓜ paarr·laa·*meng*·to
parliament

parque ⓜ *paarr*·ke *park*
— **nacional** naa·syo·*now* *national park*

parte ⓕ *paarr*·te *part (component)*

partida ⓕ paarr·*tee*·daa *departure • match (sport)*

partido ⓜ paarr·*tee*·do *party (politics)*

partir paarr·*teerr* *depart (leave)*

Páscoa ⓕ *paas*·kwaa *Easter*

passada (semana) ⓕ paa·*saa*·daa
(se·*ma*·naa) *last (week)*

passado ⓜ paa·*saa*·do *past*

passageiro/passageira ⓜ/ⓕ
paa·saa·*zhay*·ro/paa·saa·*zhay*·raa
passenger

passaporte ⓜ paa·saa·*porr*·te *passport*

passar paa·*saarr* *pass*

pássaro ⓜ *paa*·saa·ro *bird*

passas ⓕ pl *paa*·saas *raisin • sultana*

passo ⓜ *paa*·so *step*

pasta ⓕ *pas*·taa *briefcase*
— **de dentes** de *deng*·tes *toothpaste*

patinaçao ⓕ paa·tee·naa·*sowng*
rollerblading

pato/pata ⓜ/ⓕ *paa*·to/*paa*·taa *duck*

paz ⓕ pas *peace*

pé ⓜ pe *foot*

peça ⓕ *pe*·saa *play (theatre)*

pedaço ⓜ pe·*da*·so *piece*

pedal ⓜ pe·*dow* *pedal*

pedestre ⓜ pe·*des*·tre *pedestrian*

pedido ⓜ pe·*dee*·do *order (command)*

pedinte ⓜ&ⓕ pe·*deeng*·te *beggar*

pedir pe·*deerr* *ask (for something) • order*

pedra ⓕ *pe*·draa *rock • stone*

pegar pe·*gaarr* *get*
— **carona** kaa·ro·naa *hitchhike*

peito ⓜ *pay*·to *chest • breast*

peixaria ⓕ *pay*·sha·*ree*·aa *fish shop*

peixe ⓜ *pay*·she *fish*

peixeiro/peixeira ⓜ/ⓕ *pay*·shay·ro/
pay·*shay*·raa *fish monger*

pele ⓕ *pe*·le *skin*

pensão ⓕ peng·*sowng* *boarding house*

penhasco ⓜ pe·*nyaas*·ko *cliff*

pênis ⓜ *pe*·nees *penis*

pensar peng·*saarr* *think*

pensionista ⓜ&ⓕ peng·syo·*nees*·taa
pensioner

pente ⓜ *peng*·te *comb*

pepino ⓜ pe·*pee*·no *cucumber*

pequeno/pequena ⓜ/ⓕ pe·*ke*·no/
pe·*ke*·naa *little • small*

pêra ⓕ *pe*·raa *pear*

perder perr·*derr* *lose*

perdido/perdida ⓜ/ⓕ
perr·*dee*·do/perr·*dee*·daa *lost*

perdoar perr·do·*aarr* *forgive*

perfeito/perfeita ⓜ/ⓕ
perr·*fay*·to/perr·*fay*·taa *perfect*

performance ⓕ perr·forr·*mang*·se
performance

perfume ⓜ perr·*foo*·me *perfume*

pergunta ⓕ perr·*goong*·taa *question*

perguntar perr·goong·*taarr*
ask (a question)

perigoso/perigosa ⓜ/ⓕ pe·ree·*go*·zo/
pe·ree·*go*·zaa *dangerous*

permissão ⓕ perr·mee·*sowng* *permission • permit*
— **para trabalhar** *paa*·raa
traa·baa·*lyaarr* *work permit*

perna ⓕ *perr*·naa *leg*

perto *perr*·to *near*

perú ⓜ pe·*roo* *turkey*

pesado/pesada ⓜ/ⓕ
pe·*zaa*·do/pe·*zaa*·daa *heavy*

pesar pe·*zaarr* *weigh*

pesca ⓕ *pes*·kaa *fishing*

peso ⓜ pe·*zo* *weight*

pesos ⓜ pl pe·*zos* *weights*

pêssego ⓜ *pe*·se·go *peach*

pessoa ⓕ pe·*so*·aa *person*

pessoas ⓕ pl pe·*so*·aas *people*

petição ⓕ pe·tee·*sowng* *petition*

petróleo ⓜ pe·*tro*·lyo *petrol*

pharmacista ⓕ&ⓕ faarr·maa·*sees*·taa
chemist

piada ⓕ pee·*aa*·daa *joke*

picareta ⓕ pee·kaa·re·taa *pickaxe*

pico ⓜ *pee*·ko *peak (mountain)*

pifar pee·*faarr* *break down*

pikles ⓜ pl *pee*-kles *pickles*

pilha ⓕ *pee*-lyaa *battery*

pílula ⓕ *pee*-loo-laa *pill • Pill (the)*

pimenta ⓕ pee-*meng*-taa *chilli • pepper*

pimentão ⓜ pee-meng-*towng* *capsicum • pepper (bell)*

pinça ⓕ *peeng*-saa *tweezers*

pintor/pintora ⓜ/ⓕ peeng-*torr*/peeng-*to*-raa *painter*

pintura ⓕ peeng-*too*-raa *painting*

piolho ⓜ pee-*o*-lyo *lice*

piquenique ⓜ pee-ke-*nee*-ke *picnic*

piscina ⓕ pee-*see*-naa *swimming pool*

pista ⓕ *pees*-taa *track (sport)*
— **de corrida** de ko-*hee*-daa *racetrack*

pistáchio ⓜ pees-*taa*-shyo *pistachio*

planalto ⓜ pla-*now*-to *plateau*

planeta ⓜ pla-*ne*-taa *planet*

plano/plana ⓜ/ⓕ *pla*-no/*pla*-naa *flat*

planta ⓕ *plang*-taa *plant*

plástico/plástica ⓜ/ⓕ *plas*-tee-ko/*plas*-tee-kaa *plastic*

plataforma ⓕ plaa-taa-*forr*-maa *platform*

pneu ⓜ pee-*ne*-oo *tyre*

pó ⓜ po *powder*

pobre *po*-bre *poor*

pobreza ⓕ po-*bre*-zaa *poverty*

poché po-*she* *poached*

pochete ⓕ po-*she*-te *bumbag*

poder po-*derr* *can (be able/have permission)*

poder ⓜ po-*derr* *power*

poesia ⓕ po-e-*zee*-aa *poetry*

pólen ⓜ *po*-leng *pollen*

polícia ⓕ po-*lee*-syaa *police*

política ⓕ po-*lee*-tee-kaa *politics*

político/política ⓜ/ⓕ po-*lee*-tee-ko/po-*lee*-tee-kaa *politician*

poluição ⓕ po-loo-ee-*sowng* *pollution*

pomelo ⓜ po-*me*-lo *grapefruit*

ponte ⓕ *pong*-te *bridge*

ponto ⓜ *pong*-to *point*
— **de controle** de kong-*tro*-le *checkpoint (border)*
— **de ônibus** de o-nee-boos *bus stop*

popular po-poo-*laarr* *popular*

por porr *per*
— **perto** *perr*-to *nearby*
— **que** ke *because • why*

pôr ⓜ *do sol* porr do sol *sunset*

porcentagem ⓕ porr-seng-*taa*-zheng *per cent*

porco/porca ⓜ/ⓕ *porr*-ko/*porr*-kaa *pig • pork*

porta ⓕ *porr*-taa *door*

portão ⓜ porr-*towng* *gate (airport, etc)*
— **de partida** de paarr-*tee*-daa *departure gate*

porto ⓜ *porr*-to *port (sea)*

pós barba ⓜ pos *baarr*-baa *aftershave*

positivo/positiva ⓜ/ⓕ po-zee-*tee*-vo/po-zee-*tee*-vaa *positive*

possível po-*see*-vel *possible*

postagem ⓕ pos-*taa*-zheng *postage*

posto ⓜ **de gasolina** *pos*-to de gaa-zo-*lee*-naa *service station*

pouco/pouca ⓜ/ⓕ *po*-ko/*po*-kaa *little (not much)*

praça ⓕ *praa*-saa *square (town)*

praia ⓜ *prai*-aa *beach*

prancha ⓕ **de surfe** *prang*-shaa de *soorr*-fee *surfboard*

prata ⓕ *praa*-taa *silver*

prateleira ⓕ praa-te-*lay*-raa *shelf*

prato ⓜ *praa*-to *plate*

precisar pre-see-*zaarr* *need*

preço ⓜ *pre*-so *price*
— **da entrada** daa eng-*traa*-daa *admission price*

prédio ⓜ *pre*-dyo *building*

prefeito/prefeita ⓜ/ⓕ pre-*fay*-to/pre-*fay*-taa *mayor*

preferir pre-fe-*reerr* *prefer*

preguiçoso/preguiçosa ⓜ/ⓕ pre-gee-*so*-zo/pre-gee-*so*-zaa *lazy*

prender preng-*derr* *arrest*

preocupado/preocupada ⓜ/ⓕ pre-o-koo-*paa*-do/pre-o-koo-*paa*-daa *worried*

preparar pre-paa-*raarr* *prepare*

presente ⓜ pre-*zeng*-te *gift • present (time)*
— **de casamento** de kaa-zaa-*meng*-to *wedding present*

presidente ⓜ&ⓕ pre·zee·*deng*·te
president

pressão ⓕ pre·*sowng pressure*
— **arterial** aar·te·ree·ow *blood pressure*

presunto ⓜ pre·*zoong*·to *ham*

preto e branco *pre*·to e *brang*·ko
B&W (film)

preto/preta ⓜ/ⓕ *pre*·to/*pre*·taa *black*

primavera ⓕ pree·maa·ve·raa
spring (season)

primeira classe ⓕ pree·*may*·raa *klaa*·se
first class

primeira ministra ⓕ pree·*may*·raa
mee·*nees*·traa *prime minister*

primeiro/primeira ⓜ/ⓕ
pree·*may*·ro/pree·*may*·raa *first*

primeiro ministro ⓜ pree·*may*·ro
mee·*nees*·tro *prime minister*

principal ⓜ&ⓕ preeng·see·*pow main*

prisão ⓕ pree·*zowng jail* • *prison*

prisioneiro/prisioneira ⓜ/ⓕ
pree·zyo·*nay*·ro/pree·zyo·*nay*·raa
prisoner

privado/privada ⓜ/ⓕ
pree·*vaa*·do/pree·*vaa*·daa *private*

problema ⓜ **de coração** pro·*ble*·maa de
ko·ra·*sowng heart condition*

produzir pro·doo·*zeerr produce*

professor/professora ⓜ/ⓕ pro·fe·*sorr*/
pro·fe·*so*·raa *lecturer* • *teacher*

profundo/profunda ⓜ/ⓕ
pro·*foong*·do/pro·*foong*·daa *deep*

programa ⓜ pro·*gra*·maa *program*

projetor ⓜ pro·zhe·*torr projector*

pronto/pronta ⓜ/ⓕ
prong·to/*prong*·taa *ready*

proprietário/proprietária ⓜ/ⓕ
pro·pree·e·*taa*·ryo/pro·pree·e·*taa*·ryaa
landlord/landlady

proteção ⓕ **contra sol** pro·te·*sowng*
kong·traa sol *sunblock*

proteger pro·te·*zherr protect*

protegido/protegida ⓜ pro·te·*zhee*·do/
pro·te·*zhee*·daa *protected*

protestar pro·tes·*taarr protest*

protesto ⓜ pro·*tes*·to *protest*

provador ⓜ pro·vaa·*dorr changing room*

provisões ⓕ pl pro·vee·*zoyngs provisions*

próximo/próxima ⓜ/ⓕ
pro·*see*·mo/pro·*see*·maa *next*

pular poo·*laarr jump*

pulga ⓕ *pool*·gaa *flea*

pulmão ⓜ pool·*mowng lung*

punho ⓜ *poo*·nyo *wrist*

puro/pura ⓜ/ⓕ *poo*·ro/*poo*·raa *pure*

puxar poo·*shaarr pull*

Q

quadra ⓕ *kwaa*·draa *court (tennis)*
— **de tênis** de *te*·nees *tennis court*

quadraplégico/quadraplégica ⓜ/ⓕ
kwaa·draa·*ple*·zhee·ko/
kwaa·draa·*ple*·zhee·kaa *quadriplegic*

qualidade ⓕ kwaa·lee·*daa*·de *quality*

qualificações ⓕ pl
kwaa·lee·fee·kaa·*soyngs qualifications*

qualquer kwow·*kerr any*

quando *kwang*·do *when*

quanto *kwang*·to *how much*

quarentena ⓕ kwaa·reng·*te*·naa
quarantine

quarta-feira ⓕ *kwaarr*·taa·*fay*·raa
Wednesday

quarto ⓜ *kwaarr*·to *bedroom* • *room* •
quarter
— **de casa** de kaa·*zow double room*

quase *kwaa*·ze *almost*

que ke *what*

quebrado/quebrada ⓜ/ⓕ
ke·*bra*·do/ke·*braa*·daa *broken*

quebrador ⓜ **de gelo**
ke·braa·*dorr* de *zhe*·lo *ice axe*

quebrar ke·*braarr break*

queda ⓕ *ke*·daa *fall (down)*

queijaria ⓕ kay·zhaa·ree·aa *cheese shop*

queijo ⓜ *kay*·zho *cheese*

queimado/queimada ⓜ/ⓕ
kay·*maa*·do/kay·*maa*·daa *burnt*
— **de sol** de sol *sunburnt*

queimadura ⓕ kay·maa·*doo*·raa *burn*

quem keng *who*

quente *keng*·te *hot*

querer ke·*rerr want*

questão ⓕ kes·*towng question*

quieto/quieta ⓜ/ⓕ kee-e-to/kee-e-taa
quiet
quinta-feira ⓕ kween-ta-fay-raa *Thursday*
quinzena ⓕ keeng-ze-naa *fortnight*
quiroprático/quiroprática ⓜ/ⓕ
kee-ro-praa-tee-ko/kee-ro-praa-tee-kaa
chiropractor

R

rabanete ⓜ haa-baa-ne-te *radish*
rabo ⓜ haa-bo *tail*
racismo ⓜ haa-sees-mo *racism*
radiador ⓜ haa-dee-aa-dorr *radiator*
rainha ⓕ haa-ee-nyaa *queen*
rápido/rápida ⓜ/ⓕ
haa-pee-do/haa-pee-daa *fast*
raquete ⓕ haa-ke-te *racquet*
raro/rara ⓜ/ⓕ haa-ro/haa-raa
rare (uncommon)
raspador ⓜ haas-paa-dorr *razor*
ratazana ⓕ haa-taa-za-naa *rat*
rato ⓜ haa-to *rat*
razão ⓕ haa-zowng *reason*
realista he-aa-lees-taa *realistic*
recarregador ⓜ **de bateria**
he-kaa-he-gaa-dorr de baa-te-ree-aa
jumper leads
receber he-se-berr *welcome*
recentemente he-seng-te-meng-te
recently
recibo ⓜ he-see-bo *receipt*
reciclar he-see-klaar *recycle*
reciclável he-see-klaa-vel *recyclable*
reclamar he-klaa-marr *complain*
recomendar he-ko-meng-daarr
recommend
recursos ⓜ pl **humanos** he-koor-sos
oo-ma-nos *human resources*
recusar he-koo-zaarr *refuse*
rede ⓕ he-de *hammock • net*
redondo/redonda ⓜ/ⓕ
he-dong-do/he-dong-daa *round*
reembolso ⓜ he-eng-bol-so *refund*
referência ⓕ he-fe-reng-syaa *reference*
reflexologia ⓕ he-flek-so-lo-zhee-aa
reflexology

refrigerante ⓜ he-free-zhe-rang-te
soft drink
refugiado/refugiada ⓜ/ⓕ
he-foo-zhee-aa-do/he-foo-zhee-aa-daa
refugee
regional he-zhyo-now *regional*
registro ⓜ **de carro** he-zhees-tro de
kaa-ho *car registration*
regra ⓕ he-graa *rule*
regras ⓕ pl he-graas *policy*
rei ⓜ hay *king*
reiki ⓜ hay-kee *reiki*
relacionamento ⓜ he-laa-syo-na-meng-to
relationship
relações ⓕ pl **públicas** he-la-soyngs
poo-blee-kaas *public relations*
relaxar he-la-shaarr *relax*
rélica ⓕ he-lee-kaa *relic*
relicário ⓜ he-lee-kaa-ryo *shrine*
religião ⓕ he-lee-zhee-owng *religion*
religioso/religiosa ⓜ/ⓕ he-lee-zhee-o-zo/
he-lee-zhee-o-zaa *religious*
relógio ⓜ he-lo-zhyo *clock • watch*
remo ⓜ he-mo *rowing*
remoto/remota ⓜ/ⓕ
he-mo-to/he-mo-taa *remote*
renda ⓕ heng-daa *lace*
repelente ⓜ **em aspiral** he-pe-leng-te eng
aas-pee-row *mosquito coil*
repolho ⓜ he-po-lyo *cabbage*
república ⓕ he-poo-blee-kaa *republic*
requerimento ⓜ **de bagagem**
he-ke-ree-meng-to de baa-gaa-zheng
baggage claim
reserva ⓕ he-zerr-vaa
reservation (booking)
reservar he-zerr-vaarr
book (make a booking)
resíduo ⓜ **nuclear** he-zee-doo-o
noo-kle-aarr *nuclear waste*
resíduo ⓜ **tóxico** he-zee-dwo tok-see-ko
toxic waste
resolução ⓕ he-zo-loo-sowng *workout*
respirar hes-pee-raarr *breathe*
resposta ⓕ hes-pos-taa *answer*
restaurante ⓜ hes-tow-rang-te *restaurant*
retornar he-torr-naarr *return*
reverenciar he-ve-reng-see-aarr *worship*

S

DICTIONARY

revisão ⓜ he-vee-*zowng review*
revista ⓕ he-*vees*-taa *magazine*
reza ⓕ he-zaa *prayer*
rico/rica ⓜ/ⓕ hee-ko/hee-kaa *rich (wealthy)*
rin ⓜ pl heeng *kidney*
rio ⓜ hee-o *river*
rir heerr *laugh*
risco ⓜ hees-ko *risk*
ritmo ⓜ hee-tee-mo *rhythm*
rock ⓜ ho-kee *rock (music)*
roda ⓕ ho-daa *wheel*
rodoviária ⓕ ho-do-vee-*aa*-ryaa
  bus station
romântico/romântica ⓜ/ⓕ
  ho-*mang*-tee-ko/ho-*mang*-tee-kaa
  romantic
rosa ho-za *pink*
rosto ⓜ hos-to *face*
rota ⓕ ho-taa *route*
  — **de bicicleta** de bee-see-*kle*-taa
  bike path
  — **de caminhada** de kaa-mee-*nyaa*-daa
  hiking route
roubar ho-*baarr rob* • *steal*
roubo ⓜ ho-bo *rip-off*
roupa ⓕ pl ho-paa *clothes*
  — **de banho** de ba-nyo *bathing suit* •
  swimsuit
  — **de cama** de *ka*-maa *bedding*
  — **de baixo** de bai-sho *underwear*
roxo/roxa ⓜ/ⓕ ho-sho/ho-shaa *purple*
rua ⓕ hoo-aa *street*
  — **principal** preeng-see-*pow main road*
rubéola ⓕ hoo-be-o-laa *rubella*
rugby ⓜ hoo-gee-bee *rugby*
ruim hoo-eeng *bad*
ruínas ⓕ pl hoo-ee-naas *ruins*
rum ⓜ hoom *rum*

S

sábado ⓜ saa-baa-do *Saturday*
saber saa-berr *know*
sabonete ⓜ saa-bo-*ne*-te *soap*
saco ⓜ saa-ko *bag*
  — **de dormir** de dorr-*meerr*
  sleeping bag

saguão ⓜ saag-*wowng foyer*
saia ⓕ saa-yaa *skirt*
saída ⓕ saa-ee-daa *exit*
sair saa-eerr *go out with*
sais ⓜ pl **de hidratação** sais de
  ee-draa-taa-*sowng rehydration salts*
sal ⓜ sow *salt*
sala ⓕ **de espera** saa-laa de es-pe-raa
  waiting room
sala ⓕ **de trânsito** saa-laa de trang-zee-to
  transit lounge
salada ⓕ saa-*laa*-daa *salad*
salaminho ⓜ saa-laa-*mee*-nyo *salami*
salão ⓜ **de beleza** saa-*lowng* de be-*le*-zaa
  beauty salon
salário ⓜ saa-*laa*-ryo *salary* • *wage*
salmão ⓜ sow-*mowng salmon*
salsicha ⓕ sow-*see*-shaa *sausage*
sandália ⓕ sang-*daa*-lyaa *sandal*
sangue ⓜ sang-ge *blood*
santo/santa ⓜ/ⓕ sang-to/sang-taa *saint*
sapataria ⓕ saa-paa-taa-*ree*-aa *shoe shop*
sapato ⓜ saa-*paa*-to *shoe*
sarampo ⓜ saa-*rang*-po *measles*
sardinha ⓕ saarr-dee-nyaa *sardine*
saúde ⓕ sa-oo-de *health*
sauna ⓕ sow-naa *sauna*
se se *if*
secar se-*kaarr dry*
seco/seca ⓜ/ⓕ se-ko/se-kaa *dried* • *dry*
secretário/secretária ⓜ/ⓕ se-kre-*taa*-ryo/
  se-kre-taa-ryaa *secretary*
seda ⓕ se-daa *silk*
sedento/sedenta ⓜ/ⓕ
  se-deng-to/se-deng-taa *thirsty*
seguir se-*geerr follow*
segunda-feira ⓕ se-goong-daa-*fay*-raa
  Monday
segundo ⓜ se-goong-do *second (time)*
segundo grau ⓜ se-goong-do grow
  high school
segundo/segunda ⓜ/ⓕ
  se-goong-do/se-goong-daa *second*
seguro ⓜ se-goo-ro *insurance*
  — **social** so-see-ow *social welfare* • *dole*
seguro/segura ⓜ/ⓕ
  se-goo-ro/se-goo-raa *safe*
seios ⓜ pl say-os *breasts*

250

sela ① *se*·laa saddle

selo ⓜ *se*·lo stamp

sem seng without

  — **chumbo** *shoong*·bo unleaded

semana ① se·*ma*·naa week

sempre *seng*·pre always

sensível seng·*see*·vel emotional • sensible

sensual seng·soo·*ow* sensual

sentar seng·*taarr* sit

sentimentos ⓜ pl seng·tee·*meng*·tos feelings

sentir seng·*teerr* feel

  — **falta** *fow*·taa miss (feel absence of)

separado/separada ⓜ/① se·paa·*raa*·do/ se·paa·*raa*·daa separate

ser serr be (ongoing)

seringa ① se·*reeng*·gaa syringe

sério/séria ⓜ/① *se*·ryo/*se*·ryaa serious

serviço ⓜ **militar** serr·*vee*·so mee·lee·*taarr* military service

serviço ⓜ **postal rápido** serr·*vee*·so pos·*tow* haa·*pee*·do express mail

setembro se·*teng*·bro September

seu/sua ⓜ/① *se*·oo/*soo*·aa your

sexo ⓜ *sek*·so sex

  — **com proteção** kong pro·te·*sowng* safe sex

sexta-feira ① *ses*·taa·*fay*·raa Friday

sexy *sek*·see sexy

shiatsu ⓜ shee·*aa*·tee·zoo shiatsu

shopping centre ⓜ *sho*·peeng *seng*·terr shopping centre

show ⓜ show concert

sim seeng yes

simples *seeng*·ples simple

sinagoga ① see·naa·*go*·gaa synagogue

sinal ⓜ **de trânsito** see·*now* de *trang*·zee·to traffic light

sintético/sintética ⓜ/① seeng·*te*·tee·ko/ seeng·*te*·tee·kaa synthetic

sinuca ① see·*noo*·kaa pool (game)

sistema ① **de classes** sees·*te*·maa de *klaa*·ses class system

skate ⓜ ees·*kay*·te skateboarding

slide ⓜ ees·*lai*·de slide (film)

snorkel ⓜ ees·*norr*·kel snorkelling

snowboarding ⓜ snow·*borr*·deeng snowboarding

sobre *so*·bre about • above • on

sobremesa ① so·bre·*me*·zaa dessert

sobrenome ⓜ so·bre·*no*·me family name • surname

socialista so·see·aa·*lees*·taa socialist

sogra ① *so*·graa mother-in-law

sogro ⓜ *so*·gro father-in-law

sol ⓜ sol sun

soldado ⓜ&① sol·*daa*·do soldier

solteiro/solteira ⓜ/① sol·*tay*·ro/sol·*tay*·raa single

solto/solta ⓜ/① *sol*·to/*sol*·taa loose

somente so·*meng*·te only

sonho ⓜ *so*·nyo dream

sonolento/sonolenta ⓜ/① so·no·*leng*·to/ so·no·*leng*·taa sleepy

sopa ① *so*·paa soup

sorte ① *sorr*·te luck

sortudo/sortuda ⓜ/① sorr·*too*·do/sorr·*too*·daa lucky

sorvete ⓜ sorr·*ve*·te ice cream

sorveteria ① sorr·ve·te·*ree*·aa ice-cream parlour

souvenir ⓜ soo·ve·*neerr* souvenir

sozinho/sozinha ⓜ/① so·zee·*nyo*/so·zee·*nyaa* alone

subir soo·*beerr* climb

suborno ⓜ soo·*borr*·no bribe

sub-títulos ⓜ pl soo·bee·*tee*·too·los subtitles

suco ⓜ *soo*·ko juice

  — **de laranja** de laa·*rang*·zhaa orange juice

Suécia ① soo·e·*syaa* Sweden

suéter ① soo·e·*terr* jumper • sweater

suficiente soo·fee·see·*eng*·te enough

Suíça ① soo·ee·*saa* Switzerland

sujo/suja ⓜ/① *soo*·zho/*soo*·zhaa dirty

sul ⓜ sool south

supermercado ⓜ soo·perr·merr·*kaa*·do supermarket

surdo/surda ⓜ/① *soor*·do/*soor*·daa deaf

surfar soorr·*faarr* surf

surfe ⓜ *soorr*·fee surfing

surpresa ① soorr·*pre*·zaa surprise

sutiã ⓜ soo·tee·*ang* bra

T

tabaco ⓜ taa-*baa*-ko *tobacco*
tabaconista ⓜ taa-baa-ko-*nees*-taa
  tobacconist
talco ⓜ *tow*-ko *baby powder*
talheres ⓜ pl taa-*lye*-res *cutlery*
talvez tow-*ves* *maybe*
tamanho ⓜ ta-*ma*-nyo *size*
também tang-*beng* *also • too*
tampa ⓕ *tang*-paa *plug (bath)*
tampão ⓜ tang-*powng* *tampon*
tampões ⓜ **de ouvido** tang-*powng* de
  o-*vee*-do *earplugs*
tangerina ⓕ tang-zhe-*ree*-naa *mandarin*
tapete ⓜ taa-*pe*-te *rug*
tarde ⓕ *taarr*-de *afternoon*
taxa ⓕ *taa*-shaa
  — **de aeroporto** taa-shaa de
  aa-e-ro-*porr*-to *airport tax*
  — **de câmbio** taa-shaa de *kang*-byo
  exchange rate
  — **de serviço** taa-shaa de serr-*veee*-so
  service charge
táxi ⓜ *taak*-see *taxi*
teatro ⓜ te-*aa*-tro *theatre*
tecido ⓜ te-*see*-do *fabric*
técnica ⓕ te-kee-nee-kaa *technique*
técnico/técnica ⓜ/ⓕ
  te-kee-nee-ko/te-kee-nee-kaa *coach*
teimoso/teimosa ⓜ/ⓕ
  tay-mo-zo/tay-mo-zaa *stubborn*
teleférico ⓜ te-le-*fe*-ree-ko *chairlift (skiing)*
telefonar te-le-fo-*naarr* *telephone*
telefone ⓜ te-le-*fo*-ne *telephone*
  — **público** poo-blee-ko *public telephone*
telegrama ⓜ te-le-*gra*-maa *telegram*
telescópio ⓜ te-les-ko-pyo *telescope*
televisão ⓕ te-le-vee-*sowng* *television*
temperatura ⓕ teng-pe-raa-*too*-raa
  temperature
tempestade ⓕ teng-pes-*taa*-de *storm*
tempo ⓜ *teng*-po *time • weather*
tempo integral eeng-te-*grow* *full-time*
têmpora ⓕ *teng*-po-raa *temple*
tênis ⓜ te-nees *tennis*
  — **de mesa** de *me*-zaa *table tennis*

tentar teng-*taarr* *try (attempt)*
ter terr *have*
terça-feira ⓕ terr-saa-*fay*-raa *Tuesday*
terceiro/terceira ⓜ/ⓕ
  terr-*say*-ro/terr-*say*-raa *third*
terminar terr-mee-*naarr* *finish*
término ⓜ *terr*-mee-no *finish*
Terra ⓕ te-haa *Earth*
terra ⓕ te-haa *land*
terremoto ⓜ te-he-*mo*-to *earthquake*
terrível te-*hee*-vel *terrible*
tesoura ⓕ te-zo-raa *scissors*
teste ⓜ *tes*-te *test*
  — **de gravidez** de graa-vee-*dez*
  pregnancy test kit
tevê ⓕ te-*ve* *TV*
tia ⓕ *tee*-aa *aunt*
tigela ⓕ tee-*zhe*-laa *bowl*
time ⓜ *tee*-me *team*
tímido/tímida ⓜ/ⓕ
  tee-mee-do/tee-mee-daa *shy*
típico/típica ⓜ/ⓕ tee-pee-ko/tee-pee-kaa
  typical
tipo ⓜ *tee*-po *type*
tirar tee-*raarr* *take (photo)*
toalha ⓕ to-*aa*-lyaa *towel*
  — **de rosto** de hos-to *face cloth*
  — **higiênica** ee-zhee-e-nee-kaa
  sanitary napkin
tocar to-*kaarr* *touch • play (guitar) •
  ring (phone)*
tofu ⓜ to-foo *tofu*
tom ⓜ tong *tune*
tomada ⓕ to-*maa*-daa *plug (electricity)*
tomate ⓜ to-*maa*-te *tomato*
tonto/tonta ⓜ/ⓕ *tong*-to/*tong*-taa *dizzy*
torcedor/torcedora ⓜ/ⓕ torr-se-*dorr*/
  torr-se-do-raa *supporter (sport)*
torcimento ⓜ torr-see-*meng*-to *sprain*
torneira ⓕ torr-*nay*-raa *faucet • tap*
tornozelo ⓜ torr-no-*ze*-lo *ankle*
torrada ⓕ to-*haa*-daa *toast*
torradeira ⓕ to-haa-*day*-raa *toaster*
torre ⓕ *to*-he *tower*
torta ⓕ *torr*-taa *pie*
tosa ⓕ *to*-zaa *crop*
tossir to-*seerr* *cough*

trabalhador/trabalhadora ⓜ/ⓕ **de obra**
traa-baa-lyaa-*dorr*/traa-baa-lyaa-*do*-raa
de o-*braa* *labourer*

trabalhador/trabalhadora ⓜ/ⓕ **manual**
traa-baa-lyaa-*dorr*/traa-baa-lyaa-*do*-raa
maa-*noo-ow* *manual worker*

trabalhar traa-baa-*lyaarr* *work*

trabalho ⓜ traa-*baa*-lyo *work*
— **de casa** de *kaa-zaa* *housework*
— **em bar** eng baarr *bar work*

traduzir traa-doo-*zeerr* *translate*

traficante ⓜ&ⓕ traa-fee-*kang*-te
drug dealer

tráfico ⓜ *traa*-fee-ko *traffic*

tranca ⓕ *trang*-kaa *lock*
— **de bicicleta** de bee-see-*kle*-taa
bike lock

trancado/trancada ⓜ/ⓕ
trang-*kaa*-do/trang-*kaa*-daa *locked*

trancar trang-*kaarr* *lock*

transporte ⓜ trans-*porr*-te *transport*

traseiro ⓜ traa-*zay*-ro *bottom (body)*

trave ⓕ **de roda** *traa*-ve de ho-*daa*
spoke (wheel)

travellers cheques ⓜ pl traa-ve-*ler* she-kes
travellers cheques

travesseiro ⓜ traa-ve-*say*-ro *pillow*

trem ⓜ treng *train*

trilha ⓕ *tree*-lyaa *mountain path*

triste *trees*-te *sad*

troca ⓕ *tro*-kaa *exchange*

trocado ⓜ tro-*kaa*-do *loose change*

trocar tro-*kaarr* *change • exchange*

troco ⓜ *tro*-ko *change (coins)*

tudo *too*-do *everything*

tudo/tuda ⓜ/ⓕ *too*-do/*too*-daa *all*

tumor too-*morr* *tumour*

túmulo ⓜ *too*-moo-lo *grave*

turista ⓜ&ⓕ too-*rees*-taa *tourist*

U

último/última ⓕ *ool*-tee-mo/*ool*-tee-maa
last

ultrasom ⓜ ool-traa-*song* *ultrasound*

uma vez oo-maa vez *once*

uniforme ⓜ oo-nee-*forr*-me *uniform*

universidade ⓕ oo-nee-verr-see-*daa*-de
university • college

universo ⓜ oo-nee-*verr*-so *universe*

urgente oorr-zheng-te *urgent*

usuário/usuário ⓜ/ⓕ **de drogas**
oo-zoo-*aa*-ryo/oo-zoo-*aa*-ryaa de
dro-gaas *drug user*

útil oo-til *useful*

uvas ⓕ pl oo-vaas *grapes*

V

vaca ⓕ *vaa*-kaa *cow*

vacina ⓕ vaa-*see*-naa *vaccination*

vagão ⓜ **de dormir** va-*gowng* de
dorr-*meerr* *sleeping car*

vagão ⓜ **restaurante** vaa-*gowng*
hes-tow-*rang*-te *dining car*

vagarosamente vaa-gaa-ro-zaa-*meng*-te
slowly

vagem ⓕ **chinesa** *vaa*-zheng shee-*ne*-zaa
snow pea

vagina ⓕ vaa-*zhee*-naa *vagina*

vago/vaga ⓜ/ⓕ *vaa*-go/*vaa*-gaa *vacant*

vale ⓜ *vaa*-le *valley*

validar vaa-lee-*daarr* *validate*

valor vaa-*lorr* *value (price)*

van ⓕ van *van*

vapor ⓜ vaa-*porr* *stream*

varanda ⓕ vaa-*rang*-daa *balcony*

vários/várias ⓜ/ⓕ *vaa*-ryos/*vaa*-ryaas
many

vazio/vazia ⓜ/ⓕ vaa-*zee*-o/vaa-*zee*-aa
empty

vegetariano/vegetariana ⓜ/ⓕ
ve-zhe-taa-ree-*a*-no/ve-zhe-taa-ree-*a*-naa
vegetarian

veia ⓕ *ve*-aa *vein • candle*

velho/velha ⓜ/ⓕ *ve*-lyo/*ve*-lyaa
old • stale

velocidade ⓕ ve-lo-see-*daa*-de *speed*
— **do filme** do *feel*-me *film speed*

vender veng-*derr* *sell*

venenoso/venenosa ⓜ/ⓕ
ve-ne-*no*-zo/ve-ne-*no*-zaa *poisonous*

ventilador ⓜ veng-tee-laa-*dorr*
fan (machine)

vento ⓜ *veng*-to *wind*

ver verr *look • see*
verão ⓜ ve-*rowng summer*
verde verr-de *green*
verdureiro/verdureira ⓜ/ⓕ
   verr-doo-*ray*-ro/verr-doo-*ray*-raa
   greengrocer
vermelho/vermelha ⓜ/ⓕ
   verr-*me*-lyo/verr-*me*-lyaa *red*
Véspera ⓕ **de Ano Novo** *ves*-pe-raa de
   a-no *no*-vo *New Year's Eve*
vestido ⓜ ves-*tee*-do *dress*
vestígio ⓜ ves-*tee*-zhyo *trail*
vestir ves-*teerr wear*
via ⓕ **aérea** *vee*-aa aa-*e*-re-aa *airmail*
viagem ⓕ vee-*aa*-zheng *journey • trip*
   — de negócios de ne-*goo*-syos
   business trip
viajar vee-aa-*zhaarr travel*
vício ⓜ *vee*-syo *addiction*
   — de drogas de *dro*-gaas
   drug addiction
vida ⓕ *vee*-daa *life*
vidente ⓜ&ⓕ vee-*deng*-te *fortune teller*
vidro ⓜ *vee*-dro *glass • jar*
vigiar vee-zhee-*aarr watch*
vilarejo ⓜ vee-laa-*re*-zho *village*
vinagre ⓜ vee-*naa*-gre *vinegar*
vinha ⓕ *vee*-nyaa *vineyard*
vinho ⓜ *vee*-nyo *vine • wine*
   — espumante es-poo-*mang*-te
   sparkling wine
violão ⓜ vee-o-*lowng guitar*
vir veerr *come*
virar vee-*raarr turn*
vírus ⓜ *vee*-roos *virus*

visitar vee-zee-*taarr visit*
vista ⓕ *vees*-taa *view*
visto ⓜ *vees*-to *visa*
vitamina ⓕ vee-taa-*mee*-naa *vitamin*
voar vo-*aarr fly*
você vo-*se you*
vocês pl vo-*se you*
vodka ⓕ *vo*-dee-kaa *vodka*
vôlei ⓜ *vo*-lay *volleyball (sport)*
   — de praia de *praa*-yaa *beach volleyball*
volta ⓕ *vol*-taa *ride (car)*
volume ⓜ vo-*loo*-me *volume*
vôo ⓜ *vo*-o *flight*
votar vo-*taarr vote*
voz ⓕ voz *voice*

W

whisky ⓜ oo-*ees*-kee *whisky*
windsurfe ⓜ wind-*soorr*-fee *windsurfing*

X

xadrez ⓜ shaa-*dres chess*
xampú ⓜ shang-*poo shampoo*
xarope ⓜ shaa-*ro*-pe *cough medicine*
xícara ⓕ *shee*-kaa-raa *cup*

Z

zangado/zangada ⓜ/ⓕ
   zang-*gaa*-do/zang-*gaa*-daa *angry*
zodíaco ⓜ zo-*dee*-aa-ko *zodiac*
zoológico ⓜ zo-o-lo-*zhee*-ko *zoo*

E

D

F

G

KEY PATTERNS

When's (the next flight)?	Quando é (o próximo vôo)?	*kwaang·do e (o pro·see·mo vo·o)*
Where's (the tourist office)?	Onde fica (a secretaria de turismo)?	*ong·de fee·kaa (aa se·kre·taa·ree·aa de too·rees·mo)*
Where can I (buy a ticket)?	Onde posso (comprar passagem)?	*ong·de po·so (kong·praar paa·sa·zheng)*
How much is (a room)?	Quanto custa (um quarto)?	*kwang·to koos·taa (oom kwaarr·to)*
I'm looking for (a hotel).	Estou procurando (um hotel).	*es·to pro·koorr·ang·d (oom o·tel)*
Do you have (a map)?	Você tem (um mapa)?	*vo·se teng (oom maa·paa)*
Is there (a toilet)?	Tem (banheiro)?	*teng (ba·nyay·ro)*
I'd like (a coffee).	Eu gostaria de (um café).	*e·oo gos·taa·ree·aa de (oom kaa·fe)*
I'd like (to hire a car).	Eu gostaria de (alugar um carro).	*e·oo gos·taa·ree·aa de (aa·loo·gaarr oom kaa·ho)*
Can I (enter)?	Posso (entrar)?	*po·so (eng·traarr)*
Could you please (help me)?	Você poderia me (ajudar), por favor?	*vo·se po·de·ree·aa me (aa·zhoo·daarr) por faa·vorr*
Do I have to (get a visa)?	Necessito (obter visto)?	*ne·se·see·to (o·bee·terr vees·to)*